William Shakespeare: A Brief Life

ARDEN INSIGHTS

SERIES EDITORS

Peter Holland (University of Notre Dame, USA)
Zachary Lesser (University of Pennsylvania, USA)
Tiffany Stern (Shakespeare Institute, University of
Birmingham, UK)

FORTHCOMING TITLES

Shakespeare's Objects: A Guide
Catherine Richardson
978-1-3501-2356-4

Shakespeare on the Page: Books, Texts and Readers
Jeffrey Todd Knight
978-1-3501-5680-7

William Shakespeare: A Brief Life

Paul Menzer

THE ARDEN SHAKESPEARE

LONDON • NEW YORK • OXFORD • NEW DELHI • SYDNEY

THE ARDEN SHAKESPEARE
Bloomsbury Publishing Plc
50 Bedford Square, London, WC1B 3DP, UK
1385 Broadway, New York, NY 10018, USA
29 Earlsfort Terrace, Dublin 2, Ireland

BLOOMSBURY, THE ARDEN SHAKESPEARE and the Arden Shakespeare
logo are trademarks of Bloomsbury Publishing Plc

First published in Great Britain 2023

Cover design: Elena Durey
Cover image © oxygen / Getty Images

A catalogue record for this book is available from the British Library.

Library of Congress Control Number: 2022046919

ISBN:	HB:	978-1-3501-5674-6
	PB:	978-1-3501-5675-3
	ePDF:	978-1-3501-5676-0
	eBook:	978-1-3501-5677-7

Series: Arden Insights

Typeset by Integra Software Services Pvt. Ltd.
Printed and bound in Great Britain

To find out more about our authors and books visit www.bloomsbury.com
and sign up for our newsletters.

This book is dedicated to Barbara Mowat, who taught me everything I know about Shakespeare, but not nearly all she did.

CONTENTS

SERIES PREFACE

Arden Insights are lively, short guides to Shakespeare and his life, work and times. Companions to *The Arden Shakespeare Fourth Series*, they provide cutting-edge research on key topics surrounding the plays and poems, including Shakespeare's biography; Elizabethan and Jacobean material culture; theatres and performance; gender, race and sexuality; adaptations on film, television and new media; and the history of printing, publishing and reading. Supplying a fresh perspective on contexts that the play editions may not have room to explore, they give readers an enhanced understanding of the most exciting and innovative approaches to Shakespeare. In the first formal edition of Shakespeare in 1709, Nicholas Rowe gave his readers 'Some Account of the Life, &c. of William Shakespear', and *Arden Insights* continues this great tradition of Shakespeare editions by including critical contexts and discussions that bring new life to the plays and poems.

PREFACE: THE COMPLETE LIFE OF WILLIAM SHAKESPEARE

A brief word on this short book. Shakespeare lived for fifty-two years. A short life by our standards but not bad for his. However you count, in fifty-two years Shakespeare did just enough to ensure that he would live forever. For though Shakespeare stopped writing in 1616, he has never stopped being written about. Nor have the discoveries ceased about his life. This book recounts some of the most recent findings but will surely be scooped by biographies to come. The truest sentence you will read in this brief biography is that for all the attention lavished upon William Shakespeare, there are discoveries about his life yet to be made.

At 0.7 pounds, this work is a lightweight compared to the briefcases of print that have come before it, like S. Schoenbaum's heavyweight *Shakespeare's Lives* (weighing in at 2.2 pounds) or Lois Potter's recent biography (a relative welterweight at 1.5). By contrast, this book mimics short ones that told of extraordinary men and women, like John Aubrey's *Brief Lives*, written in the seventeenth century (published in 1813) – among the very first attempts to tell us something about Shakespeare's life.

The ambition of biographies like Aubrey's or this one is not comprehensiveness. Instead, this book focuses on a handful of high-definition moments in Shakespeare's life, turning – and returning – points that sometimes nudged or more often pushed him along paths that turned out to be critical to the art he made. After all, it is the art he made – not the money he earned or the men and women he loved – for which we seek him.

So this is a short book, but still long enough to cover the verifiable events of Shakespeare's life: christening, marriage, fatherhood, property acquisition, company membership, litigation, death. As that list suggests, the facts we know about Shakespeare's life would fit on the back of a postcard. But the conjectures we make of them would fill a dozen phone books. The facts tell a simple story: birth, school, work, death. But the facts do not tell us what we want to know: how a sixteenth-century boy from the English midlands became the world's most famous writer. Because what Shakespeare did between his baptism and burial was write astonishing poetry and astounding plays. This brief biography – like all the others – wrings out a few facts to try to discover the man behind, or submerged within, the art.

The facts tell us something about the writer's life, but little about his writing life. Other great authors left behind drafts, letters and occasional sketches that flesh out their finished fictions. In such cases we work backwards from completed forms to find their origins, seeking intimations of mature expression in, say, a dashed-off glimpse of Sardinia from a train, a rapturous letter written in repose, an invited lecture at an august university.

With Shakespeare we have nothing like that. No notes-to-self reading, 'King Lear = Funny hat (?)' or 'leave the key to unlock your soul hidden in the sonnets'. We have nothing like D.H. Lawrence's leftovers or Ben Jonson's table talk, just legal documents that tells us nothing of the writer's life. Except they do. They just do not say what we want them to. What they say is that Shakespeare was careful, even shrewd, even tactical, practical, reticent and wise. He may have returned to Stratford-upon-Avon for good around 1610, but he had been retiring all his life. This is not a savage Shakespeare, warbling his wood-notes wild and spending his bank notes just as wildly. He was, it seems, as ordinary in his life as he was extraordinary in his literature.

Since the bald facts of Shakespeare's life do not tell us much about the artist, we often seek him in his fictions, assuming his plays and poetry reflect, refract or illuminatingly resist the details of his life. We can certainly find something of Shakespeare in the legal documents that bear his name, but can we find him in *Hamlet*, in his sonnets, in *Cymbeline*? And if so, how and where? Who speaks for Shakespeare? Or whom does he speak through? As one critic puts it, 'It is the mark of Shakespeare's art that he eludes the most persistent efforts to make him talk about himself.'[1] If nothing else, Shakespeare always covered his tracks.

Even so, as Geoff Dyer suggests, 'Good, bad, or great, *all* writers are like inept criminals: they leave their prints on everything they touch.'[2] From these fingerprints we recreate the crime. This is, in part, why Shakespeare's work is often treated as a whodunit, or a who-wrote-it, and why many people – not all of them lunatics – have come to the conclusion that Shakespeare did not. A midland innocent, Shakespeare could not possibly have pulled off the greatest heist in history.

A more recent playwright, David Mamet, believes that to deny Shakespeare's authorship is to assert one's own.[3] Unable to author something yourself, the next best thing is to deny someone else's. If you have ever wandered through a museum, you will notice a certain posture among the patrons. They stroll with hands clasped behind their backs in a form of self-arrest. It looks like a pose of relaxed contemplation but it may be self-restraint, a check on the impulse to destroy something beautiful out of sheer envy. The history of Shakespeare's authorship is a contest between those who would put Shakespeare on a pedestal and those who would knock him off. If you cannot make a masterpiece, you might as well make a mess.

But if there were less mystery there would be fewer biographies. (And fewer forgeries, and fewer authorship controversies.) If a letter showed up over Shakespeare's signature that listed the plays that he had written, (a) it would be a forgery and (b) someone would claim it was a scheme to mask the true identity of someone else. Perhaps another person altogether named 'William Shakespeare'.

This biography does not pursue the authorship controversies that buzz like flies about Shakespeare's corpus. That has been done very well, at length, elsewhere.[4] I believe that William Shakespeare wrote the plays of William Shakespeare – though not always by himself – and that, contra Dyer, he left barely a print. Perhaps he followed his father's vocation and worked in gloves.

And so the paradox is this: the wills, bills and codicils that record the traces of Shakespeare's contact with the world seem to bear no relation to the plays and poems. What does the purchase of a Stratford orchard have to do with *King Lear*? What does his embroilment in a tedious lawsuit tell us about *Venus and Adonis*? The effect of this disconnect between life and literature is that the plays and poetry look like mysteries of nature – a leaf, a tree – that will not give up their origins. This should be enough, and it is enough. But the lack of evidence, the nothing we find when we dust for prints, makes the literary output of William Shakespeare something like the perfect crime – not just of the century but of the millennium.

We might conclude that – though dictated by form, driven by commerce, governed by convention – Shakespeare's writing always answered to art, not life. Still, surely, *something* of his personal life leaked into the ink he wrote with. But our access is compromised by the fact that Shakespeare was a fantasist, and his fantasy was of a world in which human beings enjoyed an expressive register few outside Shakespeare ever reached. He had a vision of life that exceeded life, which is just one way to describe 'theatre'.

The form he worked in also limits our access. Playwrights distribute their voice across a wide range of characters, spread it so thin that it evaporates. Put another way, Shakespeare could throw his voice so far and wide that he disappeared over the horizon. If we *could* identify this or that character with Shakespeare (my money's on Polonius), our biographies might be better but the plays would be much worse, even, paradoxically, obviating the need for a biography.

Lacking direct evidence of his creative life – other than the products of his creative life – biographies often turn to those who left more legible prints, Shakespeare's fellows, and the ways they lived and died. We can put Shakespeare in his place (and time) and see the ways that other men and women behaved in similar circumstances. This might explain Shakespeare's preoccupation with monarchical succession. His likely attitudes towards women. Even his thoughts on love and marriage. One caution here is that when we turn to what was typical of his time to learn what Shakespeare was like, we have to recall that Shakespeare was *not* typical of his time. Had he been, you would not be reading a book about him. For that matter, as Lytton Strachey wrote, 'human beings are too important to treat as mere symptoms of the past'.[5] Shakespeare was not symptomatic, he was exceptional. Just how far his exceptionalism extended is the open question. Shakespeare lived somewhere in the space between the typical and the exemplary.

Or between Stratford and London, which might be the same thing. To be crudely reductive, his Stratford life seems one of banal convention, his London one a life of extravagant adventure. This biography dwells on Stratford at both its beginning and its end since that is where Shakespeare dwelled at both beginning and end, the place he left and to which he returned. Leaving Stratford therefore constitutes one of those moments – a turning point, and a returning one – that shaped Shakespeare's fortunes. Again, he left no record of why he left, so we can only guess what drove him from Stratford or lured him to London. Tracing this journey – there-and-back-again – provides one topography of his life and work and the principal shape of the book you are reading. The contention here is that Stratford is of the essence of Shakespeare and therefore essential in understanding where he was coming from, in every sense.

Shakespeare pervades Stratford today, but the town has actually exercised some restraint. They could lay a plaque on every inch of Stratford since it could plausibly be claimed that there is not a single spot on which Shakespeare might not have walked, talked or balked at paying his fair share of taxes. Shakespeare abides in Stratford. Stratford abides in him – to the extent that authorship sceptics today call themselves 'anti-Stratfordians', as though the town's to blame. It is a bit like atheists calling themselves 'anti-Nazarites'. In any event, 'Anti-Stratfordian' is an odd term since Stratford is pretty demonstrably *there*. You can see it for yourself.

The irony then is that Shakespeare left Stratford but it is there that he remains, not least his remains. By contrast, he barely left a trace in London, other than the poetry and plays for which we remember him. Wherever he wrote his plays and poems – Stratford, London or somewhere in between – all the work was produced in London either in the playhouse or the printshop. Otherwise, London does not much remember that he was ever there. A real-estate enthusiast all his life, Shakespeare never purchased lodgings in London until late in life when he bought the Blackfriars gatehouse and then, quixotically, did not live there.

The London/Stratford binary maps neatly onto a work/ life division – aspirational London, vernacular Stratford. This is too neat since lives are never so tidy. In fact one sustaining, deliberate tension of this book is the one between the comfortable arc of Shakespeare's journey there-and-back again and the pressure the archive applies to it. Take as a minor instance the record of Shakespeare in London in November 1614. His Stratford neighbour Thomas Greene – who often referred to Shakespeare as his 'cousin', a term of endearment not kinship – was in London and notes that Shakespeare has come 'to town'. Shakespeare is supposed to be in Stratford living the comfortable life of a retired burgher, not in London seeing Greene on business.

There are other inklings of Shakespeare's restless to-and-froing from Stratford to London throughout his life. Given that playing was officially prohibited during the forty days leading up to Easter, it is quite possible that Shakespeare gave up London for Lent and spent the month and a half at home. Shakespeare may have been a commuter. Nevertheless, his departure from and return to Stratford provides the contours of his mortal life as well as of this brief biography.

There are other such turning points that this work covers. His turning definitively from poetry to playwriting in 1594. His joining that same year a company of players with whom he would work for the balance of his career. The promotion – if that's what it was – of that same company, the Lord Chamberlain's Servants, to the status of the King's Servants in 1603. Shakespeare's relations with the men he worked with and the court he served are also essential to understanding the art he created, art that bears the 'form and pressure' (*Hamlet*, 3.3.25) of commercial and courtly considerations.

He was also a family man and suffered great losses, chief among them his son in 1596. He suffered in silence, however, and this book will return to the question of Shakespeare's reticence in the teeth of personal loss. Shakespeare's death was his final return, and the incidents and aftermaths of this ultimate event provide the structuring absence that closes this study.

The life to come is brief, but, to quote the epilogue to Shakespeare's *Henry V*, in that 'small time ... most greatly lived / This star of England' (epi. ll. 5–6). Written just before the turn of the sixteenth century, Shakespeare reflects upon the life of a medieval king who got a lot done in a little bit of time. (Henry died at thirty-six. He reigned for just nine years.) The coming chapter considers the oddity that upon Shakespeare's death he did not look much like a star and his life looked less than stellar. It looked to all the world like a brief candle.

1

Shakespeare's Dead

On Tuesday 23 April 1616, Shakespeare died. And nothing happened. His widow wept. His children grieved. But school was open the next day. Folks in Stratford probably noticed – the death of the big shot in the big house who made a major fortune in a minor industry. Life went on, though, and the good people of Stratford soon returned to hoarding grain and arguing about enclosure.

Whatever splash Shakespeare's death made in Stratford it probably did not take too long for tidings to ripple around London's theatre world. For if anything is trans-historically true it is that actors love bad news. Shakespeare's death was probably a topic of morbid fascination or mordant hilarity – such a fine line in the theatre – for actors to chew on backstage at The Globe between hands of Primero. You can even hear, across the years, the jokes they might have made.

HEMINGES
So what do you think he died of?
CONDELL
Boredom, after writing *The Tempest*.

Just think how badly they felt when they found out he had willed them twenty-six shillings and eight pence each. (They paid him back in 1623 by compiling his complete works and making him immortal. Call it even.)

This is an ungenerous conceit. Pure speculation. And yet, as far as we know, upon hearing of Shakespeare's death the King's Servants did not observe a moment of silence before the afternoon show. There is no record of a heartfelt pre-show encomia, no *ad hoc* curtain-call eulogies, no retrospective season to honour the work of their former fellow. They did not name The Globe's foyer after him or erect a short statue to stand in for him. So while his fellow actors might have thrown some shade, they did not immediately stir his ghost.

The silence surrounding Shakespeare's death is striking. Just fifteen years earlier he had been the talk of the town. A cluster of references from the turn of the century suggests he had been a faddish favourite of London's chattering class. The marginal writer – in both senses – Gabriel Harvey scribbled in his 1598 edition of Chaucer's works that 'the younger sort take much delight in Shakespeare's Venus, & Adonis'.[1] By 1616 the younger sort were older types and, if still living, had put aside childish things. Fame is fickle, as Shakespeare knew, and his moment had passed. To invert Jonson's famous line on Shakespeare's fame, in 1616 William's work was not for all time, but for an age.

Shakespeare was getting his just desserts since he failed to memorialize others. His reticence in the face of his son's, father's, monarch's and brother's death in 1596, 1601, 1603 and 1607 respectively was echoed by the sound of silence at his own. Maybe it is for the best since, judging by his own epitaph – 'Good friend, for Jesus' sake forbear / To dig the dust enclosed here ….' – and the ones he allegedly wrote for others, death brought out the worst in Shakespeare.

Consider by contrast that just three days before Shakespeare died, the body of John Grimes was borne through the streets of London towards Westminster Abbey in a glittering catafalque. As was modish at the time, the funeral took place at night, the body illumined by two hundred torches, which flirted with the bejewelled fingers of the Duke of Lennox, the Lord of Roxburghe, and a score of 'grand Scottish men'[2] who showed up to turn Grimes off. Have you heard of John Grimes? Same here. Largely unknown today, the death of Grimes was as remarkable as Shakespeare's was not. Shakespeare died and no one noticed.

Sir John Grimes was a Scottish courtier at James' court, so it is not surprising that he was sent off with a bang reserved for big shots. Consider the death of another playwright, then. Francis Beaumont died about a month before Shakespeare, on 6 March 1616. He was buried just three days later in Westminster Abbey next to Chaucer and Spenser. So Francis Beaumont – esteemed at the time but little known today – was buried alongside two of England's greatest poets while Shakespeare got a spot near the altar in a sweet little church in a tiny market town.

The burial records from that pretty church tell us that Shakespeare was laid to rest on 25 April. From the inscription on Shakespeare's funeral monument we know he died two days earlier, on 23 April. The monument reads 'Aetatis 53', telling us he was 52 years old at the time of his death – having entered the fifty-third year of his life – though only just if we believe he was born on 23 April as well. Legend has it that Shakespeare died on the day he was born, with perfectly theatrical timing.

Shakespeare made his will in January of the year he died, and so he may have seen it coming. If he was in declining health, he had time to get his affairs in order but also to ready his soul. Christopher Sutton's *Disce Mori* (1600) – one of many in the era's jolly genre of books on dying – emphasized the need for a spiritual plan to ready the soul against the terrors of death. He lays out a five-point rota for spiritual preparation: the confession of sins, the acceptance of God's will, a reconciliation with the world, the forgiveness of all offences and the enjoinder that the dying accept mortality in 'good part as a preparation for death; and wholly commend himself to God's mercy through the mediation of Christ his Saviour'.[3] Shakespeare may not have followed this five-point plan to the letter, but in the early months of 1616 he had immortal matters on his mind.

He had mortal ones as well and spent some of his final months revising his will, since the original shows signs of second and third thoughts – lines crossed out, words inserted, alterations made. Among the revisions to the original will are multiple places where 'Januarie' is struck through and 'Martii' inserted above. E. K. Chambers thought that Shakespeare's solicitor, Francis Collins, drafted the will in January, but it was not signed and witnessed until 25 March or 'Martii'. Some believe the impetus for these changes was the marriage of Judith Shakespeare to Thomas Quiney on 10 February, which required some alterations.[4] One leaf makes provision for Judith 'until her marriage', which is deleted. Shakespeare's will is a re-write.

Other insertions alter his bequests to family and friends, including the insertion that leaves 'my second best bed' to his wife of thirty-five years. The 'second best bed' was a second thought. It is typical of Shakespeare's legacy that this can be read in diametrically opposed ways: as an act of petty meanness or one of sentimental valour. Perhaps it was the bed in which Shakespeare's children had been conceived and born, 'rich', as Samuel Schoenbaum put it, 'in matrimonial associations'.[5] Perhaps it was the bed in which Shakespeare was currently dying while he dictated his will. Perhaps it had come from Anne's old home at Hewlands as part of her dowry, and the Shakespeares reserved the 'best bed' for their guests. Or perhaps it was a bit of death-bed snark, a reminder to Anne that she was only ever an afterthought.

The expression shows up in other wills of the period, and we don't have to go far for examples. Thomas Combe of Stratford, whose family had multiple links with Shakespeare's (his grandfather left William five pounds in *his* will), bequeathed his wife all 'tables bedsteads ... except the best Bedsteads which I will give and bequeath unto my said son William with the best Bed'.[6] The parallel is close but not exact. Like Shakespeare, Combe did not leave his wife the best bed, but then, unlike Combe, Shakespeare had no son by 1616. This bequest was not unique to Shakespeare, then, but – like so much else in the will – a matter of convention.

It is the only explicit mention of Anne, however, which, yet again, yields competing explanations. Anne stood to automatically inherit one-third of the estate, and so she went without saying. But she seems to have gone without saying for most of Shakespeare's life. In any event, this much is clear: Shakespeare and Anne knew exactly what 'the second best bed' meant and we never will.

The will opens with the date in Latin before the standard preamble identifying the testator and calling him sound of mind and body. Next it moves to Shakespeare's youngest daughter Judith, then his sister Joan Hart, then his nephews and other friends and family. He makes a generous gift of ten pounds to his lawyer, Francis Collins, who had acted for Shakespeare several times before. This is far more than the twenty-six shillings, eight pence Shakespeare left his fellow actors. It tells us something about Shakespeare that one of his favourite people was his lawyer. What it tells us probably depends on what you think of lawyers.

Then followed details about provisions for Susanna Hall and a long digression about the descent of his estate through the male line (this didn't work out). Then more personal bequests above the signature of Shakespeare and his witnesses – or, to be precise, of 'Shackspeare' as his name is spelled throughout. Speaking of names, it is apparent from Shakespeare's sonnets that he was acutely aware of the punning potentials of his own given one. The irony may not have been lost on him that his final writing project was to write and re-write his 'will', thus alerting him to the fact that he was on the brink of becoming a buried pun.

Shakespeare's legatees may have been excited about his comparatively ample will (a deal of property and 350 pounds in cash), but the first recorded reaction to it was one of disappointment. The Revd Joseph Greene, writing in 1747, couldn't believe his eyes: 'So dull and irregular, so absolutely void of the least particular of that spirit which animated our great poet; that it must lessen his character as a writer, to imagine the least sentence of it his production.'[7] Everyone's a critic. But a will is a legal document, a way to disperse one's worldly possessions not to unpack the contents of the heart. As a legal document it does what legal documents do, adhere to the standards of the form as dictated in the handbooks of Henry Swinburne and William West, legal writers who left templates for drawing up what West called 'a very perfect form of a Will'.[8] Howsoever altered, wheresoever revised, Shakespeare's last piece of writing was perfectly conventional.

He probably died surrounded by friends and family. Perhaps his last words were for his children, since dying, advised the puritan counsellor William Gouge, gave parents the chance to bestow on their children one 'last blessing'.[9] In 1600 Francis Tate described how the recently deceased were 'laid forth, as they term it, upon a floor in some chamber, covered with a sheet, and candles set burning over it on a table day and night, and the body continually attended and watched.'[10] Shakespeare's family may have done the same.

Death mingles the routine with the ritual, and so after they covered his body his family said some prayers and paid the bells of Holy Trinity to change their tune. New Place was in the middle of town, and so the household was attuned to a variety of rings. Harvest bells to summon the reapers, the 'pancake bell' on Shrove Tuesday. The old year was rung out with a muffled peal and the new year announced by an open one. The 'Passing-bell' was rung when a person was near death, and so perhaps this bell was the soundtrack to Shakespeare's last moments. Once death had come, a different bell was rung, called the 'knell', to inform the neighbours and 'to remind them of their duty to pray for the departed soul'.[11]

William Shakespeare's husk was laid in the earth before two days had passed. In an age before refrigeration, getting the body below ground was a pressing matter. The vicar of Raynham, Essex, was charged with negligence in 1624 for permitting a body 'this summer to lie three days unburied after it was dead until it did stink'.[12] Embalming was reserved for aristocrats. Their bodies needed to be preserved while preparations were made for funerals of great pomp. This was no mean feat. Sir

Thomas Browne, in his *Hydriotaphia, or Urn-Burial* (1658), notes that, 'to keep the corpse seven days from corruption by anointing and washing, without exenteration [removal of the organs], were an hazardous piece of art'.[13] Shakespeare's body might merely have been wrapped before it was drawn across the cobbles to his final resting place inside Holy Trinity Church, the last of his many journeys.

The funeral service itself probably conformed with the 1552 Book of Common Prayer – updated in 1604 by the order of James I – and possibly included a prayer cycle called 'the office to the dead'. The cycle of prayers includes the phrase, '*Timor mortis conturbat me*', or, colloquially, 'I am scared to death of dying', a deathless pun Shakespeare might have liked. Seven years later, when Heminges and Condell collected Shakespeare's plays, they called the book an 'office to the dead' in its preface, imagining the book as a memorial to Shakespeare's death. They could not have known it would ensure he lived forever.

The funeral was likely attended by Shakespeare's living relatives, a dwindling number by that point. A number of poor townsfolk may have turned out in hope of a customary gift, sometimes a ribbon or even gloves, which were in Shakespeare's family line since his father had manufactured them. They might at least have stuck around for 'a drinking' at the expense of Shakespeare's family, a funeral custom that followed the service. Still, remarkably, even this wake did not make a ripple. As a testament to his death, we have only the curate's word for it in the parish registry from 25 April, 'Will Shakspeare gent'.

'Gent' stands for 'gentleman'. And that 'gent' remembers something that was evidently important to Shakespeare, his pricy acquisition of a coat of arms in 1596. Aristocrats were permitted heraldic displays at their funerals, but Shakespeare was not an aristocrat. Nevertheless, lower gentry in the seventeenth century often aped the custom, which prompted the College of Arms to grump that if any such arms be 'set up or erected at any ... burial or interment without such authority and assent ... then it shall be lawful for [the heralds] to raze, deface and pull down the same being so used'.[14] Still, the surviving Shakespeares might have displayed the family seal at his funeral, safe in Stratford from the reach of the College of Arms.

In addition to a display of arms at a funeral, aristocratic and gentle families were allowed to erect ornate memorials over the tombs of their loved ones. In 1625, Henry Pettit's family was still quarrelling over the design of his funeral monument two months after he'd been buried in the church at Denton, Kent. In most cases, however, the dead joined the community of departed Christians in the churchyard, their individual lives absorbed into the anonymity of death. Families might erect temporary memorials, which bishops would tidy up after a respectable period. As will be treated at greater length in this book's penultimate chapter, 'Shakespeare's Head', Shakespeare eventually got his own monument, an effigy on the wall that looks down upon his body, keeping a close watch lest violators ignore the grave warning, 'Good friend, for Jesus' sake forbear ....' A curse that proved ineffective, but that story is to come.

*

So in the English spring of 1616 Shakespeare was interred at the head of the nave in Holy Trinity Church in Stratford-upon-Avon. Shakespeare was gone, but he would not be forgotten. The question is whether he'd been, in his reclining years, forgotten but not gone. That is, what was Shakespeare's reputation at the time of his death? Was anybody still reading Shakespeare or seeing his plays around the time of his demise?

Let us return to that backstage scene of Shakespeare's former fellows learning of his death. How long had it been since they'd staged one of Shakespeare's plays? Did any feature within the repertory of the King's Servants in 1616? If so, what plays would be the most likely candidates? There was a living link to Shakespeare through his one-time collaborator John Fletcher, who was the man of the moment. (If we were to take the temperature of the time, however we shake the thermometer, it almost always comes up Fletcher.) If, at news of Shakespeare's death, the King's Servants had wanted to revive a play that satisfied both nostalgia for Shakespeare and the taste for Fletcher, they had *The Two Noble Kinsmen* or the now-lost *Cardenio*. If you wanted to wager on Shakespeare in 1616, then, you might bet on *Kinsmen* or *Cardenio*, though it is not clear that those plays would have struck anyone as 'Shakespearean', since his star had been eclipsed by the younger Fletcher. But this is just guesswork, since there is no record of a play by Shakespeare appearing on the commercial stage in England in 1616.

To find such a record, we have to go to court, whose accounts tell us what the King's Servants were playing at the time. They were playing their hits since revivals were favoured at the courts of James and Charles. From 1616 to 1642, the King's Servants presented *twice* as many revivals as new plays at court. They opted for the tried and true over the novel and new. Shakespeare's *Twelfth Night* appeared at Whitehall on 6 April 1617 with *The Winter's Tale* presented the very next night. Neither play was very fresh, with *Twelfth Night* dating back to the beginning of the century, when James I of England was still James VI of Scotland.

This mini-revival of Shakespeare at court in the spring of 1617 was his first appearance there since a *Cardenio* for the Ambassador of Savoy nearly five years earlier on 8 June 1612. What broke the five-year fast? That half-a-decade of Shakespearean silence at the court of James? It's possible to fantasize some nostalgia, even a wistful memorial impulse in the revival of two Shakespeare titles at court, on back-to-back days, almost exactly a year after his death. Did anyone notice that he wasn't there?

To answer the question of whether Shakespeare's name still had any purchase on the theatrical imagination in the years of his death, we can turn from boards to books and consider Shakespeare's fortunes in print. If there were any booksellers who thought to profit from Shakespeare's death in 1616, they were awfully slow about it. Had a Londoner heard about Shakespeare's death in 1616 and wanted to pick up a playbook from the bookstalls of St Paul's to remember him by, the pickings were pretty slim. A survey of Shakespeare playbooks in 1616/17 does not take very long. No new quartos of Shakespeare's plays appeared between *Troilus and Cressida* and *Pericles* of 1609 and *Othello* in 1622. As with theatrical revivals, we have to look to reprints to find the few titles that might still be available in 1616/17, warehoused or otherwise.

In the five years before his death, a handful of reprints appeared: *Pericles*, *Titus Andronicus* and *Hamlet* in 1611; *Richard III* in 1612; *1 Henry IV* in 1613; and *Richard II* in 1615. Let's be generous and imagine that *Richard II*, *1 Henry IV* and *Richard III* – all reprinted within four years of Shakespeare's death, all for Matthew Law – caught the eye of the nostalgic Shakespeare shopper in 1616. These three plays were Shakespeare's most popular in print, if we judge by reprints alone. One quick conclusion about Shakespeare's reputation in 1616 was that he was history. Indeed, these three titles might have telescoped the extent to which Shakespeare was a figure from the past. All date from before 1595 and were therefore nearly twenty-five years old in 1616. These quartos produce a forced perspective, one that antiqued Shakespeare, marbleizing his literary profile. That profile is of Kid Shakespeare, Elizabethan poet and playmaker – the writer of erotic juvenilia and Tudor propaganda.

The only two known allusions to Shakespeare in 1617 reinforce the impression that he was stuck in the past. The poet John Taylor mentions Falstaff in a Theophrastian description of a hang-man. And Geffray Mynshul, confined to the King's Bench for debt, conflates *The Merchant of Venice* and *The Jew of Malta* to describe his plight: 'If with the Jew of Malta, instead of coin, thou requires a pound of flesh next to thy debtor's heart, wilt thou cut him in pieces?'[15] Neither man mentions Shakespeare by name, neither seems to know he is dead, but the two plays they remember date from the 1590s. By 1616, Shakespeare had already become posthumous.

We turn next to the Stationers' Register, the book trade's repository of copyright information, to see if any enterprising publisher thought to re-issue Shakespeare in 1616 to bank upon his death. But there is nothing to be found between 1 March 1614 (for *The Rape of Lucrece*) and 8 July 1619 (for *The Merchant of Venice*), though on 16 February 1617, William Leake transferred his rights to *Venus and Adonis*, along with twenty-nine other non-Shakespearean titles, to William Barrett. The presence of *Lucrece* in the Stationers' Register reveals the two titles by Shakespeare that *did* appear the year of and after his death. An octavo of *The Rape of Lucrece* was issued in 1616, printed for Roger Jackson, and the very next year *Venus and Adonis* was printed for William Barrett. In the immediate aftermath of his death, Shakespeare appeared in print with the titles with which he began his printed career, with narrative poetry not verse drama.

So if a book browser wandered past Jackson's shop near the conduit on Fleet Street, they would find a copy of *The Rape of Lucrece* advertising the name of William Shakespeare, followed by the unlikely proposition that it was 'newly revised'. As for the title page of the 1617 *Venus and Adonis*, it does not mention Shakespeare at all. In the year of 1617, the single title by Shakespeare to appear in print lacked his name, except at the end of its dedicatory epistle. So he appears in print in the year after his death with the same anonymity with which he began.

His posthumous reputation got off to an ignominious start, then, if we take 'ignominy' literally to mean 'no name'. The publication of Shakespeare's early poems in the immediate aftermath of his death traces an analogous circularity of both his body and his body of work. They both display a striking tendency to end up right back where they started from.

If London's theatre makers were not thinking much about Shakespeare in 1616, he was thinking about them. As noted, in his will he left '26 shillings 8 pence apiece' to Burbage, Heminges and Condell 'to buy them rings'. The will was 'proved' in the Prerogative Court of Canterbury in London by John and Susanna Hall on 22 June 1616 and sometime after that the money was conveyed some 100 miles south-east from Stratford to the City of London (reversing the flow of capital from London to Stratford that subsidized Shakespeare's splendid standard of living in his later years). By 1616, far from 'Shakespeare our contemporary' or 'Shakespeare for all time', or the BBC's 'Man of the Millennium' in 1999, Shakespeare was 'an Elizabethan playwright'. One, it seems, condemned to the relative obscurity that Beaumont and Fletcher enjoy, or suffer, today.

*

The moment of silence did not last. Still, immediately following his death in 1616, Shakespeare was entering an odd phase, a brief but unique stretch between the death of the writer and the birth of the author, a literary purgatory between the decomposition of Shakespeare's biological corpse and the re-composition of his bibliographical corpus.

In the years following his death Shakespeare's reputation caught fire, first as a flicker then as a flame. That flame burst into full fluorescence in 1709, when Shakespeare was really born, or born again. If, like Nicodemus, we are sceptical about the phrase 'born again', we can agree that in 1709 Shakespeare was re-born, not of water and the spirit, but by editors and anecdotes. For 1709 is the year Nicholas Rowe got together with Jacob Tonson to publish *The Works of Mr. William Shakespear* in six volumes – kicking off the great century of Shakespearean editions, in which the editorial quibble was fully weaponized. Among its many other innovations, Rowe's 1709 edition contained the first formal biography of William Shakespeare, completed with the aid of research done by the actor Thomas Betterton, whom Rowe sent to Stratford to visit Shakespeare's old haunts and stir a ghost or two.

Rowe was not just an editor, he was a resurrectionist. And once he had exhumed Shakespeare, he baptized him in anecdotes. He gave us Shakespeare the deer poacher,

Shakespeare the truant student, Shakespeare the country rascal who lit out for London with the law on his heels, thirsty for all that London had to offer.

To compound an exaggeration with an irony, Shakespeare biography begins when the story of his life achieved escape velocity from fact. For Rowe launched Shakespeare's biographical tradition with a flurry of dubious anecdotes. At the time, Rowe modestly suggested that, 'the knowledge of an Author may sometimes conduce to the better understanding his Book' and allowed that his readers might be 'fond … of discovering any little Personal Story' about the life of the author.[16] Among Rowe's many editorial innovations, the most enduring is the idea that Shakespeare's life might matter to his art, and to us.

Rowe was right more often than he was wrong. Readers do like little personal stories about writers. The more personal the better. Rowe also knew that there are things more true than truth, and tied a few tall tales to Shakespeare's legacy that still get retold in each new tale of his life. The deer-stealing incident; the William the Conqueror punchline; and an aging queen who should like to see Falstaff in love (and thus Shakespeare writes *The Merry Wives of Windsor*, etc.) – anecdotes taken up later in this book. Why scramble after facts about the life of a fictionalist? Facts might matter more to the life of a statesman or scientist – an Attlee or a Curie – but the mundane matter of when and where is not what Rowe was after.

This biography begins at the end of Shakespeare's life so that we might take a look back and see how he got there, how he ended up right back where he started, in Stratford-upon-Avon. The return to Stratford produces a life that reclines into myth so comfortably as to ease even the sceptical scholar. The early departure, the late return. Public success, private loss. A twilight of plays about family reunions, a death at home in the biggest house in town, the one he walked by as a boy on his way to school.

The next chapter treats Stratford in full, since Stratford is so critical to the story. Not for the fact that Shakespeare left but that he came back. This makes of his life not an arc but an orbit, and the constant return of Shakespeare's life, that perfect circle, implies that he might go on forever while his equals have come to an end.

There is some truth to the comfort of this familiar story. As Jeremy Lopez has written about something slightly different, 'we accept the risks inherent in this assumption' – that the circle of Shakespeare's life conforms with the curve of his art – 'because we understand that the interpretive rewards are potentially great'.[17] We can read the plays against Shakespeare's orbital life and see the boisterous energy of his early plays – juvenile experiments like *Titus Andronicus*, clockwork farces like *The Comedy of Errors* – maturing into his great tragedies before mellowing into the late Romances, suffused with redemption, restoration and the relationship between fathers and daughters.

The truth is more complex and Shakespeare's life probably seemed more rough than smooth to him, with the loss of family and friends, disappointments of the bed and board that seem to leak into his work from time to time. This book ruffles the familiar story here and there, throwing a few wobbles into Shakespeare's wheel of life, even puncturing it now and then. What follows courts a tension between the alluring ease of a coherent story and some pesky but pertinent archival facts that lodge in the story like a rock in your shoe. Within the smooth prosody of Shakespeare's earthly sentence there is a parenthetical tale to tell, something quirkier, jerkier. A worm in the damask. A wasp in the bloom.

*

If you visit Holy Trinity Church today you are greeted by an unnerving sign that reads, 'Shakespeare's Tomb is Open'. Thankfully, the church is open but the tomb is closed. Shakespeare is buried inside, right up against the altar itself, in an old church encircled by tombstones. Shakespeare died as he lived, centre stage, surrounded by groundlings.

No one seems to be counting, so it is hard to know whether more folks visit the gravesite or the birthplace, though the latter seems a lot busier, as coach upon coach of schoolchildren and their weary wardens nod their way through the dinky house. The sites of birth and death are less than a mile apart, which can leave the impression that Shakespeare did not get very far, though he managed to accomplish quite a bit in-between, which is what concerns the chapters that follow.

Shakespeare is dead in Holy Trinity Church, but he did not die there. That almost certainly happened at a third site, roughly in-between the birthplace in Henley Street and the gravesite in Holy Trinity. If Shakespeare died at home, he did so at New Place, at the corner of Church Street and Chapel Lane, right across the street from the Guild Chapel. It is important at this late point in Shakespeare's life – but early point in this study – to acknowledge that this is speculation. He may not have died at home in bed surrounded by family and friends. Shakespeare might have died anywhere in Stratford or its surroundings, dropping of a massive infarction while bollocking a tenant over unpaid tithes, say. Less romantic, just as likely.

You can visit New Place today though the house is long gone. There's a nice garden where the house once stood, with plaques that tell you what was once there. You might leave feeling a bit like Shakespeare's first audience, your pockets lighter, having given something for nothing, feeling like you've been sold a pup. But you can stroll the grounds and imagine what it looked like back in the day. You will probably pass over or under the spot where Shakespeare's heart beat one last iamb. Imagine that moment. Just think of it. Maybe as Shakespeare expired, breathed his last breath, he thought of everything he had not said, of everything he had left unwritten. Just possibly, in his last lucid moments, just before he passed from earth to eternity, he gave a rueful smile, since he realized he alone had the perfect words to describe it.

2

Earth unto Earth

Stratford-upon-Avon is a small town in the English midlands smack in the middle of the county of Warwickshire. It lies along the River Avon which flows from Northamptonshire through Rugby, Warwick, Stratford-upon-Avon, Evesham, Pershore and Tewkesbury before joining the River Severn. It was chartered as a market town by Richard I in 1196, but people had made Stratford home since the time of the Anglo-Saxons. Hunters. Gatherers. Nomads. Then farmers and shepherds. Then merchants and artisans and now artists, actors and educators among the shopkeepers and labourers. Around the time of Shakespeare's birth, it had about 1,500 residents. Today, Stratford's chief industry is tourism. Its town motto is 'people were shorter back then'.

That last bit is not strictly true, but visitors to Shakespeare's birthplace today bow their heads, and not just in reverence. The dinky scale of the town's Shakespeare meccas means you're always in danger of banging a forehead on history's lintel. Out on Church Street, massive coaches, shuddering juggernauts, idle in front of Shakespeare's school house, fouling the midland air. Due to Stratford's omnipresent pastness, they don't even look modern. They look futuristic. Interstellar ships making a brief touch-down for a look-in at the birthplace of earth's exemplary ambassador.

The bus windows are always tinted, probably to hide the blush since there is something embarrassing about a literary pilgrimage to such a tiny place. Still, the tourists look happy enough, cheerfully shouldering their way through the school house, the churchyard, the birthplace, the giftshop. Stratford today is a requisite stop on the island tour, from Big Ben to Little Will.

The scale of central Stratford today is roughly something like ¾ to 1, the scale of nostalgia. (It was just this scale that the 'imagineers' at Disney World employed when they built a 'Main Street' for their first theme park in Florida, since the past is always receding in our memory.) What's vital – though difficult – to imagine about Stratford today is that its scale to the young William Shakespeare was one-to-one, the scale of life. At least until the late 1580s, when it may have become too small for him, and he set off for London to create something much larger than life.

Stratford today has the quality of a double-exposed snapshot, as though the lens has been open for 400 years. We gain a sense of what it looked like on all those yesterdays, with this important qualification. Stratford may look 'cute' to us, a picturesque postcard of the merrie olde past, but Shakespeare would not have found it so. Wattle and daub looked as modern to Shakespeare as bricks and mortar do to us. Whatever else he felt about Stratford, he would not have found it cute, quaint or maybe even merrie. How Shakespeare found Stratford, why he left it and why he came back is what most immediately concerns the chapter that follows.

*

John Shakespeare was dwelling in Henley Street, Stratford on 29 April 1552 when he was fined one shilling for making a *sterquinarium* there. If you are unfamiliar with the term, *sterquinarium* is a Latin word for an English dunghill. One of the earliest references to the Shakespeares of Henley Street is a load of crap.

That Henley heap might clear the air – or foul it – of any sense of twee when we contemplate the Stratford into which

Shakespeare was born. Consider that just three months after his baptism was recorded in the parish registry, the same hand writes '*Hic incepit pestis*', or 'Here began the plague' beside the entry for Oliver Gunne's burial on 11 June 1564. In the year he was born, the plague wiped out one in eight of the local population. Shakespeare was born into a world of danger.

Merely being born, then – the least impressive and most important thing he ever did – was a stroke of good luck. And Shakespeare's luck is just one recurring theme of his life. Consider for instance that in the year he was born the profession that would make him immortal – 'playwright' – did not properly exist yet.

It was also good luck that Shakespeare did not die as a child. Infant mortality was horribly high at the time. In the few words that John Aubrey spares Shakespeare in his *Brief Lives*, written in the late seventeenth century, he spends some on this odd sentence. After noting that Shakespeare was a butcher's son (he wasn't), Aubrey writes that, 'There was at that time another Butcher's son in this Towne, that was held not at all inferior to him for a natural wit, his acquaintance and coetanean [i.e., Shakespeare's contemporary], but dyed young.'[1] This odd note introduces us to Shakespeare's twin, or his shadow, equal in age and promise but not in luck or health. This shade follows Shakespeare throughout his life – and across this book – a spectre of contingency, a ghost of luck, to remind us that things might have gone otherwise, not least his life. Shakespeare was lucky just to be alive.

In the years of his youth, Stratford was a provincial market town, one of a handful of business centres in Warwickshire. It had paved streets and gardens around some of its houses. It was surrounded by open fields and enclosed pastures. Access to London and Oxford was available on roads which carriers travelled regularly, conveying goods and letters.

The surrounding towns, hamlets and holdings had been 'Warwickslands' in times past, land belonging to the Earl of Warwick, though the area had been known as 'Warwickshire' as early as the year 1000, after 'warwick' meaning 'dwellings by the weir'. (A 'weir' is a low dam, and even today Stratford is contoured by a confluence of river, dams and bridges, which chivvy and cover the water.) Stratford sits on the edges of the Cotswold Hills, an area of sheep raising before and in Shakespeare's time.

However small Stratford seems in hindsight, it was the 'urban' hub that held a number of radiant places together, a market for its agricultural surroundings. As an urban centre, Stratford was full of urban industries: weaving, dyeing, tanning, shoe-making, glove-making, smithing, rope-making, carpentry, and on and on. The people of Stratford were mainly wrights, makers of this and that. Shakespeare's future as a 'playwright', a maker of plays, owes some debt to the handy townsmen and women among whom he was raised, whose occupations were with the handmade, the homespun, the artisanal.

Shakespeare's father was a glover, whittawer and wool dealer, who cured and whitened skins and then shaped them into gloves. When his son William later wrote about the 'dyer's hand' in sonnet 111, he could recall his father's hands, stained, not whitened, by his trade. Shakespeare's hands as he aged, darkened by ink not dye, may have come to resemble those of John Shakespeare.

John's wife, William's mother, was named Mary Arden, daughter of Robert Arden, a well-off landowner who left his daughter property, which his son-in-law John (whom he probably never knew) expanded upon, buying up land in Stratford upon his marriage. John was evidently proud of the union with the Ardens, enough so to claim it as evidence for his petition for gentle status in the late 1570s.

Shakespeare's parents were at the height of their prosperity during his infancy, though their fortunes declined when he was in his teens. In 1571 John was appointed as chief alderman of Stratford, not long after he applied for a coat of arms. We do not know how much money John and Mary amassed or how much William eventually inherited, but he got some of their ambition for bourgeois comfort and station.

The street on which Shakespeare was born, Henley Street, was – and still is – quite wide, a stark contrast with those of the London where he'd come to live, where the cantilevered buildings reached out to one another, shading the street below. Henley joined the high street at its lower end, and so was close to the places central to Shakespeare's life: the school house, the Guild Chapel and New Place – all less than a five-minute walk from his home.

Henley Street was wide but John and Mary Shakespeare's house was narrow, not much bigger than a creche. (Two up, two down. No mod cons.) During Shakespeare's youth his parents expanded upon it, buying adjacent property to accommodate their expanding family, with a workshop attached for his father's industry.

Shakespeare's origins are humble, then. Not impoverished, just modest. There is nothing in his origins that accounts for what he turned out to be. As far as we know, bees did not settle upon his infant lips, presaging the honey that would flow from hence, as legend has it they did with Plato. William was the third child of a comfortably set up couple who lived, worked and died in a small, pretty, marketplace town in the English midlands.

Be it ever so humble, the home on Henley Street was already called the 'birthplace' by the time of the Shakespeare Jubilee in 1769, a coronation of Shakespeare as national poet staged by that era's first actor, David Garrick. (The jubilee – during which it rained so hard that Stratford-upon-Avon became Avon-upon-Stratford – celebrated the bicentennial of Shakespeare's birth, but Garrick was late for his cue. It's symbolic of the way that Shakespeare's life stretches towards myth, and away from facts, that the 'bicentennial' of his birth was celebrated 205 years after it.)

At that celebration, an eastern room on the first floor of the Henley house was indicated as the 'birthroom' by a painting hung before its windows 'representing the sun breaking through the clouds'.[2] (There is an English almanac for 1564 composed in Salisbury by Henry Lou. Though Salisbury is one hundred miles south of Stratford, Lou predicts for April: '[on the] three and twenty and four and twenty day cloudy wind'.) Whatever the weather when Shakespeare was born, the 'birthroom' probably depicted a false dawn. It's not certain that Shakespeare was even born in this house, much less this room, but history has christened this place as the 'birthplace', a verdict confirmed by all those idling coaches.

Shakespeare was the third child of John and Mary, who had extensive family connections in the area. He never knew his oldest sister, Joan, who was born in 1558 but died shortly thereafter. Then came Margaret in 1562 who also shortly died. Then came William and his younger siblings Gilbert in 1566, another Joan in 1569 ('thrift, Horatio, thrift'), Anne in 1571, Richard in 1574 and Edmond in 1580. If we are tempted to read in these names intimations of Shakespeare's characters – all his Margarets, Joans, Richards and Edmonds – we need to check that impulse against the Elizabethan tendency to name every boy William, Henry or John and every girl Joan, Anne or Meg (every Tom, Dick and Harry in England was named Tom, Dick or Harry).

This can make a mischief of genealogy, and many an English antiquarian has mistaken a father for a son, an aunt for a niece. Such errors can make for great drama – tragedy for the Greeks, farce for the English – but bad biography. There were other Shakespeares in the area, some related some not to William, but the sequence of Shakespeare's siblings is clear. He was the first son, the third born and the oldest surviving child of John and Joan's brood of eight.

'William Shakespeare', then. A perfectly fine name though not a perfectly fitting one. There are, by contrast, artists whose names exactly express their work. If you came across a poet named 'Wordsworth' in a novel, you would throw it across the room. And even Charles Dickens would not have named a post-modern architect 'Rem Koolhaas'. But the martial swagger of 'Shake-spear' does not suit the reticent writer of that name.

In fact 'Shake-spear' would better fit a playwright who had actually appeared in battle, like Shakespeare's fellow writer Ben Jonson, who trailed a pike in the low countries before writing two or three of the greatest comedies in English. The anodyne 'Jonson' doesn't do him justice. This is a writer, after all, who killed an actor in a duel. (Jonson wouldn't be the last playwright to harbour murderous fantasies about an actor.) For that matter, William's father was named 'John', so he was more of a 'John's son' than Ben. Whatever else Shakespeare and Jonson exchanged – plays, pleasantries, quips and barbs – they should have changed names. They might at least have shared a common admiration for their perfectly named colleague, Christopher Mar-low, counterfeiter, street-fighter, spy, punk.

What is evident from Shakespeare's family record is that he grew up in a crowded house. If he took to wandering the open fields around Stratford or along the rivers that wound through it – observing the midland flora that bloom throughout his plays – it may have been to find some space to think without tripping over a younger sibling. Maybe he finally left for London to find some peace and quiet.

*

Shakespeare was baptized on 26 April 1564. The 1559 Book of Common Prayer states that, 'When there are children to be baptized upon the Sunday, or holy day, the parents shall give knowledge over night, or in the morning, afore the beginning of Morning prayer, to the curate.'[3] The 26th of April 1564 fell on a humble Wednesday, not a holy Sunday. It was not even a Saint's day. John and Mary may have rushed to baptize Shakespeare. They had buried two children already.

Maybe their third child and first son was weak. If so he was sprinkled with holy water not dipped in the font. The Book of Common Prayer instructs the curate that '*if the Child be weak, it shall suffice to pour water upon it, saying the foresaid words.* I Baptize thee in the name of the Father, and of the son, and of the holy Ghost. Amen.' These were the first formally cadenced, scripted words that Shakespeare heard.

The curate then made the sign of the cross upon Shakespeare's forehead, saying:

> we receive this Childe into the congregation of Christs flock, and do sign him with the sign of the crosse, in token that hereafter he shall not be ashamed to confess the faith of Christ crucified, and manfully to fight under his banner against sin, the world, and the devil, and to continue Christs faithful soldier and servant unto his lives end. Amen.

It is a lot to ask of a three-day-old.

We do not often think of Shakespeare as 'Christ's faithful soldier', manfully battling sin under Christ's fluttering banner. While God – and the gods – shows up often in his works, 'Christ' rarely does. Shakespeare was probably not 'ashamed to confess the faith' in a crucified Christ. Rather, it was the state Protestantism of Shakespeare's lifetime that muted more overt expressions of faith in Jesus.

When Jesus does show up in Shakespeare's plays it is to amplify a sentiment a character feels strongly about. Justice Shallow in the second part of *Henry IV* responds to Falstaff's 'We have heard the chimes at midnight' with, 'Jesus, the days that we have seen!' (3.2.215, 219).[4] Here 'Jesus' serves to intensify nostalgia: Shallow yearns for yesterday. Perhaps Jesus was a figure of hindsight for Shakespeare as well. In 1559 Elizabeth I passed a royal injunction for the 'removal of all signs of superstition and idolatry from places of worship'. When Shakespeare was just four, his own father served as bailiff and authorized payment of two shillings for 'defacing images in the chapel'.[5] Under John Shakespeare's authority, images of the last judgment – the 'Doom' in Old English – were whitewashed over in the Guild Chapel.

John Shakespeare may have done some whitewashing of his own. While he publicly enforced the edicts of state Protestantism, he privately practised a closet Catholicism – if, that is, a discovery made in 1757 turned out to be authentic.

On 29 April of that year a bricklayer named Joseph Moseley was retiling the roof of Shakespeare's birthplace, then in the hands of Thomas Hart, a descendent of Shakespeare's sister Joan. The bricklayer found six stitched leaves of paper between the roof and the rafters, a handwritten profession of faith now known as the 'Spiritual Last Will and Testament of John Shakespeare'. Such testaments circulated in the sixteenth century in print and in handwritten forms, designed to be carried by Roman Catholics should they perish without a priest on hand to deliver the last rites. The birthplace copy allegedly featured John Shakespeare's name inserted into the blanks left in the original document.

The story of the discovery features a paper trail that casts its authenticity into doubt. Moseley passed it to a Stratford alderman, who thirty years later allowed it to be copied, and eventually it reached the scrupulous Shakespeare editor Edmund Malone. Malone had his doubts – Malone *always* had his doubts – but published it anyway, though he later retracted his belief in its authenticity. The original was lost along the way – because of course it was – so if we believe that John Shakespeare put his name to his faith and hid it in his rafters, we have to put our faith in a third-hand copy of a now-lost testament.

Whether the testament was real or not, it would not be odd for John Shakespeare to have professed the old faith. From the time of Shakespeare's birth through his death and beyond, English Catholicism was always there, just beneath a thin veneer of Protestant whitewash. Shakespeare could be forgiven if, before folding his hands in prayer, he lifted a finger to the wind to see which way it was blowing, from Rome or from Geneva. It seems he decided to keep his cards close to his doublet, or concluded that it's unwise to play cards in a gale.

Discovered in 1804, uncovered and restored in 2016, the images in the Guild Chapel can be seen clearly today. Shakespeare may have seen them but would have been too young to remember the image of Jesus perched on a rainbow, flanked by Mary and John the Baptist. To Christ's left is the Kingdom of Heaven, on his right the Mouth of Hell, depicted as a fanged serpent. Painted atop the Chancel arch, the image made the stakes clear to any and all worshippers.

But it was not just the day of doom his father had whitewashed when Shakespeare was a child. On the chapel's lower west wall, behind wooden panelling, is a well-preserved painting of the 'Earth upon Earth' poem. An allegory of life and death, the poem was a familiar one at the time. Even if it was covered up in 1568, Shakespeare read it elsewhere. It was inscribed upon walls and tombstones across England as well as on the first or final leaves of manuscripts. In a modern transcription, the Stratford version runs, in part,

> Earth upon earth wins castles and towers
> Then says earth unto earth, 'This is all ours!'
> When earth upon earth has built up his bowers
> Then shall earth for earth suffer many hard showers.
> I counsel earth upon earth that is wondrously wrought
> While earth is upon earth he should turn his thought
> And pray to God upon earth that all earth wrought
> That all Christian souls to your bliss may be brought.[6]

The point of this cheerful poem is that whatever you may come to in life in the end you come to this. Death. Dearth. Earth. Man is made of earth and to earth he will return.

We hear an echo of this poem in Hamlet's oddly forensic curiosity about what happens to the body after death: 'Alexander died, Alexander was buried, Alexander returneth into dust, the dust is earth, of earth we make loam, and why of that loam, whereto he was converted, might they not stop a beer-barrel?' (5.1.206–10) Throughout his poems and plays Shakespeare has a strong sense of the transient, of where we come from, what we're made of and to what we all return.

When John Shakespeare whitewashed the walls of the Guild Chapel, Shakespeare did not know anything of transience yet, nor anything of the Doom, Catholicism, Alexander or beer barrels. But he would learn it soon, right next door to the Guild Chapel in a little school room where he would learn to tell his alpha from his omega.

3

Shakespeare at School

Draw up a manual called 'How To Train A Playwright' and you could do a lot worse than the schooling William Shakespeare enjoyed – or occasionally suffered, since corporal punishment was part of the curriculum. (One preacher at the time suggested that God invented buttocks to ensure that schoolboys learned their Latin. It's not for nothing that hornbooks were shaped like paddles.) Shakespeare's education included an immersion in the classics, an introduction to the grammars of both Latin and English, a rigorous programme of rhetorical training and even, quite possibly, some Latin dramatics. A Norwich statute of 1566, issued when Shakespeare was in his terrible twos, outlines the aim of grammar school learning, which was to tutor every boy, 'To say his catechism and to read perfectly both English and Latin, and to write competently.'[1] Shakespeare's Latin was not perfect, but Time has affirmed the competence of his writing.

Grammar school lasted from dawn to dusk, six days a week, a grinding regimen that Shakespeare unwistfully remembers when Jacques in *As You Like It* speaks of a 'schoolboy … creeping like snail / Unwillingly to school' (2.7.145–7). Sundays were 'off' from school but not from church, and so on Sundays Shakespeare crept from Henley Street to Holy Trinity, passing the school room on the way – from the frying pan into the fire. From the age of six or seven until around the age fourteen this was his daily bread, a diet of words both secular and sacred.

The grammar school curriculum was stunningly ambitious at the time. In 1636, the teacher Charles Hoole wrote a tract on the state of English schools entitled *A New Discovery of the Old Art of Teaching School*, whose long subtitle concludes, *Shewing how Children in their playing years may Grammatically attain to a firm groundedness in an exercise of the Latin and Greek Tongues* (published in 1661). We might ask if there was anything at all playful about these playing years (Shakespeare's playing years were yet to come). At one point Hoole describes what a country education might have looked like in the late sixteenth century:

These [boys] were first put to read the Accidents [books of grammar], and afterwards made to commit it to memory; which when they had done, they were exercised in construing and which it was required to say four Lessons a day: but of the other forms, a part and a Lesson in the fore-noons, and a Lesson only in the after. The second form was to repeat the Accidents for Parts; to say fore-noons Lessons in *Propria quae maribus*, *Quae genus*, and As in *praesenti*, which they repeated *memoriter*, construed and parsed; to say an after-noon's lesson in *Sententiae Pueriles*, which they repeated by hart, and construed and parsed; they repeated their tasks every Friday *memoriter*, and parsed their Sentences out of the English.[2]

On and on it staggeringly goes through the seventh, eighth and ninth form, the last wholly occupied with Greek.

It was in these latter forms that Shakespeare met Ovid, Cicero and Virgil. If he made it to the seventh form, according to Hoole, he read Seneca's tragedies and translated them into English. While Shakespeare's own tragedies are not particularly Senecan, his familiarity with the form is evident. Schoolboys advanced through the forms by accomplishment not age, so Shakespeare may have worked his way through an impressive canon of English grammar, Greek testaments and Latin authors by the time he left school for good.

Shakespeare's plays make light of his grammar school education in scenes like *Merry Wives*' Latin lessons (featuring a schoolboy named 'William') or *Love's Labour's Lost*'s pedantic schoolmaster. But there is nothing of university life, such as in Christopher Marlowe's *Doctor Faustus*, which is a campus novel masquerading as verse drama. And that is for the obvious reason that Shakespeare did not go to university (unlike the author of *Faustus*). Few boys did at the time; only one boy born in Stratford in the year of Shakespeare's birth went on to university. He later entered the church.

However imperfect Shakespeare's Latin may have been, it is worth pausing to consider how extraordinary – and non-inevitable – it was that Shakespeare and his school chums turned off Church Street into a long, low, wattle-and-daub building, climbed the winding stairs to a vaulted school room and walked right in on ancient Rome. Cicero, Ovid and a host of antique others were the companions of Shakespeare's early life. It explains why his plays join that living classicism of the age, in which the fall of Troy seems as recent as the rise of the Tudors. In which the Tiber flowed into the Thames. It helps explain why the weather that warms so many of Shakespeare's plays is Mediterranean, not English.

In fact, despite his later dabbles in English history, it was not really the legends of England's past that fired Shakespeare's imagination. Where, for instance, are the adventures of Arthur in Shakespeare's plays? He and his knights errant have wandered off somewhere. Other than the odd reference to 'Arthur's bosom' as Falstaff's final resting place, you might think that nothing had been written between the moment Ovidius Naso put down his pen and Shakespeare picked up his. When Shakespeare thinks of a hoary old king, he thinks of Priam not Arthur. When he thinks of a young hero he thinks of Paris not Lancelot. Still, his imagination was a synthetic one, and so the classical past and his homely present filled up the same room. And thus in *A Midsummer Night's Dream* the trades union of Athens are full of men named Nick, Peter, Robin and Tom.

It is hard to overestimate the importance of Latin to Shakespeare's English. Two or three supremely lucky things happened to Shakespeare in 1564, then. He didn't die. Christopher Marlowe was born. And Arthur Golding Englished Ovid. For Golding's translation of Ovid's *Metamorphoses* appeared in the year of Shakespeare's birth. Now by the end of his school days, Shakespeare *could* have read Ovid in Latin – or *should* have been able to, if his schoolmaster did not spare the hornbook – but Golding guaranteed that he would not have to. Scholars have estimated that 90 per cent of Shakespeare's classical allusions are lifted from Ovid's tales.[3] Shakespeare was mad for Ovid all his life, from his first works to his last, and it was largely thanks to Arthur Golding.

It was also thanks to his teachers, so when we praise Shakespeare today we should spare them a thought. For to continue Shakespeare's string of good luck – which didn't run out until 1616 – Stratford's schoolmaster was unusually well-paid, 20 pounds per annum. Much more than the 12 pounds, 5 shillings at Warwick, better too than even the emoluments of a fellowship at Oxford or Cambridge. This handsome salary guaranteed a run of highly competent, or at least highly qualified, instructors to tutor Stratford's sons (though not its daughters).

Depending upon when exactly Will started school and precisely how long he stayed there, Shakespeare's schoolmaster was either Simon Hunt (*c.* 1571–5) or/and Thomas Jenkins (1575–9) – fellow of St John's Oxford. If Shakespeare stuck it out past the age of fifteen, he learned from John Cottam (1579–81). Did any of them glimpse a glimmer of genius in young Will Shakespeare (somehow one pictures him already balding)? Did any of them later stand in the yard of The Globe, taking in *Lear* or *Twelfth Night*, nudging strangers and muttering, 'taught him, didn't I?' What would it be like to plausibly claim that you taught Shakespeare everything he knows?

Forced to choose just two books that shaped Shakespeare – his desert island reading – we land on the *Metamorphoses* and the English Bible. For though Shakespeare, as Ewan Fernie points out, was not an 'orthodox or systematic religious

thinker'⁴ – like a Dante or a Milton – he was alive to the cadences
of the English Bible. This began at school and at church in
Stratford. (Recall that the catechism and Latin grammar were
both on the syllabus.) The two buildings – the Guild Chapel
and the school house – are right next door to one another,
just across the lane from New Place, where Shakespeare would
later live. He was born on Henley Street, but his imagination
was hatched just a few blocks away in a first-floor room next
to the Guild Chapel and right across the street from where he
would later breathe his last.

*

The school room segregated its students by forms, not age,
though the younger boys probably sat together conning their
ABCs while the older boys worked on their Latin and Greek.
One of those older boys was Richard Field, just a few years
ahead of William. He would leave for London when his
learning was done to serve for six years under the Huguenot
printer Thomas Vautrollier. Richard Field married Vautrollier's
widow in 1589 and inherited his thriving business, a common
occurrence in the world of print. It was Field who would print
Shakespeare's first works, three editions of his *Venus and
Adonis* (1593–6) and *The Rape of Lucrece* (1594) as well.

Field also produced a number of important English and
foreign works, including Holinshed's *Chronicles*, possibly
providing Shakespeare a lending library when he finally
turned up in London. Field may be the answer to the otherwise
puzzling question of how Shakespeare accessed the many,
varied and pricey books he plundered for his poetry and plays.
Field and Shakespeare may not have spent break-time plotting
what they would do when they got out of school (a long con
to reinvent English literature), but Richard Field blazed a trail
to London and possibly provided some initial connections for
William when he followed him there.

Looking at Stratford's King Edward VI school today – still
in use though much expanded – you cannot actually imagine
Shakespeare going to school there, much less conjugating

Latin verbs. But you can imagine what kind of student he might have been. In the commendatory poem that Ben Jonson contributed to the 1623 folio of Shakespeare's work, the second most famous thing he says is that Shakespeare had 'small Latin and less Greek'. (The most famous thing he said was that Shakespeare was 'not for an age but for all time'. One of the crueller ironies of literary history is that Ben Jonson's best known line is a compliment.)

Shakespeare probably did not best his school chums at Latin declensions, rattling off his 'hics' and 'hocs' without a hitch or halt. Ben Jonson's gift, or curse, was to always tell the truth, and as an ardent classicist he was in a position to judge Shakespeare's learning. If Shakespeare did not master Latin and Greek, however, he learned the sound of his own voice, one culled from a canon of masterful stylists.

Shakespeare had an excuse for his small Latin, which might have been larger had he not left school early – perhaps as early as 1577, at age thirteen – for he received another education in his early teens, one that likely forced him from school. That lesson was in economics, as his father's fortunes faltered. The crash had been coming for some time. On 4 July 1565, when William was just a year old, John Shakespeare had been tipped to join the fourteen bearded burgesses and other aldermen who administrated the borough of Stratford. More obligation than honour, public service came with a price. Officials were expected to make annual contributions to the Stratford coffers – up to ten pounds per annum for the bailiff. Public life apparently crushed the private gains John Shakespeare had made. In 1583 he was included in a suit filed by John Brown and 'pursued to the point of arrest'. The warrant was dropped because John Shakespeare was found to have 'nothing of which he could be distrained'.[5] By the early 1580s John Shakespeare had nothing left to lose.

*

Had Shakespeare been a better student would he have been a lesser playwright? Nicholas Rowe implied as much, claiming in the first biography of Shakespeare in 1709 that Shakespeare's

'Fire' was kindled by his 'Ignorance of the Ancients' and fuelled by his 'Imagination'.[6] This is an exaggeration, but Rowe is right in the sense that Shakespeare was a magpie reader, feathering his nest with threads of Ovid, patches from the Bible, yarns from Aesop. He follows no one thinker in particular but that did not prevent him from getting somewhere.

Consider at random Hamlet's suggestion that 'there is nothing either good or bad, but thinking makes it so' (2.2.250–1). We could hear in this posit an echo of the riddles of Heraclitus ('nature loves to hide') or the obscurities of Parmenides, his hexameter musings on 'What is' and 'What is not'. Or we could imagine Shakespeare weighing in on Protagoras' famous maxim that 'man is the measure of all things', taking up a pro-Protagoras and anti-Aristotelian position on truth. But this makes Shakespeare into a doxographer, not a dramatist. There is nothing dogmatic in Shakespeare's philosophy. It is of here and everywhere, a vagrant philosophy. His learning was greedy and appropriative, expedient and absorbent. His mind was catholic, even if his faith was not.

After a long day spent construing and parsing, construing and parsing, Shakespeare made the short walk back to the house on Henley Street, filled with the sound of siblings and the smell of his father's work. Along the way he passed New Place, which he may have eyed with envy as he to-and-froed to school each day. Of course, schoolboys often have other things on their minds than property acquisition. Like the conjugation of Latin verbs. As he would write some years later in *Romeo and Juliet*, 'Love goes toward love as schoolboys from their books, / But love from love, toward school with heavy looks' (2.2.156–7). Shakespeare probably escaped the daily grind in the pages of Ovid's *Metamorphoses*, but his next turning point was from books to love. For some time between the end of his schooldays and when he left for London he met a young woman at market or at church. For better or worse, her name was Anne Hathaway, unless it wasn't.

4

Anne Hathaway, aka

It's about a twelve-minute walk from Stratford to Shottery, eight if taken at a dead sprint – if, for instance, you're being chased by your future father-in-law. Let's split the difference and suppose Shakespeare took it in ten. As Juliet puts it, lovers go towards love a whole lot faster than schoolboys on their way toward school.

Where did Shakespeare meet his future wife, aka Anne Hathaway, who lived out of town in a charming cottage that you can tour today for £10.50 ('disappointing for the entrance fee' gripes an Irish visitor on tripadvisor.com)? Probably not at school, which was mostly an all-male enclave though some provisions were made for the education of girls at the time.[1] Maybe at church, 18-year-old Will making moon eyes at 26-year-old Anne during the collect. Maybe upon some Mayday outing or civic feast or holiday rite. Or introduced by their parents since John Shakespeare was friendly enough with Richard Hathaway to pay off some of his debts in 1566. No one knows, but the fact remains that William met Anne sometime before 1582, and the marriage was clapped up quicker than you can say 'unlaced stomacher'.

Many years later, in 1609, when Shakespeare's sonnets were printed, they include a poem he could have written during his courtship of Anne. It suggests that among the things that attracted him to Anne was her name, which he found pregnant with meaning (to get ahead of ourselves).

Those lips that Love's own hand did make,
Breathed forth the sound that said 'I hate',
To me that languished for her sake:
But when she saw my woeful state,
Straight in her heart did mercy come,
Chiding that tongue that ever sweet
Was used in giving gentle doom;
And taught it thus anew to greet;
'I hate' she altered with an end,
That followed it as gentle day,
Doth follow night, who like a fiend
From heaven to hell is flown away.
      'I hate', from hate away she threw,
      And saved my life, saying 'not you'.[2]

She married him anyway. The penultimate line – '"I hate", from hate away she threw' – tells us her last name 'Hathaway' opened with some 'gentle doom'. It was pronounced 'hate' not 'hath'. This spared Shakespeare some smutty jokes from fellow actors that his wife 'hath a way' about her. It also suggests that she married Shakespeare out of pity, which Olivia in *Twelfth Night* calls a 'degree to love', though possibly not the highest one.

One of the oddest things Shakespeare did was to beget a child before he begot a play. Unique among his fellow playwrights, he was a family man well before he had a livelihood. The Shakespeares welcomed their first daughter to the world about six months after they wed. People were shorter back then, but gestation periods were not. Anne was pregnant when they wed, so the marriage could have been made in haste, not heaven.

Marriages were less formal then than now. Marriage certificates, as we now know them, did not exist yet. Elizabethan custom allowed that a 'troth plight' before friends – an exchange of vows – had the force of a civil ceremony. If William and Anne plighted their troth in front of friends, then this means that by custom – if not law – the Shakespeares were wed when they first went to bed. Anne's pregnancy may not have been a scandal.

Still, it's not hard to find stern warnings against pre-marital sex at the time. In the *Commendations of Matrimony*, the rector of St Anne's, Aldersgate warns couples not to 'fleshly meddle together as man and wife afore such time as that matrimony be approved'.[3] By the time the Shakespeares formalized their wedding in a church, they'd evidently done some fleshly meddling.

That was not the only irregularity. The records of the wedding obscure where they should enlighten, since the registry has Shakespeare marrying a woman named 'Anne Whately of Temple Grafton', whereas the bond reads 'Hathwey' of Stratford. Marriage often changes a woman's last name, but that usually happens after the marriage, not before it.

On balance, the archives point to Anne, daughter of Richard Hathaway of Hewlands, Shottery, as Shakespeare's wife. So unless Shakespeare had a penchant for marrying serial Annes, there is an error here. Some honest clerical goof up that confused the names of parties and places. The diligence of scholars has revealed that the clerk who wrote 'Anne Whately' elsewhere mixed up 'Edgock' for 'Elcock' and 'Darby' for 'Bradeley.' The crude homonyms of 'Hathaway' and 'Whately' might be a clue. Maybe Anne had a cold and 'Hathaway' came out 'Whately' through clogged midland sinuses.

Anne's pregnancy and the confusion of names are still not the only irregularities surrounding Shakespeare's marriage. William was young – not Juliet-young, but a minor – and so needed his father's consent. He was only eighteen at a time when young men normally waited until their mid-twenties (until they'd served an apprenticeship or their fathers died and they'd inherited the means to set up a household). In fact, William was one of just three known teenage bridegrooms to marry in Stratford between 1570 to 1640. Anne was twenty-six and so just a bit older than was common for women at the time of marriage. William was quite young to be getting married, Anne slightly old.

For whatever reason, they were in a hurry to be wed and canon law required that the 'banns' be read three times in church on successive Sundays. The same canon law forbid the reading of the banns between Advent and Epiphany, however, and the window had closed. On 28 November, therefore, Fulke Sandells and John Richardson – farmer friends of Anne's deceased father – rode the twenty-one miles west to Worcester to fetch a special dispensation, and not only because William was so young but because the couple lacked the banns. The Bishop of Worcester, the firebrand reformer John Whitgift, approved a bond that bound Sandells and John for £40 as surety for the marriage to indemnify the Bishop against future damages should anything go awry with the marriage. The way was cleared for Anne and William to meddle fleshly on the windy side of canon law.

That they married is clear from the records. *Where* they married is not. The errant clerk may have got Anne's name wrong but the place of the wedding right. Perhaps the marriage *was* in Temple Grafton, overseen by a hawk enthusiast named John Frith who was 'Unsound in religion', according to a 1586 survey of the Warwickshire clergy.[4] (In *As You Like It*, Touchstone the clown opts for an 'unsound' priest to preside at his marriage since 'not being well married, it will be a good excuse for me to leave my wife' [3.3.84]. Shakespeare would leave his wife over and over and over again, but that is yet to come.) Baptized and buried in Holy Trinity Church, Shakespeare was not married there. It is one of the only family matters he ever conducted outside of Stratford.

Back to Juliet for a moment. What's in a name? A good question, and so here's another: Why does history not call Shakespeare's wife 'Anne Shakespeare' but always 'Anne Hathaway'? Is there some reluctance to couple Shakespeare? Must singular men remain single? The fact is that Shakespeare was a married man from the age of eighteen until death did him part, and he shared his life with a wife named 'Anne Shakespeare'. In fact, 'Anne' and 'Agnes' – pronounced 'Annis' – were used interchangeably in the period. In 1581, Richard

Hathaway left money to a daughter 'Agnes', then unmarried. It is quite possible that the woman known to history as 'Anne Hathaway' was called 'Agnes Shakespeare' by her husband and her friends.

Still, history has tried to preserve Anne in her maiden state or make of her an unfortunate accessory to the blameless poet. In the terms of many scholars and artists, their wedding was a shotgun affair between the reluctant Will and grasping Anne due to their 'antenuptial fornication' as one commentator put it with, somehow, demure crudity.[5] Anne is a regrettable appendage, Shakespeare's beard.

'Antenuptial fornication' is far from the worst of it, for history has roughed up Anne for her temerity in marrying William Shakespeare. A sorry sample includes Samuel Schoenbaum, who calls Anne the 'fading siren of Shottery';[6] Augustine Skottowe, who concludes that Shakespeare 'Neither bettered his circumstances, nor elevated himself in society by the conversion';[7] Thomas Campbell who castigates Anne Hathaway for 'decoying her man into a match made which (since he was a stripling and she a mature woman) does her no credit';[8] and John Britton, who suggests that Anne mothered bastards along with her legitimate children. Anne's 'unfaithfulness' shows up again in James Joyce's *Ulysses*. She is described, crudely and cruelly, in Bill Cain's play *Equivocation* (2009) as 'constantly rutting'. (*Constantly?*) Richard Grant White sniffs that Anne 'came to [Shakespeare] with a stain upon her name .... Should we not wish that one of them, even if it were he, had not died before that ill-starred marriage?'[9] This chilling scenario of better-dead-than-wed is only worsted by a popular biography series that tells students that Shakespeare 'married a pregnant orphan named Anne Hathaway' without noting the important detail that it was Shakespeare who got her pregnant.[10]

The misogyny behind the treatment of Anne stinks to heaven. Firmly put, there is no evidence that the marriage was an unhappy one, not the second best bed, not the fact that Shakespeare spent many years in London, not the absence of merry connubiality in his plays (though the Macbeths seem to get on okay). In truth, there is little evidence to the state of the marriage of William and Agnes. They did spend the last five years of William's life together in a big house in Stratford, close to their two surviving children. If we seek evidence of their relationship, this evidence must be weighed.

William Shakespeare was not financially independent at the time of his wedding. In fact Anne was a minor heiress who brought more to the table than he. 'Anne Hathaway's cottage' – as it is now known – was not a cottage. It was a substantial farmhouse on a substantial farm, and her father left her nearly seven pounds to be delivered on her wedding day. What did Shakespeare have going for him? He still lived at home on Henley Street and may not have entered upon a trade as yet. In his popular biography of Shakespeare, Anthony Burgess writes that young William offered (cover your eyes) 'auburn hair, melting eyes, ready tongue, tags of Latin poetry', but melting eyes don't pay the bills when baby needs a new pair of shoes.[11]

Shakespeare 'got Anne in the family way' in another sense then – for once she welcomed a daughter and a set of twins not long after, there were four adults and seven children now living on Henley Street, turning a full house into a crowded one. Four adults and four kids under the age of three. Every member of the family was in the family's way. The noise must have been as constant as the laundry.

Those seven children included Shakespeare's siblings but also his daughter Susanna, born and then baptized on 26 May 1583, and the twins Judith and Hamnet, baptized on 2 February 1585. Hamnet and Judith were named after a baker and his wife, Hamnet (or Hamlet) and Judith Sadler, who served as godparents to their namesakes. The temptation to think that Shakespeare had Hamlet the Dane on his mind all his life runs into this more banal explanation, though Shakespeare may have been struck by coincidence when he later came across the story of Hamlet, prince of Denmark. It is revealing that Shakespeare named his first and only son after a friend, and not himself.

And so Anne and William raised three children during their years on Henley Street. Whatever William did to earn a crust during these years, it was to help fill the mouths of three young children. He may have left Stratford for London not to find peace and quiet but to find some cash. His marriage had done little to lift the fortunes of the family Shakespeare. Anne had a dowry but hers was another mouth to feed, along with the three children. However happy the marriage, it wasn't a profitable one. The 'lost years' – treated below – may have been hard ones.

*

There is a real possibility that Anne or Agnes Shakespeare never saw a play that her husband wrote. Never turned up on an opening night to natter over drinks at the after party. It is hard to get a sense of the social status of the wife of a working playwright at the time. Her husband was absent a great deal of the time, but the money made its way home. The household at New Place might have been the source of at least mild curiosity among the folk of Stratford. A thriving homestead powered in part by capital from the capital. The coins of London apprentices, merchants' wives and larking law students flowed in a steady stream, against the current, from London to Stratford. Paying for new leading on the sloping roof, pewter bowls for dipping fingers greasy from supper, linens and lace for Shakespeare's daughters. Theatre is a commercial practice that persuades audiences to turn over something for nothing, and all those afternoons of leisurable nothings materialized 100 miles to the north-west in the beds and board of New Place, managed successfully by William's wife, Agnes Shakespeare.

5

The Lost Years

The list of jobs Shakespeare allegedly held during his 'lost years' is almost longer than the list of jobs he didn't. Teacher, servant, clerk, actor – the number of theories is directly inverse to the absence of evidence. We have little enough sense of what he did between school and marriage, but we have even less of what he did for ten years between wedding Anne and living in London. We spot him one last time at the twins' baptism in 1585 (if he went). But then he slips into the shadows until 1592, when fellow playwright Robert Greene insults him by calling him 'upstart crow beautified with our feathers' (treated below in '*Enter London*'). Greene's insult tells us that Shakespeare had made a name for himself in London by the early 1590s, even if that name was mud. But how he got from here to there – Stratford to London – is unknown ('horseback' is the literal answer, also treated below).

He may have helped his father make gloves for seven years. He may have taught school or tutored toffs. He may have served as household help or toured as an actor. These notions are not mutually exclusive. He could have helped his dad out around the shop, served as assistant (or 'usher') to the schoolmaster, done a turn as a lawyer's clerk before he fell in with a cry of players in need of a pair of reliable legs and lungs. He was certainly a husband, father and provider for three young children, but for nearly one-eighth of his life – critical years, formative ones between the ages of twenty-one and twenty-eight when many literary prodigies fire up and flame out – biography draws a blank.

The popular idea that Shakespeare was a schoolmaster comes from John Aubrey, who interviewed William Beeston about fifty years after Shakespeare's death. Beeston's father Christopher had been an apprentice actor with Shakespeare's company in the 1590s. (If you're keeping track, that makes this information third-hand, and should be treated as cautiously as a third hand.) Beeston told Aubrey that Shakespeare 'had been in his younger years a schoolmaster in the country'. As noted in 'Shakespeare at School' above, his plays are sprinkled with school-house scenes and feature the odd schoolmaster, some of them very odd, like Holofernes in *Love's Labour's Lost*. Holofernes is never lost for words though often lost in them. He is a prototype of the 'absent-minded professor' whose brain dizzies with linguistic niceties but who cannot tie his shoes. It could be a caricature of one of his own teachers. It could be a self-portrait.

If Shakespeare did teach school, he probably worked with 'petties', children too young for grammar school, since he lacked the university education needed to teach older children. If so, none of his charges ever thought to brag about the fact – at least not for the record – that they'd been taught by Shakespeare in their infancy ('I knew him when he was *nothing, a teacher!*'). But Shakespeare's celebrity was only ever minor during his lifetime, and even his longest-lived pupil would have died well before his fame truly ascended. The evidence that Shakespeare was a teacher is thin but about as deep as it gets during Shakespeare's seven-year apprenticeship in anonymity.

The great eighteenth-century editor of Shakespeare, Edmond Malone, thought he was a law clerk not a teacher in these years, which has endeared Shakespeare to lawyers ever since. Legal work was plentiful in Shakespeare's time since litigation was England's favourite pastime until the rise of football. Shakespeare's facile fist would have come in handy with the great drifts of paperwork that litigation leaves behind.

Still, had Shakespeare served as a lawyer's clerk, he would have witnessed any number of wills and thus recorded his name upon at least *some* of them. And yet, tireless searches of Stratford records have uncovered no such documents. On balance, teachers and lawyers vying for a Shakespearean lineage are playing to a scoreless draw, though teachers might just squeak through on penalties.

A less plausible but more provocative theory of Shakespeare's location during the lost years has flickered across the last century. That theory suggests that Shakespeare was a household servant in Lancashire in the home of Alexander Hoghton of Lea Hall, near Preston in the north of England. In Hoghton's will of 3 August 1581, he includes a clause that one of his servants, a 'William Shakeshafte', would pass into the service of his brother-in-law, Thomas Hesketh, upon his death. In the preceding clause, Hoghton also disposes of 'his instruments belonging to musics, & all manner of play clothes' to Hesketh should his own brother Thomas not wish to 'keep & maintain players'.[1] So Hoghton had a servant named 'William Shakeshafte' who was a musician and possibly an actor in the early 1580s. Was this musical William Shakeshafte William Shakespeare of Stratford?

The theory gains in intrigue due to the family's Catholic sympathies. Acting for Catholics does not make one an active Catholic, but the theory has some obvious attractions. It picks two locks for the price of one, locating Shakespeare during the lost years and revealing his 'true' religion. One mark against this theory is that William's surname was 'Shakespeare' not 'Shakeshafte'. Names *were* fluid in this era of orthographical promiscuity. In fact Shakespeare's name appears in multiple forms across the age – Shaksper, Shakspere, Shaks, Shakspe, Shakspeare – and those are just his own signatures. But 'Shakespeare' and 'Shakeshafte' are manifestly different names though they have obvious similarities (every spear is a shaft, though not every shaft is a spear).

For that matter, the name 'Shakeshafte' was a common one. Between 1530 and 1630, around 120 'Shakeshafte' baptisms, marriages and burials occurred in Lancashire alone. It would not be odd to find a young player named 'Will Shakeshafte' in Lancashire in the 1580s who was a wholly different person from 'Will Shakespeare' of Stratford. There are also discrepancies in ages, leading one scholar to conclude that 'William Shakeshafte' is not our budding playwright. The 'more likely but distinctly less-exciting scenario' is 'that William Shakeshafte was a middle-aged man born and bred in Lancashire'.[2]

On balance, Shakespeare probably did not play the Vice or the *viol de gamba* to while away long winter nights in Lea Hall, Lancashire. But the Shakeshafte theory has one thing going for it that other theories lack. It accounts for the fact that sometime during these seven years Shakespeare became an actor. But how? When? And with whom? The 'upstart crow' wasn't fully fledged by the time Greene accused him of feathering himself with borrowed plumes, but at some point during his 'lost years' Shakespeare left the nest and learned to sing.

Of all the moments we might most want to witness – the moment Shakespeare first met Richard Burbage, the moment he first scrawled the words 'who's there?' at the top of a sheet of paper, the moment he and his fellows opened The Globe Theatre – of all those moments we might wish to watch the very first time he stepped before an audience to recite some words that he'd taken to heart. This could have been on any number of 'stages': a hastily mounted market-place scaffold, at the head of a school room before tittering boys, the fire-lit great room of a landed lord, the guildhall of a provincial town before a murmur of snoring burghers, etc. Wherever it happened, whatever kind of 'play' it was (morality, interlude, Whitsun pastoral) at some point during the 'lost years' Shakespeare became an actor.

To understand how Shakespeare became Shakespeare, we have to pause and take a look at the theatre industry in Shakespeare's youth. A glib account of the 'theatre industry in Shakespeare's youth' would be that there wasn't one, not in the sense we mean it. This is not to say there was not theatre. To the contrary. Theatre was *everywhere* when Shakespeare was a boy. Maskings, mummings, dancing, drumming, quasi-liturgical drama, feast-day frivolities, pedagogic drama performed in Latin, skimmingtons, ridings and other shaming rituals. Even the magnificent cycle dramas – allegedly suppressed after the Reformation – were still performed annually at Coventry, just twenty miles north-east of Stratford, until 1578. Elizabethan England was a culture of performance. Kid Shakespeare could hardly avoid the stuff.

But what about 'professional' drama? Things you would pay money for? Powerful Earls and Lords might patronize companies who toured the land, broadcasting their patron's image and retailing their agendas. The Earls of Leicester, Sussex, Oxford, Derby and more all had companies trouping the country in their livery. These patrons did not profit directly from the drama, but patronage had its privileges. Think of a corporate sponsor of a football club today, whose economic return is more ambient than immediate. A Lord might 'profit' by having his company selected to play at court, where politics were always oblique. This was a time where a courtier might stage a costly masque to signal his displeasure at the persecution of the Presbyteriat. 'Professional' theatre was produced not for profit but for posturing, not for the cause of art but in the service of courtly advancement.

For all the theatrical activity at court, there were scores of playing companies all over England in the employ of sub-aristocratic patrons. Think only of Hoghton's will and the players he maintained. This is private and domestic drama not the public and 'professional' kind. It is also local. The players probably performed for Hoghton's and then Hesketh's neighbours, an expression of reciprocal hospitality. There were likely dozens of such companies throughout the land, attached to great houses, touring locally, leaving little behind in the way of archival records. The line between 'professional' drama and the amateur kind is, in this period, blurry to the point of invisibility.

The more powerfully patronized theatre companies in Shakespeare's youth might be made up of half-a-dozen lead actors, as many hired men, and a few boys to play the ladies and to fetch the drinks. They travelled England's highways and byways on foot and by horse. Ben Jonson's Tucca in *Poetaster* describes life on the road as having 'to travel with thy pumps full of gravel … after a blind jade and a hamper, and stalk upon boards and barrel heads to an old crack'd trumpet' (3.1.144–5). So much for the glamour of show biz.

Such companies visited Stratford under the flag of their patron. In fact the 'lost years' were good ones for Stratford if you were a theatre fan. Between 1572 and 1583 alone, thirteen companies played in Stratford – the finest in the land: Leicester's Men, Warwick's Men, Worcester's Men, Strange's, Essex's, Derby's and Lord Berkeley's Men. Five companies visited Stratford in 1587 alone, one of which, the Queen's Men, received twenty shillings for their pains, a handsome payday. Any one of these mobile companies could have punched Shakespeare's ticket out of town.

Shakespeare had privileged access to these actors since his father was the first Stratford bailiff to allow visiting players to perform there. Maybe Shakespeare took in his first play standing between his father's knees – John Shakespeare's tanned hands covering Will's ears at the bawdy bits – watching a group of travelling actors perform the 'Bailiff's play', a gratuity offered in exchange for the right to play for profit in the town.[3] Two of John Shakespeare's sons entered the trade – William and his younger brother Edmond – and so John Shakespeare seems to have been not wholly hostile to the art.

So in addition to (or instead of) working in gloves, teaching school, drafting deeds or playing the lute, he may have been a strolling player during his lost years (not a wandering one. Minstrels wander, players stroll). However he met them, he probably got his start travelling the provinces with a group of actors and eventually made his way into the large group of players travelling under the Queen's name.

For in 1583, just after Shakespeare married Anne or Agnes, Queen Elizabeth plundered a few of the touring companies to form an all-star-troupe of her own, the 'Queen's Men', the finest band in all the land. The Queen may or may not have liked plays, but she did not form the 'Queen's Men' out of her fondness for verse drama. If she did like plays, she could simply summon a troupe to court at her whim. One of her favourites, the Earl of Leicester, for instance, had a group of players who often entertained at court. In fact it was Leicester's troupe, among a couple others, that she raided when she formed the Queen's Men, taking half of the known names for her new company from Leicester's old one. There's no record of how he took it. He was probably publicly polite and then went home to grumble to his pheasants.

The Queen had Sir Francis Walsingham, her spymaster and all-round fixer, form the company. To do so, he consulted the Master of the Revels, Edmund Tilney. As Master of the Revels it was Tilney's job to arrange entertainment at court each Christmas, and he probably knew which actors pleased the Queen and which ones got up her nose. But the Queen's Men were not formed to pass the time between courses of figgy pudding. They were put together primarily for touring. The Queen and Walsingham understood the political advantage of advertising the Queen's largesse throughout the land via a group of talented players touring under her pennant.

So the Queen's Men were built for speed, a road show, a rolling-thunder review that retailed the Queen's munificence and beneficence – as well as her brand of moderate Protestantism – across her realm. They owned plays of *The Famous Victories of Henry V*, *King Leir* and *King John*, plays that Shakespeare later rewrote. It is therefore likely that sometime between 1585 and 1592 Shakespeare joined the company. These plays lived in his mouth and memory until he had the time and talent to put them into his own words.

At least one question nags this theory. How did Shakespeare ascend from grammar school drop-out to an actor in the Queen's Men, a gang of all-star players culled from the cream of the crop? He may have had his chance in 1587, when the Queen's Men visited Stratford. One of their leading men, William Knell (whose name also had some 'gentle doom' about it), had just been killed in a fight in June, and the company reached Stratford not long after that. Knell's end may have been Will's break.

It is not likely. Had the Queen's Men showed up in Stratford down a man and tapped the glover's son, it would be like calling a fan from the stands to start for Manchester United. A less romantic but more likely version is that Shakespeare cut his teeth with another company and then made his way into the Queen's Men before the end of the 1580s.

During Shakespeare's infancy and adolescence, theatre in England was a combination of amateur dramatics conducted at the local level – on one hand – and a practice controlled by a coterie of aristocrats on the other. Chalk it up to luck once more. The job he ended up doing did not exist when he was born, but by the time he did it, it did.

*

However divergent, all the theories of Shakespeare's lost years find him in the word trade, pushing them across the page, coaxing them from the mouths of school boys, memorizing lines from *Clyomon and Clamydes* and then mesmerizing audiences from Bristol to Bartlow. But in a rare turn for Shakespeare biography, the most romantic explanation requires the least guess work. Since Shakespeare became a playwright, it stands to reason that he entered the trade during his 'lost' years. We can flirt with romance just far enough to imagine that Shakespeare first travelled to London with a group of players, singing dirty ballads while they descended the Great North Road, laying bets on who would be first to spy one of London's hundred steeples, prompting a player to cry out what remains, to this day, London's allure: 'A spire! A spire!'

This story deserves a dash of cold water, since the romance of Shakespeare's 'lost years' is curdled by a couple of facts. In Michaelmas Term 1588 the name 'William Shakespeare of Stratford' shows up twice in a bill of complaint brought before the Queen's Bench in Westminster. He is identified further as the son of 'John Shakespeare', suggesting that William's first trip to London might not have been as a strolling player but as the literate agent of his father's lawsuit.

There was an unwritten rule of Elizabethan jurisprudence that all legal matters must immediately assume the most complicated form of themselves possible. Thus, the suit brought by John Shakespeare against Edmund Lambert in 1588 is of fiendish complexity (and it's one of the simpler suits that Shakespeare got entangled in during his life). It was a family matter and therefore a nasty one. Edmund Lambert was husband to Joan Arden, Shakespeare's aunt on his mother's side. When Shakespeare's father ran out of money in the late 1570s he tried to raise some cash by mortgaging to Lambert a piece of property called 'Asbies' that his wife owned. The arrangement quickly devolved from complicated to complex to a Queen's Bench complaint and dragged on for years, making Christmas awkward for everyone.

On 26 September 1587 Edmund Lambert's son John agreed to pay the Shakespeares twenty pounds for an outright title to Asbies. Since William was heir to his father, he is named in the agreement. But the deal was sealed by a handshake only, and the money never materialized. Shakespeare's father chased the twenty pounds through the Stratford Court of Record but could not catch up to it. And thus, a complainant's bill of 1588 names '*Johannes Shakespeare et Maria uxor eius, simulcum Willielmo Shakespeare filio suo*' ('the said John Shakespeare and Mary his wife, together with William Shakespeare their son').[4] The case was delayed – they always were – and shows up as late as 1597 when the Shakespeares reopened the interminable affair in the court of Chancery.

The immediate question is whether William travelled to London alone or with his father to press the case in 1588 (perhaps he checked in with school chum Richard Fields to see how he was getting on). If the 24-year-old William made his maiden voyage to London in 1588, he could have visited The Rose on London's Southbank or The Theatre in Shoreditch to see what the capital had to offer. He could have taken in

Marlowe's *Tamburlaines*, Greene's *Friar Bacon*, Kyd's *Hamlet* or a score-and-a-half of other plays that live in the archive now known as 'lost'.

This *nouveau* drama may have looked quite different from the stuff he'd been served in Stratford, though this sets up a contrast between the taste of urban sophisticates and the musty fare of country bumpkins. What might have impressed Shakespeare as novel were not the plays but the playhouses. Perhaps these purpose-built playhouses instilled some confidence in young Shakespeare that there was something to this theatre game. It was always real estate that most impressed Shakespeare.

Whatever he did for these seven 'lost' years, besides raise a family alongside Anne, Shakespeare was *not* one of those precocious children who dazzle their parents and irritate others with their early onset genius. Mozart whistling concertos before he had his teeth. Da Vinci working out the physics of flight before he could even walk. Or consider Shakespeare's exact contemporary, Galileo Galilei, re-ordering the universe before he had turned thirty. While Galileo was peering at the stars through a homemade telescope in Pisa, William was fumbling with Anne's laces in a Warwickshire hedgerow.

The nearer parallel to Shakespeare is, again, Christopher Marlowe, who provides a startling contrast. He completed his canon by 1593, while Shakespeare was just getting started. So while Shakespeare may have been wiping the noses of schoolboys in Stratford, Marlowe was writing both parts of *Tamburlaine*, his *Faustus*, *Edward II*, 'Hero and Leander' and more. (He was, at the least, reading Lucan at Cambridge when Shakespeare was wedding Anne.) Shakespeare's career was not to be the parabolic flight of Marlowe, however, the Elizabethan Icarus. Shakespeare was something of a late bloomer. But if his literary output started relatively late, he wrote at a steady clip once he got up to speed, roughly two plays per annum for almost twenty years. He was the tortoise to Marlowe's hare.

The 'lost years' were not lost on Shakespeare. They are lost to us only because during these years Shakespeare failed to make a mark. He and Anne had no more children (for whatever reason). He did not publish (on page or on stage). He did not purchase any real estate (because he had no money). And he did not sue anyone (because he had no leverage). Though these years may have been crowded with incidents, he made no contact with the world that left an indelible imprint, an archival scrap for future ages to make a meal of. Something may yet emerge to tell us what he got up to, but the trail goes cold in the mid-1580s before heating up in 1592. By then Shakespeare had made enough of a splash on the London stage to take the starch out of Robert Greene's collar.

6

Stratford in the Rear View

Stratford's Avon seems, impossibly, to have no depth, only surface. The bridges that span it look less like bridges than braces, holding the two banks in place lest the river nudge them still further apart. Its flow reminds us of the passage of years, all those currents that have passed between the banks since the time Shakespeare walked them, dowsing for the right words. The Avon is also suggestive of Shakespeare's departure from Stratford, since he, like the Avon, made a measured exit from the town.

Of all the turning and returning points in Shakespeare's life, his departure from Stratford is the most significant. In many respects, this is *the* moment that matters the most. Shakespeare leaves Stratford for London where his future waits for him. And yet, maddeningly or marvellously, this is the period of Shakespeare's life about which we know the least. We are forced to choose the term we prefer to describe his exit: Shakespeare departed, moved, fled, escaped, lit out, made his way, journeyed, re-located …. Do we say he 'fell in with a group of strolling players'? Or that he 'fled the dullness of provincial Stratford'? Or he left, 'determined to make his fortune in London'? How passive, active, desperate, aspirational was W.S. at this time? A man on the make or a boy with a problem?

Was he Dick Whittington or Tom Joad? Sal Paradise or Bilbo Baggins? Because Shakespeare wasn't leaving for good. His was a journey of there-and-back-again. And again. And again.

(Here the Avon comparison breaks down since it only flows one way. We might look to the Thames, a tidal river that has it both ways.) Perhaps the to-and-fro from Stratford to London and to Stratford once again is indicative less of a restless soul than what we would call today 'compartmentalization'. London for work, Stratford for life. Not to say that Shakespeare never wrote in Stratford, perhaps in the back garden at New Place, scribbling a bit and growing quietly drunk on home brew as the evening fell.

We should not make too much of this there-and-back-again business, as if Shakespeare was one of Tolkien's hobbits. (Tolkien was dismayed by Shakespeare, by the way. He thought that Shakespeare got his elves all wrong.) Speaking of Tolkien, in a review of his *Fellowship of the Ring*, W.H. Auden wrote, 'All quests are concerned with some numinous object, the waters of life, the grail, buried treasure, etc.'[1] If we want to think of Shakespeare as a quester, what was he seeking in London? Immortality? Immorality? Or did he just want to make his daily bread, and send some crumbs back home to the family? Or escape from the crowded house on Henley Street?

Washington Irving imagines Shakespeare dreaming of himself in the 'temple of fame', then waking from the dream, determined to 'make for London'.[2] The Austrian psychoanalyst (the other one) Otto Rank claimed that, 'many poets commence their poetic careers with a flight which for them signifies emancipation from parents and siblings …'. Still others suggest he 'absconded to the Capital' to escape the clutches of the village seductress or criminal prosecution from a landed tyrant.[3] A more sober scholar concludes that, 'no one knows when, how and why Shakespeare left his wife and family in order to perform on the stage in London …'.[4] We do not even know that Shakespeare left Stratford 'in order to perform on the stage'. He may have left in order to get his dad's twenty pounds back.

The view of his 'escape' from Stratford is coloured, even technicolored, by one of the most vivid anecdotes about Shakespeare's youth – that he was caught red-handed poaching deer. The 'facts' are as follows, according to Nicholas Rowe's 1709 biography. Shakespeare fell in with a crew of local toughs who, for a lark, liked to poach Sir Thomas Lucy's deer on his Charlecote estate, four miles up the Avon from Stratford. Shakespeare was caught up the creek and Rowe concludes,

> he was prosecuted by that Gentleman, as he thought, somewhat too severely; and in order to revenge that ill Usage, he made a Ballad upon him. And though this, probably the first Essay of his Poetry, be lost, yet it is said to have been so very bitter, that it redoubled the Prosecution against him to that degree, that he was obliged to leave his Business and Family in *Warwickshire*, for some time, and shelter himself in *London*.[5]

A lithograph from 1869 shows Shakespeare before Sir Thomas Lucy, in which the young Shakespeare is already balding. He would have been about twenty-three.

Rowe was just amplifying an echoing anecdote. It shows up first – though anecdotes have no origin – in the accounts of a wandering clergyman, Richard Davies, who in the late seventeenth century noted it in his memorandum. He suggests that 'Shakespeare was much given to all unluckiness in stealing venison and rabbits', particularly from Lucy, which eventually made him 'fly his native country to his great advancement'.[6] Perhaps young William was just desperate to feed the many mouths in Henley Street.

There's an element of Robin Hood to this tale that's wildly attractive. Shakespeare sticking it to the big shot by ventilating his deer, then shooting like an arrow from disgrace to fame. The story provides an outlaw origin for the journey up to London, where the rest is history (and comedy, and tragedy …).

The anecdote is also at odds with what we elsewhere know of the even-keeled Shakespeare, one scrupulous about the law, though not above dodging the tax man. Margreta de Grazia has pointed out the non-conformity between Shakespearean anecdotes and the documentary evidence for the conduct of his life. 'Why is the Shakespeare of the anecdotes at such variance with the Shakespeare of the biographies?' she asks.[7] She concludes that Shakespearean anecdotes emphasize his wild side – deer poaching, heavy drinking, citizen fornicating – not as a form of biography but as a kind of literary criticism. Our sense of Shakespeare's pen – so fluid, so quick, so altogether unblotting – requires and so produces a writer whose ungoverned actions match his ungovernable art. Shakespearean anecdotes don't give us the life he led, they give us the life we need.

When Shakespeare left Stratford for London, it was probably not like Dick Whittington and his cat, Bilbo and his ring, or Clyde Barrow on the lam from the law. His trip was neither a chancer nor an epic. It may have simply been a business trip. These aggrandizing explanations of his flight out of Stratford disguise how un-epic a journey it was. Even by foot it isn't much of a quest from the Midlands to London. It probably took Shakespeare just a day or two to get from Stratford to the capital, or just a little bit less than it takes today to get from Heathrow to Stratford by public transportation.

There were two good roads from Stratford to London, which carters and carriers travelled often. The vast majority of treks at the time were taken on foot, in woollen stockings and leather shoes, which sold in vast numbers. If Shakespeare first went to London with a group of players, he likely took it like Ben Jonson's Tucca, on foot behind a wagon loaded with theatrical gimcrack and grotty costumes.

In later years, on solo sojourns, he might have hired a horse, which were as available then as rental cars today. If he was feeling thrifty and didn't want to spring for overnight lodging, he could have just managed the trip in a day. The English traveller Fynes Moryson, just two years younger than Shakespeare, remarked that the English 'ride from day break to the evening without drawing bit, neither sparing their horses nor themselves, hence is the Proverb, that England is Hell of Horses'. If so, Shakespeare would have required a series of post horses picked up from ostlers along the way. No single mount could have covered that distance in a day.[8]

It is more likely that Shakespeare broke the trip in two. If legend holds, he did so in Oxford, where he lay at the sign of the Bush. There was a wine-house he favoured called the Crown Tavern fronting the Cornmarket just off the High Street, close to the main highway from Stratford. The wineshop was run by John Davenant, a sober wine merchant (never trust a sober vintner, a thin baker or lethargic barista). His wife was apparently as pleasant as he was melancholy, however, and anecdotes suggest that Shakespeare stopped over in Oxford for more than a tipple.

The story shows up in multiple versions across the late seventeenth and early eighteenth century. It was boosted by the son of the establishment, the playwright William Davenant, who boasted that Shakespeare was his biological father. Existing in multiple versions, a canonical form was told at dinner by Alexander Pope in the mid-1750s and recorded by William Oldys:

> If tradition may be trusted, Shakespeare often baited [lodged] at the Crown Inn or Tavern in Oxford, in his journey to and from London. The landlady was a woman of great beauty and sprightly wit; and her husband, Mr. John Davenant, (afterward mayor of that city) a grave melancholy man, who as well as his wife used much to delight in Shakespeare's pleasant company. Their son young Will Davenant (afterwards Sir William) was then a little school-boy in the town, of about seven or eight years old, and so fond also of Shakespeare, that whenever he heard of his arrival, he would fly from school to see him. One day an old townsman observing the boy running homeward almost out of breath, asked him whither he was posting in that heat and hurry. He answered, to see his *god*-father Shakespeare. There's a good boy, said the other, but have a care that you don't take *God's* name in vain.[9]

The anecdote pulls off the neat trick of being simultaneously cute and smutty. The keeper of the Bodleian library, Thomas

Hearne, noted the anecdote as well and dryly glossed the gag after recording that Shakespeare was Davenant's godfather, 'In all probability he got him.'[10]

William Davenant was a splendid writer, the author of poetry, panegyric and plays, including *The Wits*, *The Siege of Rhodes*, *The Playhouse to be Let* and many more. He also wrote a tragedy called *The Unfortunate Lovers* (1638) but found nothing unfortunate in the love between Shakespeare and his mother. As unsober as his father was abstemious – the grape fell far from the vine – he liked to retell the anecdote when he'd had a few. William Davenant was willing to be a bastard if it meant that Shakespeare was his father.

When he was not enjoying a layover in Oxford, or at home in Stratford, or at work in London, Shakespeare was on the road, a word he uses to mean a highway in *1 Henry IV*. Such usage was rare before the seventeenth century. 'Way' and 'path' were more common, derived from the Saxon *weg* and *pad*. Other common words include port ways, trade-ways, and market-ways, which led to market towns. 'Drift-ways' was used for the movement of livestock. 'Church-ways' for a road that led to a church. Throughout his life, Shakespeare made his *weg* and *pad* back and forth from Stratford to London and home again, home again. He also toured as an actor on many occasions. Maybe he even composed as he rode, the jogging nag providing the backbeat.

There is a weird moment in *The Merchant of Venice* when Gratiano, who thinks he has just learned that his new wife has been unfaithful, says that such behaviour is like 'the mending of highways / In summer, where the ways are fair enough' (5.1.263–4). (One baffled early editor concluded that, 'the aptitude of this comparative illustration is not, at first view, very discoverable'.[11]) The line is proverbial and means that highways are in good shape in the summer and do not *need* mending. It is the timing of the infidelity that Gratiano really minds. His wife might have waited until the honeymoon was over before engaging in some retaliatory infidelity. But behind this 'comparative illustration' is the experience of a seasoned traveller. William Shakespeare was well acquainted with the condition of England's roads, at all seasons.

(Much later in life, in 1611, back in Stratford, Shakespeare was a chief signatory and financial contributor 'towards the charge of prosecuting the bill in Parliament for the better repair of the highways'. It did not succeed. There is a certain poignancy to highway repair bills that go nowhere.)

The essential, even pivotal thing about Shakespeare leaving Stratford is that it meant he would return. He seems to have been that kind of writer, that kind of man. Not like, say, D.H. Lawrence, permanent-pilgrim, wandering, questing, uncertain wherever he went except in the certainty that he did not want to be there. Shakespeare was not a restless soul, he was a reticent one, and the reticent come home again. The point of a birthplace is to leave, however, as every hero knows. The closed logic of Shakespeare's career takes its shape from his Stratford exit. And his London entrance.

7

Enter London

There is a church at the edge of Trafalgar Square called 'Saint Martin-in-the-Fields'. It's right across St Martin's Place from the National Portrait Gallery, which owns the 'Chandos Portrait' of Shakespeare, the one with the earring that makes him look cool. The steps of the Portrait Gallery are a good spot to take in Saint Martin-in-the-Fields and ponder the incongruity of its name. For in addition to not being square, Trafalgar Square is not in the fields. Trafalgar Square feels like the centre of the biggest city in the world. It isn't either one of those things, but it sure seems that way today.

St Martin's is no longer in the fields, but it obviously once was. Around the time Shakespeare was born the area between St James's Palace and the village of Charing Cross was a stretch of open land, with three or four houses at the east end of Pall Mall. The church of St Martin-in-the-Fields was probably built during the reign of Henry VIII. It was named for an Hungarian priest, St Martin, who was Bishop of Tours in the fourth century. The 'fields' bit derives from its location outside the walls of the City of London. Today, the oddity of thinking of Trafalgar Square 'in-the-fields' reminds us that in the late 1580s Shakespeare wasn't 'Shakespeare' yet but then neither was London 'London'.

To consider Shakespeare's career in London, let us take the measure of the place in 1600. Estimates are just that in a pre-census era, but London had a population of about 85,000 around the year Shakespeare was born. But he was part of a population boom fuelled by folks just like him who moved to London from rural England. So Shakespeare was part of a demographic rip-tide that doubled the city's population during the sixteenth century to nearly 200,000. (That includes the suburbs that eddied about the city.)

By today's standards, that means that by 1600 London was the size of thriving metropolises like Amarillo, TX, and Swindon, UK. As far as the 'City itself', the square mile within the ancient walls, it may have housed around 75,000, or fewer than the number who crowd into a stadium to watch Arsenal play Liverpool.

In terms of landmass, the 'City of London' then as now referred to just the single square mile within the walls built by the Romans around 200 AD (and a handful of wards just 'without' the walls). By contrast, Heathrow airport is almost five square miles. Manhattan is nearly twenty-three. You couldn't quite pitch a stone across the 'City of London', but it wouldn't take long to walk from the Tower on the East End and out Newgate on the west, had you wanted, say, to wander in the fields and say a prayer to St Martin. Tudor London was so parochial that Trafalgar looked like wilderness.

Considered by Shakespeare's standards and not ours, London was massive. Shakespeare grew up in a town of 1,500. The largest city in England after London was Norwich, with just 10,000 folks. Shakespeare may have visited Norwich while trailing a wagon full of props and costumes. Even so, London was an order of magnitude larger, rivalling Paris for the title of the biggest city in Europe.

Stratford may have been too small for Shakespeare, but London might have been too large. And it was always getting larger. It may have struck Shakespeare as a building site, for it was always expanding, spilling over the Roman belt that girdled the ancient city, blurring the formal boundary between city and suburb, creating an early modern sprawl that troubled court figures and city officials. John Stow, London's most thorough chronicler, complained that the walls and ditches that defined the City were being filled in, erasing the outlines of the city's limits. As London's waistline expanded, Elizabeth tried to impose a strict diet. But there was no curbing the city's appetite for growth.

The immigration that fed London was both national and international. There were over 7,000 'aliens' – resident but un-naturalized natives of other countries – registered in London in 1573,[1] and so Shakespeare encountered a range of people that Stratford lacked. Book-binders from Bruges, tailors from Toulouse, gun-makers from Genoa. There were 'moors' who dwelled in Cheapside and made steel needles. Jews – or 'Muranos' – lived and worshiped in Clerkenwell. For every Tom, Dick and Harry that Shakespeare grew up with in Stratford he found a Giles, Jacques and Eastfanyo in London.[2]

It was also a city of youth. High mortality rates, driven by disease, depressed the average age (as well as the average inhabitant, to judge by the fashion for melancholy at the time). The highest proportion of Londoners were, like Shakespeare, under the age of thirty. London was big, young and bursting at the seams.

Youth will be served, but they have to wait first. The Elizabethan world was, as the historian Keith Thomas explains, 'organized along the gerontocratic premise that old men should rule and young men should serve; at all levels, from parish to playhouse to palace'.[3] But what did 'old' or 'young' mean 'back then'? In 1588, average life expectancy at birth was just thirty-seven. This figure skews low due to infant mortality, however. If you made it to twenty-five you might expect to live a lengthy life, though not by modern standards. (King Lear puts his age at just above eighty – 'neither more nor less' – which means that he's a freak.) Shakespeare was not a particularly young man when he arrived in London, then, whether he was in his mid or late twenties. But he was surrounded by men and women around the same age.

Londoners were young, but the City was old. Today, inside this vast, sprawling, modern metropolis is a tiny, tidy, ancient one. You can still feel it as you wander down Egg Street, past

Credit Suisse and Deutsche Bank. You might wonder why the street arcs so elliptically, so very like an egg. It bends to circumvent the Roman coliseum that was once there, well below the surface even of Shakespeare's London. In the bowels of Guild Hall today you can get a glimpse through a pyrex window of London's first theatre deep below the city streets. Throughout the City proper – that bare square mile of Shakespeare's life and times – glimpses of the ancient city blink out their ancient light like dying stars.

As Shakespeare walked through London, say from Shoreditch to the South Bank, he'd pass through something like a geological cut that revealed a strata of time. London was full of picturesque dumps. This is a check to a romantic view of jolly old, wattle-and-daub London, full of merry men and women with broken teeth but full hearts. Shakespeare's London was decrepit and shitty, befouled by the waste of people and animals, crowded, noisy, dark and damp. Which is to say, exciting.

Shakespeare encountered a world of difference in London, then. But what difference did it make? Faced with this teeming, theatrical City, Shakespeare turned his back on it. There is nothing in his works like a *Chaste Maid in Cheapside*, *The Cripple of Fenchurch Street*, *The Blind Beggar of Bethnal Green*, *The Boss of Billingsgate*. When his titles indicate a setting, it is an elsewhere – Venice, Verona, anywhere but here. Even his merry wives live in Windsor not Wapping Street. The exception is the Eastcheap scenes in his *Henry IV* plays. A bit of local colour nestling like a Russian doll inside a history play. Even here, however, there is a temporal displacement. Falstaff's tavern bills are reckoned in sixteenth-century currency, but the time stamp is medieval. In the midst of this modern city, Shakespeare glimpsed the past, as though modernity was all a bit too much for him. He never wrote a play set in his own midst.

When Shakespeare does mention London in his plays, the references are Easter eggs for his audience to find. Take a single moment from *Taming of the Shrew*, written not long after Shakespeare arrived in London. Petruchio's first words, 'Verona, for a while I take my leave', establish the play's Italian setting. Yet at the end of 4.3 Petruchio orders Grumio to 'bring our horses unto Long-lane end; / There will we mount, and thither walk on foot' (ll. 183–4). Long Lane was in London, a street that led from the Barbican to Smithfield Market. The instructions imply an urban setting with enough congestion that Petruchio and his party need to walk to the end of the street before mounting their horses. (It was something of a running joke, or a galloping one, in the drama of the time to mention the horses stabled just off stage. Take *Macbeth*, where Banquo and Fleance are riding back to Macbeth's castle on a starless night of ominous foreboding. Naturally, they dismount and walk the last mile.)

The mention of Long Lane in *Shrew* might explain why all of Petruchio's servants have English names. Consider that, in Padua, people are named Katherina, Bianca, Baptista, Petruchio, Grumio, Gremio, Hortensio, Lucentio, Tranio, Biondello and Vincentio. At Petruchio's place, they are named Curtis, Nathaniel, Philip, Joseph, Nicholas, Peter, Walter, Adam and Ralph. For variety's sake, Petruchio calls for his favourite spaniel, 'Troilus'. No wonder Kate is tired. They seem to have walked from Padua to Paddington.

This instance in *Shrew* is part of a peculiar Shakespeare habit of name-checking London in unlikely plays and places. *Twelfth Night* is set in Illyria, an elegant name for what is, today, a Balkan state, but the best lodging available is at 'The Elephant', an inn on London's Southbank. In *Comedy of Errors*, set on the Mediterranean coast, the 'Porpentine' is the name of a disreputable restaurant where Antipholus (of Ephesus) likes to dine. It was also the name of a house in Southwark. Then there is the 'Bunch of Grapes' in *Measure for Measure*'s Vienna and perhaps even the 'Sagitary' in *Othello*'s Cyprus. Shakespeare's mind was often in the Mediterranean, but his stomach lived in London.

Shakespeare was never a Londoner, however, not officially at least. To be a citizen of London was to be a member of a guild. There wasn't one for players or playwrights, but many of Shakespeare's fellows joined guilds, not as their primary trade but for the social perks they offered. Take a contemporary playwright, John Webster. He was a Merchant Taylor and 'Citizen of London'. Or Anthony Munday, a Draper. He wrote civic pageants and celebrations for the installation of the Lord Mayors, annually plucked from one of the twelve great companies of London (Mercers, Grocers, Drapers, etc). And while Shakespeare liked to write himself a 'gentleman' (see Chapter 11), Middleton advertised the fact that he was London's chronologer, appointed to record memorable events in the city's life. Appointed to the role in 1620, he signed a commendatory poem to John Webster, '*poeta and chron. Londinius*'.

Shakespeare's relative neglect of London makes him exceptional, since so many of his fellow playwrights cast London in the lead. Middleton, Dekker, Heywood and Jonson ... their plays are rife with London settings and ripe with London types. But Shakespeare never wrote a Lord Mayor's pageant, never bought a London lodging that he lived in, never brought Anne and the kids down to see the sights (as far as we know). In 1612, deposed in a legal dispute, he identified himself as 'William Shakespeare of Stratford upon Avon'.

London was wasted on Shakespeare, then. He wrote *in* London, not about it. It gave him a market, not material. Luckily, Shakespeare's timing was as good as ever. There was an audience hungry for new fare and Shakespeare was just getting cooking.

*

So Shakespeare moved to London. Whether he was alone or in company, penniless or flush, in flight or in hope, we cannot say. What we can say is that he joined a community of playmakers, actors, writers and entrepreneurs. So as we try to get a fix on the scale of London, we need to size up an even smaller 'city' within the city, the community of men in the theatre trade. How many men were immediately occupied with the practice of putting on plays for money in the 1590s? And how many men and *women* were collaterally involved in the pursuit? The scholar David Kathman compiled a *Biographical Index of English Drama Before 1660*, an annotated list of all playwrights, actors, patrons, musicians and miscellaneous other people active in English drama before 1660.[4] His index runs to over 1,000 names but includes people like Arthur, Prince of Wales, who, though he was patron of the Prince's company from 1494 to 1501, cannot be said to have been very active in the daily practice of staging plays for money around the turn of the sixteenth century.

In their collection *Playhouse Wills, 1558–1642*, E.A.J. Honigmann and Susan Brock locate about 145 wills of actors, managers, musicians, playwrights, theatre owners and investors within a briefer span of years.[5] This is a limited collection of materials; they could only include what survives, which is obviously not everything. In his book *Actors and Acting in Shakespeare's Time*, John Astington compiled an index of the 'principal actors' from 1558 to 1660 and located 172 of them.[6] Also not a lot. As Galileo and Shakespeare were discovering, the world was a small one.

It takes more than actors to put on a play (just don't tell them that), and so a rough count of how many players were professionally employed around 1588, say, does not give us a sense of how big London's theatre world was when Shakespeare got to town. Whatever the actual numbers, it seems safe to conclude that there are more people writing about the early modern theatre industry today than there were writing for the early modern theatre industry in 1600. It was a small world in which Shakespeare made a big splash.

*

Shakespeare wrote several scenes of young men arriving in a big town. We see Petruchio showing up in Padua, 'to seek [his] fortune farther than at home / Where small experience grows …' (1.2.50–1). Small experience may have grown in Stratford, but so did Shakespeare's small family, which he seemingly abandoned for much of his adult life to live and work in London. He must have been largely an absentee father, content to nurse his career in London while Anne Shakespeare sheltered his Stratford brood.

And yet there is less life of Shakespeare left in London than in Stratford. Fewer material traces of his domestic life and time there. No single surviving domicile associated with his presence survives. This is not surprising, though it is revealing. Shakespeare lived like a drifter in London, a transient, a bachelor. The traces of him are not found in private homes, but in public houses: The Theatre, The Globe, The Blackfriars, playhouses in which he probably spent the bulk of his time. Among the wonders of Shakespeare's writing career is that he authored a deathless canon of drama and did it all in rented rooms.

Shakespeare moved often, and we know where and when because he left a trail of unpaid taxes, staying one flat ahead of the tax man. Perhaps one of the most 'universal' things about Shakespeare is that he never paid a bill until he absolutely had to, and sometimes not even then.

When Shakespeare first settled in London, he lived in the northern suburbs, outside the 'City', close to The Curtain and The Theatre playhouses. A few years later, in 1596, he was dodging taxes in the parish of St Helen's, Bishopsgate, still close to the northern playhouses. It was an eccentric district, one that attracted both theatre makers and foreigners. Drama thrives on difference, and Shakespeare would have witnessed all around him Londoners who hailed from France, Germany and the Netherlands. There were men, women and children from the continent of Africa as well as in London in these years, as the archival work of Imtiaz H. Habib revealed, with families clustered around Tower Hill.[7] London was as international as Stratford was parochial.

Perhaps after finding lodgings the first thing Shakespeare did when he moved to London was see a play by Christopher

Marlowe. It's a good thing he'd already unpacked because what he saw – or what he heard – might have made him hightail it back to Stratford on the first rented horse. Among the most courageous things that Shakespeare ever did was, faced with Marlowe's plays, decide to emulate, not exit.

It was in London, and around this time, that Shakespeare made a transition from player to playwright, a transition spread out over many years since he was still acting in the early 1600s, according to a 'cast list' for Ben Jonson's *Sejanus* in 1603. Of course Shakespeare may have been working on plays during his 'lost years', either in Stratford or on the road, scribbling drafts on the back of tavern bills while he strolled the provinces. But it was in London that his first plays bloomed.

He had good models to build upon, both those plays that he had performed in and the new ones sprouting all around him like dandelions in summer. In fact, the real hard work of building an English dramatic repertory had already happened when Shakespeare put his hand to it. Shakespeare was a second-wave writer, following those plays of Marlowe, Kyd, Nashe and Greene. The second wave is the best wave to be part of, since the first wave always breaks upon the shoals.

As luck would have it – and Shakespeare's luck always held – Marlowe, Kyd, Nashe and Greene had all cleared the way for Shakespeare by 1593, building the *weg* and *pad* that he was now there to mend. Dumb luck or brilliant plan, Shakespeare arrived in London in the middle of an entertainment boom not seen since early Athens and unrivalled until Hollywood in the 1920s. He was ready for his close-up.

8

Shakespeare, Playwright

Most images of authorship are studies in solitude. The writer alone with his thoughts – always 'his' thoughts – nibbling his quill, staring into the middle distance, inviting, or daring, the muse to inspire him. Hair tousled, lips pouted, doublet every-so-slightly undone, the author alone communes with the immortals.

This is not how Shakespeare wrote. He wrote surrounded by books and tools. Those sources he sifted – chronicles, novellas, poetry and plays – and those instruments he used to mine them – goose quills and sharpening stones, pounce and paper. Writing was manual labour, work done by hand and with hand tools. Shakespeare may never have suffered from writers' block, but he no doubt had a bout or two with writers' cramp. When the epilogue to *Henry V* calls him our 'bending author' it means that Shakespeare is taking a bow somewhere. But it might give us a quick glimpse of Shakespeare at work. Not staring moodily into the middle distance but hunched over a table, scouring borrowed books, sharpening his quill, pausing now and then to unbend his back.

Writing was a craft in Shakespeare's time. Hamlet mentions to Horatio that he worked hard to unlearn how to 'write fair' since neat handwriting was not a sign of learning but of labour. When a German visitor refers to John Davies of Hereford as 'the most famous writer of his time', he meant the most famous penman, or calligrapher.[1] In these terms, based upon a small sample, Shakespeare was a terrible writer.

Turns out it is easy to write like Shakespeare. Take a piece of paper, a small penknife and a straight edge. Incise faint lines across the page's width, marking the lateral score that will rationalize the words. (Before it can be written, it has to be ruled.) Now fold the paper length-wise into three lanes. The far left will be for speech prefixes. Those can wait. The middle one is for dialogue. If it is verse, the words will stay in their lane. If prose they might drift into the slow lane on the left (or the right in the US). That's where we can stick any stage directions that occur to us, whether they are instructions or invitations. ('In scuffling, they change rapiers', from *Hamlet*, is a playwright with a notion of how the fight needs to go. The actors can work out 'they fight' for themselves.) And that is all there is to it. Anybody can write a play. It's as easy as lying.

As for those speech prefixes, it appears they came *after* the dialogue was written. So though we write and read from left to right (in the West), Shakespeare wrote his plays from the inside out, filling the centre lane with dialogue and then returning to populate the left lane with characters. There is only one surviving sample of a scene in Shakespeare's hand, three pages of a manuscript play called *The Book of Sir Thomas More*. In the *More* fragment, the members of the crowd are simply 'other' or 'all'. We get the sense that the words came first, before the characters. Today, play texts always give us a *dramatis personae* before the play, as though characters preexist the play. It is possible for Shakespeare that his characters spoke themselves into existence, the product not the producers of their words. There are seven character lists in the 1623 folio. In every instance they follow not precede the play.

Shakespeare did not write alone, then, but in good company, surrounded by written materials and materials for writing. But he may have been surrounded by men and women as well. For if Shakespeare was frugal he could have written in taverns by the borrowed light of tavern keepers while he took a meal. If so, he may have written with voices in his ears and not just in his head. Thomas Heywood's *The Fair Maid of the Exchange* paints a picture of a writer at work under just these circumstances. The disabled hero of the play, named 'Cripple', describes how he came by his literary facility.

CRIP. ... I could make enquiry
Where the best witted Gallants use to dine,
Follow them to the tavern, and there sit
In the next room with a calves head and brimstone,
And over hear their talk, observe their humours,
Collect their jests, put them into a play,
And tire them too with payment to behold
What I have filched from them.

$(3.2.120–7)^2$

This is every writer's dream, charging people for words you filched from their tavern talk. The film critic David Thompson notes that, 'Among other things, filmmaking converts light from nature to product'.[3] In Elizabethan England, playwrights took words, which are everywhere, and converted them into a commercial good. If you could pick the right ones and get them in the right order, people would pay to listen.

This helps us get a fix on how and where Shakespeare wrote. But what was it like when he put pen to paper? Did Shakespeare nod along to the beat of his own line? Bobbing his head in time to his metre? Did he hum along like Glenn Gould at the keyboard? Or let out an occasional yelp like the jazz pianist Keith Jarrett when he really hit his stride? In the first folio Heminges and Condell say that what Shakespeare thought, 'he uttered with ... easiness'. Uttering can mean a lot of things (including passing bad cheques), but Heminges and Condell might mean that Shakespeare wrote out loud, transcribing his plays from his own tongue. Shakespeare was his own amanuensis. Or maybe he held his breath until he surfaced at the end of a passage like a deep-sea diver returning to the surface, riches held aloft in an outstretched hand, dripping with meaning.

For there are passages in Shakespeare so saturated with sense that it sometimes seems he was lifting words from the paper rather than placing them there. But at some point, like every writer, he stared at a blank page. The value of Shakespeare's scrap of the *Book of Sir Thomas More* – if it is indeed Shakespeare's – is that it lets us imagine him working, searching, discovering, failing – as he surely often failed – to find the right word. It asks us to imagine the terror of the open page. The way that a writer can get off course before making a correction. The way that first impressions are overwritten by second thoughts.

Ben Jonson snarked in *Timber* (printed in 1641) that, 'the Players have often mentioned it as an honour to Shakespeare, that in his writing, (whatsoever he penned) he never blotted a line. My answer hath been, Would he had blotted a thousand'.[4] This is mean – and hilarious – but incorrect. Shakespeare's contribution to *Sir Thomas More* shows him blotting and crossing out as he wrote, engaging in what scholars call *currente calamo* correction. This translates as 'the current pen' or 'with the pen running out', a sense of writing in the heat, off the cuff, or the top of the head, or the tip of the tongue, subject to change and correction. The strike-throughs do not result from measured reflection or studious revision. They show us Shakespeare at work, changing his mind, Shakespeare re-writing Shakespeare. The comfort of this document is that it turns out that even Shakespeare did not always write as well as Shakespeare wrote.

*

Scholars have recently put some pressure on the story being told here, that Shakespeare was an actor before he 'turned his hand' to writing. That he toured the provinces as a player before settling down in London to the serious work of literature. Biographers, who are writers after all, have probably fallen prey to an implicit bias that sees Shakespeare 'maturing' from a player into a writer.

He did do one or the other first, in purely technical terms. That is, he first put pen to paper or first played upon the stage. But there is a chicken-or-the-egg quality about the question (though not all actors turn into writers. Just as not all eggs grow up to be chickens. Some become omelettes). The quibbling over which came first obscures the fact that the roles were not as distinct then as they are today. In fact it is a sure sign of decadent art forms that they tend towards ever greater specialization. It is only recently in the theatre that you could describe someone non-risibly as a 'wig wrangler'. The theatre today proliferates separate jobs that were once combined. And so to hair-split over whether Shakespeare was first an actor or first a playwright misses the point that he was both, at least until later in his career when he stopped acting but kept on writing.

The quarrel over which came first obscures the fact that Shakespeare did not step from the stage into the garret, from the company of players to the solitude of the study. To return to the opening point, images of authorship today are romanced by isolation, when playwriting in the early 1590s was a collaborative trade. G.E. Bentley estimated that upwards of half of the plays in the period were written by more than one playwright.[5] Whether in taverns or in rented rooms, Shakespeare did not write alone. He collaborated, especially early and then late in his career, when he was first coming into his powers and then again when he was losing them.

The co-labour of collaborative writing suggests that it saves labour, though some writers will tell you that co-authorship doubles, not halves, the work. The fact that we can say the two writers might 'share' or 'divide' the work between them captures the friction of co-writing. The antithetical words – 'sharing' and 'dividing' – telegraphs the tensions that can inhere in co-writing.

The case of Beaumont and Fletcher yields a productive contrast with Shakespeare and Middleton. This dazzling duo did not divide, they shared. A contemporary reports of the two that they

> lived together on the Bank side, not far from the Play-house, both bachelors; lay together ...; had one wench in the house between them ...; the same clothes and cloak, &c., between them.[6]

This is a vision of co-writers as two halves of a whole –
a four-handed ampersand who shared one woman, one
wardrobe and a singular vision of drama. (The shared clothing
suggests, inadvertently, a shirts-and-skins scenario with
Beaumont or Fletcher shivering shirtless while the other wore
the cloak.) The duo were so inseparable that they feature in
one of the funnier anecdotes of the time. A version from the
1830s outlines the broad contours: 'There is a story related of
Beaumont and Fletcher, that while consulting over a bottle of
wine in a tavern, about the catastrophe of a tragedy;–one said,
"You kill the king and I'll poison the queen." A waiter, who
had been listening at the door, immediately took the alarm,
and went for a constable to apprehend them.'[7] So there was
one downside to public plotting.

The model of Beaumont and Fletcher – who finished one
another's meals and sentences – was probably untypical. Co-
writing at the time more often took the form of writers working
separately from the same plot, presumably in their own homes
and in their own clothes. A 'plot' of the play outlined the broad
structure – think of a Hollywood 'treatment' for a film. One
writer might take on an act while another writer, or writers,
worked on other bits. Shakespeare may have been assigned
a scene or two of a play about Henry VI, working on it in
a rented room in Bishopsgate while other hands turned out
other parts across town.

Some of the madcap inconsistencies of plays in the period,
the vaudevillian juxtaposition of scenes of high tragedy
with those of low comedy, may result from different writers
working in different rooms upon a common project. It is often
mentioned that the King James Bible – produced in 1611 by a
team of learned scholars – is the only work of literary genius
ever produced by a committee. But many of the finest plays of
this period were also produced by a gang of writers, together –
but, often, separate.

So Shakespeare collaborated at the top and tail of his career.
(Half of Shakespeare's final ten plays are collaborations and the
final results are not in. Scholars are still counting.) The three

plays about Henry VI are among the earliest that 'Shakespeare wrote', but the quotation marks here indicate that Shakespeare did not write these plays in the singular sense the phrase implies. There is considerable dispute about their authorship, but the Henry VI plays are collaborations, committee work, and the question of just who wrote what is one of scholarly dissent (and therefore delight). There is an authorship controversy, just not the one the anti-Stratfordians think.

*

Our best early evidence about Shakespeare-the-playwright comes from the thinly veiled – in fact translucent – insult that Robert Greene lobbed at him in a book called *Greene's Groatsworth of Wit*. Some scholars now think the pamphlet was written by Henry Chettle, a printer turned writer (which is a bit like a taxidermist turned hunter).[8] If Chettle, he thought it wise to publish under the name of Greene whom, he knew, would not object. Since he was dead. It reads:

> there is an upstart Crow, beautified with our feathers, that with his Tigers heart wrapped in a Players hide, supposes he is as well able to bombast out a blank verse as the best of you: and being an absolute *Johannes fac totum*, is in his own conceit the only Shake-scene in a country.[9]

The taunt alludes to a line, 'O tiger's heart wrapped in a woman's hide' (1.4.137), found in a play we now call *Henry VI, Part 3* (*c.* 1591–2) but which was known at the time – if its title was known at the time – as *The true tragedie of Richard duke of Yorke, and the death of good King Henrie the sixt.* Greene's jibe locates Shakespeare in London by at least 1592 and it seems he'd been there just long enough to irritate people. For the insult and the response gives us a sense of how the fledgling writer struck his peers. He struck 'Greene', at least, as a plagiarist, a jumped-up Johannes come-lately filching feathers from his betters.

(The obvious irony is that the image of the upstart crow is lifted from Aesop's fable of the bird in borrowed feathers, who is exposed by those from whom he stole his plumes. And so Greene [or Chettle], without so much as a footnote, plagiarizes Aesop to indict Shakespeare for plagiarism.)

The French philosopher Michel Foucault argued that authorship emerged as a form of punishment. He meant that we invented authorship not when we needed someone to credit but when we needed somebody to blame. Shakespeare became an author when another author charged him with authorship. Once liable to critique by other writers, his professionalism emerged from his alleged violation of professional protocols. Greene confers authorship on Shakespeare by accusing him of writing in bad faith.

The most interesting thing about Greene's attack is that other writers rallied to Shakespeare's defence. This is all the more remarkable since the insult is buried in an enormously long, somewhat incoherent prose account of a prodigal son (that is, people actually *read* it). Greene's insult produced a bit of a flap, with at least two writers speaking up for Shakespeare. This suggests not only that Shakespeare was working in London by the late 1580s, but that other writers had taken note. Even Robert Greene had noted the bits that Shakespeare contributed to *Henry VI*. In other words, even without computational analysis he identifies the 'tiger's heart' as quintessentially Shakespearean. He not only creates Shakespearean authorship, then, he turns what might be a collaborative play into Shakespeare's by blaming it on him.

If the line is 'Shakespearean', what makes it so? Well there is the arresting incongruity of the metaphor itself, the monstrous idea of a human woman with a beastly heart. There is the careful antithesis of a 'tiger's heart' and a 'woman's hide' with its slightly tweaked alliteration (a Shakespearean characteristic is to flirt with the formulaic but eventually refuse it. It could have been a 'wolf's heart' in a 'woman's hide', though that wouldn't scan). And 'wrapped' is striking. The main idea of the metaphor is that the woman's 'hide' is a skin that cloaks a tiger beneath. For us there's the sense of gift wrapping, too, the horrifying idea of a beautifully wrapped present that turns out to be a box of live snakes. It's a good line, even a great one. Greene liked it so much that he hated its writer.

*

What Shakespeare wrote in a rented room in London during the late 1580s and early 1590s is the reason you are reading this book. Because it is not the town that Shakespeare was born in or the wife that he wed, or the rooms he rented or the men he met that occasion this biography: it is the plays that Shakespeare wrote. And these early years in London were the years of the *Henry VI* plays, of *Titus Andronicus*, *Taming of the Shrew* and *The Two Gentlemen of Verona*. Collaborative English histories, co-written Roman tragedies and solo Italian comedies.

The early histories and *Titus Andronicus* are stage bangers, full of 'love, blood, and rhetoric' (to borrow a feather from Tom Stoppard's *Rosencrantz and Guildenstern are Dead*). They picked up Marlowe's gauntlet, responding to his smash hit *Tamburlaine the Great*. In fact audiences thought *Tamburlaine* was so great that Marlowe wrote a second part: 'the general welcomes Tamburlaine received, / When he arrived last upon the stage / Have made our poet pen his second part' (epi. 1–3). Both parts are full of amazing images and vicious language and the other way around. If the three *Henry* plays do not match up to the two *Tamburlaines*, at least Shakespeare outlasts Marlowe on points. If you can't beat them, write more than them.

With Shakespeare's first plays, we should pause to consider the condition of English drama at the time. Not the state of drama as a commercial affair – its companies, its playhouses, its touring practices, its personnel arrangements, its licensing laws. All of this is important enough, and even occasionally interesting, but what was the state of English drama in the

1580s? Why did Shakespeare write about what he wrote about when he decided that what he wanted to write was a play?

One imaginative breakthrough of all literary, graphic and plastic arts is the expansion of subject matter, the range of things an artist might think possible or appropriate to treat. Think of medieval art, where artists could not imagine anything else to paint but images of the Madonna and child. Medieval dramatists, for that matter, restricted themselves to biblical matters or – when they were feeling daring – the plight of man's soul in this miserable and transitory world. *Everyman* was once *avant garde*.

It finally occurred to someone to ask, how about a play about an earthly king, not a heavenly one? Once dramatists released the brakes on drama, things really started to roll. There are not *that* many years between the anonymous *Everyman* and Ben Jonson's *Every Man Out of His Humour*, but the plays are apples and oranges. English drama really began to bear fruit, that is, once dramatists considered that every man (and even every person) might make for good material. The medieval dramatist thought life was a vale of tears. To the Renaissance dramatist it was a bowl of cherries.

The range of Shakespeare's early plays – from attic maniacs like Titus Andronicus to moody medieval kings like Henry VI to randy Italian bounders like Petruchio – shows us a world of writing with an exalted sense of possibility, one in which Shakespeare could really stretch out.

However skilfully put together, the seams sometimes show in Shakespeare's early plays. Take the baggy dramaturgy of the three Henry plays, a series of dramas in search of a protagonist as Shakespeare and his co-writers audition various historical figures for the lead before, finally, settling on Richard, Duke of Gloucester, who got his own spin-off called *Richard III* a few years later.

They also reveal Shakespeare's reading at the time. The *Chronicles* of Raphael Holinshed and Edward Hall; Seneca, Plautus and above all Ovid, always Ovid. As noted, Shakespeare might have borrowed the more expensive books from Richard

Field, even using his shop as a lending library. This reading complemented his grammar school curriculum and mingled with the plays he'd memorized on the road. His learning and his experience coalesced into his craft.

They are also hugely laddish plays. The cast lists of the three Henries read like rugby rosters, and the curdled comedies of *Shrew* and *Two Gents* find brides settling for unsettling grooms. The women of the Henry plays are termagants and witches, a 'she wolf' of Anjou, a lunatic witch of Orleans. The heroine of *Shrew* is so attractively spirited that she has to be 'tamed' through sleep deprivation and starvation. We don't usually call that comedy. We usually call that torture. As for *The Two Gentlemen of Verona*, at the end of that play Valentine forgives Proteus for trying to rape his fiancée and – no harm, no foul – says he can have her if he wants. Suffice to say the title overestimates by two how many 'gentlemen' there are in Verona.

The cast of characters might reflect the company Shakespeare kept in London, which was also largely male. London at the time may have had as many as 115 men for every 100 women (odds reflected in Shakespeare's romantic comedies, which often feature supply and demand imbalances between the sexes). So among other things, Shakespeare's move from Henley Street to Bishopsgate absented him from daily, intimate contact with women – a household with a mother, wife and two daughters – and introduced him to a working life largely comprised of men. In London his world was one of fellow actors and writers, whose livelihood depended upon well-off male courtiers, whom they courted hard.

On the basis of this early work we can conclude that Shakespeare was not a 'naïve' or primitive artist. His early plays are squarely within the tradition he inherited and set out to solve formal problems, not social ones. How to convert the mathematical rigour of Plautine farce to the native English idiom? How to compress a wide swath of chronicle history into the cramped space and time of the commercial stage? From these early formal adventures, Shakespeare grew in eccentricity, developing an elliptical, almost enigmatic art. However odd, the plays are always powered by a dense poetic energy, compact and arresting images, daring linguistic deployments, bizarre and adventurous syntax. It's all there in the early work.

The painter George Braque wrote that 'one's style is one's inability to do otherwise'. At this point in his writing life, however, Shakespeare could only do otherwise; that is, he was writing like other people in order to discover how to write like himself. Some years later another playwright, Alan Bennett, wrote, 'Art comes out of art; it begins with imitation, often in the form of parody, and it's in the process of imitating the voice of others that one comes to learn the sound of one's own.'[10] What Bennett means is that you find your voice by throwing it. Shakespeare was often at his best when trying to sound like Christopher Marlowe, for instance, whose voice he could never get out of his head.

These were the working conditions – this was the neighbourhood – in which Shakespeare made a scene in the late 1580s and early 1590s. But Shakespeare's budding career as a playwright was nipped by the plague that struck London in 1593. The privy council issued an order in January of that year stating 'it appears the infection doth increase', thus 'we think it fit that all manner of concourse and public meetings of the people at plays, bear-baiting, bowlings and other like assemblies for sports be forbidden'.[11] In addition to wondering at the company plays kept at the time (we don't often mention Shakespeare and bowling in the same breath), we can marvel at the foresight of the Privy Council. Even without the insights of modern epidemiology, they called for social distancing. History's hindsight sometimes views the closing of the theatre as a disruption to Shakespeare's literary career. We might think more soberly about these timely interventions and the souls saved by the forbidding of public gatherings during London's many plagues. Close a theatre, save a life. Any one of which is worth a dozen plays.

But for a brief respite the next winter, the theatres were closed for nearly a year and a half. During this time Shakespeare seems to have contemplated a different path – as a patronized poet rather than a company playwright. This was forced upon him by the closure of the theatre, but he had made some important connections in London, ones that would sustain him for a couple of years while he turned his hand from plays to poetry.

9

Shakespeare, Poet

Players may stroll but they don't often climb. Actors were *actually* mobile, not socially so. True, some grew rich, like Richard Burbage and Edward Alleyn. But Burbage's family was in real estate, and Alleyn married the step-daughter of the owner of the theatre he worked in. If a young man wanted to climb the ladder of success, he would not join a playing company, though by doing so he might get to see a bit of the world, or at least Norwich.

Still, by the nature of their work, players came into contact with a wide range of people, the ordinary at their ordinaries, courtiers at court. So while Shakespeare's closest neighbours were actors and aliens, his social network was wider than the average man's. In his first years in London, he met, or courted, a powerful man who harboured him when the plague came. For his pains, or his pounds, that courtier was immortalized by Shakespeare in a dozen or more sonnets and served as patron to two wildly successful narrative poems.

The sonnets may not be the key to Shakespeare's soul – as Wordsworth claimed – but they might unlock his place in London society, the circles, or, better, triangles in which he moved. For in the sonnets are all the elements of a dramatic genre he never tried, city comedy. A rich patron, a rival writer, a shady lady, envy, money, jealousy, passion. Perhaps the 'key' to the sonnets is to read them as a treatment for an Elizabethan sitcom (*The Inklings, A Bit of Ruff, Three's Company*) or a proto-version of a Noël Coward bedroom farce, *Earls and Others*.

The sonnets were written at different points across Shakespeare's career, so if they form a 'sequence' it is a gappy one. Shakespeare's sonnets were printed in 1609 but the collection gathered poetry written at different stages of his life. They certainly do not all date from the early 1590s. As noted in Chapter 4, sonnet 145 might even have been an early ode to Anne (or Agnes). But the first seventeen sonnets are addressed to a beautiful young man and open a window – a stained glass one – into the luminous world in which Shakespeare moved in the early 1590s. For somewhere around this time, possibly at a court performance, Shakespeare met Henry Wriothesley, the Earl of Southampton, who became a vital patron to his art. But that art was not plays but poetry.

With the theatre closed from 1593–4 Shakespeare may have thought that his literary career might lie as a private poet not a public playwright. Patronage might have looked like the surer bet. His *Venus and Adonis* and *The Rape of Lucrece* were printed in '93 and '94 by his old schoolmate Richard Field, both with fulsome dedications to the Earl of Southampton. If Shakespeare and Field ever spent a Stratford lunch break contemplating a takeover of English literature, there is some irony that it's Richard Field's name, not Shakespeare's, that appears on the title pages of *Venus and Adonis* and *Lucrece*.

Venus and Adonis and *The Rape of Lucrece* were written during troubled times. For it wasn't just the theatre that was on the rocks. If Shakespeare got his nose out of a book for a moment in the 1590s, he would have caught a whiff of a country still nervous about Spain and fraught, as always, by uncertainty over Elizabeth's successor. (One of the downsides to being a monarch is that everyone around you is always planning for your death. Kings and queens are the walking dead.) Throughout 1592 and into 1593 rumours of a Spanish invasion crackled over the air waves. Philip II was invading through Scotland, the Spanish fleet was anchored off Portsmouth, an armada was even now sailing up the Thames. Elizabeth's response was always the same: murmur some rumours and arrest some Catholics.

In the summer of 1592, then, as the plague increased so did Armada sightings. On 7 August the Privy Council ordered all leading recusants returned to prison. Six days later they arrested every prominent Catholic lawyer in London. Between Armada anxieties and outbreak of plague, the atmosphere might not have seemed ripe for a career in the theatre. As for Shakespeare, he kept calm and read Ovid.

If the early plays – the locker-room histories, the horror-show *Titus*, the misogynist comedies – are apprentice work, though exciting ones, his Ovidian epyllion *Venus and Adonis* and *The Rape of Lucrece* are highly refined and still highly readable. They were also highly popular, continuously in print through his life and even beyond. As treated earlier, the year after his death saw yet two more editions of the poems. In the early 1590s, Shakespeare had reason to believe that he could make a living writing light pornography for London lawyers.

> … on his neck her yoking arms she throws:
> She sinketh down, still hanging by his neck,
> He on her belly falls, she on her back.
>
> Now is she in the very lists of love,
> Her champion mounted for the hot encounter.
>
> (*Venus and Adonis*, ll. 592–6)

Then as now, hot encounters equal cold cash. Passages like this one shifted major units at the book stalls of St Paul's Churchyard. It went through sixteen editions by the 1640s, many of which only survive in one copy. The poem was literally read to death.

The poem delivers but Adonis doesn't. Venus spends 1,200 lines trying to get him to have sex with her. She makes ethical arguments (he owes the world a copy of himself), arguments by precedent (Mars lost his mind over her) and arguments from nature (bees do it). Nothing avails. The poem's an early version of 'He's just not that into you'. Young Adonis just wants to go hunting, which he does and is fatally gored by a boar. So let that be a lesson to you.

But it wasn't just the poem's light smut that made it so appealing. Take a sexy sixain like the following as an instance of Shakespeare's art.

Touch but my lips with those fair lips of thine, –
Though mine be not so fair, yet are they red, –
The kiss shall be thine own as well as mine.
What seest thou in the ground? Hold up thy head;
    Look in mine eye-balls, there thy beauty lies;
    Then why not lips on lips, since eyes in eyes?

(ll. 115–20)

Every word but one is but a single syllable. They tinkle across the stanza like cocktail jazz. The diction is homely, the rhythm is light, the mode is conversational. As one early reader, William Reynolds, dismissively put it, there's 'much ado with red and white', and he's not wrong.[1] But the poem also contains some of the best dialogue Shakespeare had written to that point. This is Ovid recast in easy-going English, immediate, amusing, arousing, wonderful.

We also see Shakespeare's preoccupation with who a kiss belongs to, the kisser or the kissed, which he'll revisit when Romeo meets Juliet. Whether or not he was looking forward to writing plays again, he's writing like a playwright here. In short, it was not titillation alone that made *Venus and Adonis* such a hit with London's readers. As with Christopher Marlowe's *Hero and Leander* (printed in 1598) it's a sure-handed translation of a Latin classic into companionable English verse.

If *Venus and Adonis* primarily appealed to the horny young law students of Lincoln's Inn, Shakespeare reached a wider, or wiser, audience with his *Lucrece*. Gabriel Harvey noted in 1601, 'The younger sort takes much delight in Shakespeares Venus, & Adonis: but his Lucrece, & his tragedy of Hamlet,

Prince of Denmark, have it in them, to please the wiser sort.'[2] One of these things is not like the other and it is *Hamlet*. In 1601, the smart set could only have seen *Hamlet* performed since it was not in print yet, but there is the slightest possibility it circulated in manuscript since Harvey is talking here about book-readers not play-goers. And those readers snapped up *Lucrece* as they had devoured *Venus and Adonis*.

The poems captured the imagination of London's literary class, but Shakespeare had one main reader in mind, a 'younger sort', the 19-year-old Southampton, to whom Shakespeare dedicated both works. Flattery did not bring out the best in Shakespeare. As sparkly as *Venus and Adonis* is, the dedication is dull as a butter knife.

Right Honourable,

> I know not how I shall offend in dedicating my unpolished lines to your Lordship, nor how the world will censure me for choosing so strong a prop to support so weak a burden; only if your Honour seem but pleased, I account myself highly praised and vow to take advantage of all idle hours till I have honoured you with some graver labour. But if the first heir of my invention prove deformed, I shall be sorry it had so noble a godfather and never after ear so barren a land, for fear it yield me still so bad a harvest. I leave it to your honourable survey, and your Honour to your heart's content, which I wish may always answer your own wish and the world's hopeful expectation.
>
> Your Honour's in all duty,
> William Shakespeare.[3]

Thus the 29-year-old Shakespeare to his 19-year-old patron. It is hard to imagine anyone – least of all the writer and the reader – taking such a suck-up seriously. But the dedication is purely conventional, from its tortured double negatives to its laboured agricultural conceit. Shakespeare describes *Venus and Adonis* as the 'first heir of my invention' (somewhere in Stratford-upon-Avon, Hamnet Shakespeare's ears were burning) though at this point he could claim at least co-authorship of a handful of plays. But it is important to the project of the poem that it appears to be Shakespeare's inaugural offering. And the project here is profit.

The 'graver labour' Shakespeare promises in the first sentence is a poem Shakespeare called *Lucrece*, subsequently known as *The Rape of Lucrece*, which is every bit as serious as *Venus and Adonis* is lubricious. Whereas the first poem offers an older female aggressor (and a larger one as well, since at one point she tucks Adonis neatly beneath her arm), the longer *Lucrece* portrays the cataclysm unleashed by male sexual aggression. In its chilling, almost forensic description of Tarquin's approach to Lucrece's chamber, it fires the imagination. In its anguished, almost unbearable account of Lucrece's conscience after the assault, it moves the heart.

> His falchion [sword] on a flint he softly smiteth
> That from the cold stone sparks of fire do fly;
> Whereat a waxen torch forthwith he lighteth,
> Which must be lodestar to his lustful eye;
> And to the flame thus speaks advisedly:
> 'As from this cold flint I enforc'd this fire,
> So Lucrece must I force to my desire.'

(ll. 176–82)

He is the hammer. She is the stone. The image it sparks illumines the reader's imaginations and lets them peer into the dark purposes of Tarquin's intent.

The poem features other interests, other oddities, and not just the 'Night-wand'ring weasels' (weasels?) that 'shriek' to see Tarquin stumbling in the dark (l. 307). There are echoes of Thomas Kyd ('O shame to knighthood ... O foul dishonour ... O martial man ...' [ll. 197–9]), as well as echoes of Shakespeare, echoing himself: 'Oh rash false heat, wrapped in repentant cold'

(l. 48). The line metrically mirrors 'A tiger's heart ...'; both lines turn upon the flange of 'wrapped'. It's as if Shakespeare chucks one last rock at Greene's casket, ringing one more change on his infamous line. Lucrece's midnight anguish is also a preview, or a call back, to the turbulent inner dialogue of Richard III, waking from a nightmare with his identity halved (5.3.178). Taken together with *Venus and Adonis*, *Lucrece* shows a writer of considerable, almost unimaginable range, flexing across forms and styles, tones and registers.

Lucrece is dedicated to Southampton as well, and if the first dedication reads like a cover letter for a job the writer hasn't landed yet, the second reads like an annual report: 'What I have done is yours; what I have to do is yours, being part in all I have, devoted yours.' Shakespeare updates Southampton on his work and promises some more to come. What it doesn't read like is a resignation letter, and so why Shakespeare returned to playwriting remains a mystery. Of course, he didn't really 'return' at all. He probably never left it. Much of *Titus Andronicus* was written during these couple of years, when Shakespeare was enthralled with Ovid. (The play probably premiered on 24 January 1594.[4]) But when he promised Southampton that 'what I have to do is yours', he probably didn't mean *Titus Andronicus* or any of the plays to come. If there were plans in store for more patronized poems, they didn't pan out.

Dedicated poems are a kind of literary shakedown, an art of handsome robbery, and Shakespeare's first biographer, Nicholas Rowe, thought that 1,000 pounds dropped from Southampton's pockets into Shakespeare's hands. This is an unlikely amount, but it's probable Shakespeare received something for his pains since he had enough capital to invest in a playing company soon after.

Perhaps stung by Greene's invective, shaken by Marlowe's death and unsettled by the plague, Shakespeare took a hard look at the literary landscape and contemplated a future as a cosseted poet not a company playwright. If so, the vision was short-lived. Probably bolstered by Southampton's largesse (whatever the amount), Shakespeare invested in a company of players around 1594. And not just a company of players, but *the* company of players, one that would sustain his work, ensure his livelihood, and cement his legacy. Once he first wrote for the Lord Chamberlain's Servants in 1594, he never wrote for another company for the rest of his life.

That couldn't have been obvious in 1594, when the commercial theatre was in disarray. Why, in short, plays over poetry when the latter was working out so well? A cynical reading is that Shakespeare sold out. His decision to write plays was driven by his desire to make money. Turned his back on fickle fame and chased the money instead.

If there is any truth to this, it is far more complicated than the explanation that Shakespeare's return to plays from poetry was a cold-eyed money grab. If the plays were written for money alone they were much better – and certainly much longer – than they needed to be. Also, it could not have been obvious that the path to prosperity lay in plays not poetry. And so 1593–4 is another one of those turning points, or returning ones, when Shakespeare made an important decision – or it was made for him; Southampton may have cut him off – that pointed his future in one direction over the other, a return to the public playhouse from the allure of patronized poetry. Before he returned to the theatre, however, he had turned some heads with his narrative poems.

*

Lyric poetry is the closest literature comes to being a performing art. (A playscript is just an accessory to the act.) Lyric poetry is written in the first person, and *for* the first person to come across it and try it on for size. Something you might sing in the shower or recite while you garden. No other form of literature comes close. However fine the novels, nobody hums Tolstoy while stirring the risotto.

And the sonnet is a form of lyric poetry, a form scored for the expression of personal crisis. Take the exultant *Amoretti* of Spenser, written to celebrate his marriage and published in 1595. Or the anguished *Astrophil and Stella* of Sidney, an extended song of insomniac heartbreak. Both are sixteenth-century sonnet sequences written on the heights or from the depths of human experience. They are the cries of an 'I' calling out to the world of emotions too loud to be quiet.

Shakespeare's sonnets are not like that. The first mention of 'I' does not come until the tenth sonnet, and there it refers to the speaker's persuasive powers, not his inner life. The speaker's voice is controlling, persuasive, even hectoring, sometimes impassioned but oddly detached, giving little of himself away at first. Indeed the first handful of sonnets seem written to spec; their theme is a single young man reluctant to marry. It is hard to imagine the muse visiting Shakespeare in his garret and saying, 'fool, look in your heart and write seventeen sonnets persuading the Earl of Southampton to reproduce'. Unless Shakespeare was being paid – or otherwise persuaded – to write them, it is hard to understand what occasioned these poems.

Whatever else we might conclude about Shakespeare, he was the kind of man mothers turned to when they wanted to convince their sons to marry. At least twice in his life Shakespeare played the go-between with two reluctant lovers, first with Southampton and later when he lodged on Silver Street (treated later). In these terms, Shakespeare was Cassio of *Othello*, who 'very oft' went between Othello and Desdemona and is left standing, but only barely, when the smoke clears.

This might seem a strange conclusion since Shakespeare's own marriage is often alleged without much evidence to be a cold thing, but if Shakespeare was not a personal fan he was a marriage artist in both his work and life. How often did he find himself at the point of a romantic triangle, for which, his comedies reveal, he had a nearly Euclidean fondness? The first seventeen sonnets show Shakespeare playing Venus to an English Adonis, possibly the Earl of Southampton, prevailing upon him to marry and reproduce as a courtesy to a world starved for beauty.

We call Shakespeare's sonnets a 'sequence' today, which suggests a coherent and controlling plan of attack. But as mentioned at the outset, the composition of the sonnets stretched over many years, occasional writing only latterly gathered into a sequence. But the first seventeen date from the mid-1590s and directly address the young Earl, or *a* young earl, since as with everything Shakespeare touched he left some mystery there.[5]

The Elizabethan court was a high-stakes dating game, one that put the 'alliance' in dalliance. Henry Wriothesley, the third Earl of Southampton, was about as eligible as they came back then, rich, titled, curled and cultured. A portrait from the early 1590s survives of Southampton, though for nearly four centuries art historians thought it was a woman, only lately concluding that it pictures the androgyne Southampton. They can be forgiven for not knowing whether it was a woman or a man since Shakespeare couldn't tell either, and he worked for him. In sonnet 20 he calls the young man – Southampton? – the master-mistress of his passion and blames nature for making him a man, cheating him by 'adding one thing to my purpose nothing'. If it's not one thing, it's another.

There were some designs for, and on, the third Earl of Southampton, but there were others for the third Earl of Pembroke, William Herbert, as well, whom Aubrey called 'a most magnificent and brave peer, and loved learned men'.[6] Scholars consider him an alternative candidate to Wriothesley since he apparently also took a dim view of marriage, and the first handful of sonnets may have had designs on him. He has the advantage on Wriothesley in that when the sonnets were published in 1609 they were dedicated by the publisher, Thomas Thorpe, to a 'Mr. W.H.' as 'the only begetter of these ensuring sonnets'. (This has proved a runic cypher across the ages. It's alleged to be an impertinence for Thorpe to address Pembroke as a 'Mr.', but he and his brother Philip were the dedicatees of the 1623 folio and so have a Shakespeare connection.)

The dating of the sonnets is a vexed matter. If the first twenty printed in the sequence were written first, Pembroke was a pup when Shakespeare wrote them, urging procreation upon the recipient. Pembroke was born in 1580, and so was barely pubescent when they were penned. For that matter, the 'begetter' of the poems need not be the young man to whom a handful are addressed.[7]

Whether addressing the 'master-mistress' Southampton or lover 'of learned men' Pembroke, the poems are frankly homoerotic. The master scholar of the sonnets, Stephen Booth, once wryly observed that Shakespeare was 'almost certainly homosexual, heterosexual, or bisexual'. He may have understated the matter, leaving out 'pan' and 'omni'. These sonnets along with Shakespeare's depiction of same-sex love in his plays raise the question of whether Shakespeare was gay. To a certain extent, the question doesn't mean anything. The question 'doesn't mean anything' because its terms are ours, not his. The predicate would have been indecipherable to the proper noun about whom we are asking.

The closest equivalents to 'homosexual' in Shakespearean time were 'bugger' and 'sodomite', but neither is very specific. 'Buggery' also referred to bestiality. In addition, 'sodomy' covered a variety of heterosexual acts. Elizabethan thinking did not ask a man who had sexual relations with another man to imagine himself to be fundamentally different from his peers. It asked him to think about himself as fundamentally the *same* as his peers: that is, a sinner.

Perhaps most surprising to readers today is that frank expressions of male-to-male affection are not a dirty secret in the plays, poetry and prose of the sixteenth and seventeenth century. Not something to be covered up by a polite fiction, or furled in euphemism. It is hiding in plain sight. We are so used to treating such expressions as a taboo, or an embarrassment or an indictment, that we are tempted to think that they must be talking about something else when they talk about love. For centuries, scholars said that when a man said he 'loves' another man in Shakespeare's England, he just meant they were pals. Turns out the Elizabethans did have a word for the love of a man for another man and that word was 'love'.

Following Bruce Smith, perhaps it is best to conclude that the primary question that Elizabethan and Jacobean men asked themselves was not 'am I a homo- or heterosexual', but 'where do my greater emotional loyalties lie, with other men or with women?'[8] (And women asked the same question, with the terms reversed.) Shakespeare's romantic comedies are absolutely laced with this question, in fact structured upon it. In Shakespeare's romantic comedies, there is nearly always an odd man out, a friend of the male ingénu who's left standing at the altar when his buddy ties the knot. This figure is the shadow of heterosexual marriage, the trailing image of friendship that marriage leaves behind. This leads to what we should call the 'Antonio codicil', which is predicated on the idea that if your name is Antonio in a Shakespeare play don't bother to register for candle-sticks.

Taking the order of their printing as the sequence of their writing would lead us to conclude that, late in the game, Shakespeare turned from a fair youth to a 'dark lady'. It is more likely that the sonnets and their subjects overgrew one another in densely tangled ways, and Shakespeare got stuck in the underbrush. We are introduced in sonnet 127 to a dark complexioned woman of whom Shakespeare writes:

> In the old age black was not counted fair,
> Or if it were, it bore not beauty's name;
> But now is black beauty's successive heir ....

> (ll. 1–3)

Shakespeare's project here is to recuperate blackness, convert it from a 'bastard shame' (l. 4) to a beauty mark, but whom is he writing about? Scholars have advanced various candidates: Lucy 'Negro', a notorious prostitute who ran a Clerkenwell brothel; Emilia Lanier, of Italian descent; and a host of other dark-haired beauties. The jury is out.

Rather than ask who Shakespeare meant by 'black', we might ask what Shakespeare meant by the word. Further, we could ask how Shakespeare taught the world what it means by 'black'. Kim Hall has argued:

> Descriptions of dark and light, rather than being mere indications of Elizabethan beauty standards or markers of moral categories, became in the early modern period the conduit through which the English began to formulate the notions of 'self' and 'other' so well known in Anglo-American discourse.[9]

The difference between 'self' and 'other', as Hall notes, was written in black and white, and Shakespeare played a large part in that.

If read as an extended narrative, the so-called 'dark lady' sonnets depict a tortured affair when Shakespeare's love for a man and a woman got a bit complicated. Seems the one met the other and forgot to tell Shakespeare. It is not at all clear how Shakespeare got tangled up with a beloved male friend and an alluring 'dark lady', but the love triangle the poems describe is, in fact, oblique not Euclidean. And it's likely that Shakespeare formed the obtuse angle in the three-sided affair and felt the difference acutely. The sonnets treat searchingly a world from which Shakespeare was ultimately excluded. If there is bitterness in them, it is that of a eunuch at a brothel.

Gabriel Harvey, whose praise of the sonnets is quoted above, does not mention what the 'younger sort' or the 'wiser sort' thought of Shakespeare's sonnets. That assessment fell to Francis Meres, who noted in 1598 that, 'the sweet witty soul of Ovid lives in mellifluous & honey-tongued Shakespeare, witness his Venus and Adonis, his Lucrece, his sugared Sonnets among his private friends, &c.'.[10] In 1598, then, in Shakespeare's first rave review, Meres talks a bit about Shakespeare's plays, but he leads off with his poetry, which is telling. His reputation was as much, or more, as a poet than a playwright in the years just before the turn of the century.

This first reference – in print – to Shakespeare's sonnets reveals to us that they are not in print. Meres is describing manuscript publication. That is, Shakespeare's sonnets enjoyed a coterie of readers who passed handwritten copies of them about. This was not at all unusual, and it helps explain why a couple of sonnets leaked into verse miscellanies in the period. But it wouldn't be until over a decade later that the sonnets made it into print (although saying they 'made it into print' suggests that the print is the apotheosis of all writing. It isn't, or at least, it wasn't). By the time his sugared sonnets were printed in 1609, the poetic Shakespeare had just finished a run of plays including *Timon*, *Macbeth*, *Pericles* and *Coriolanus*. He was about to turn to what we now call 'Romances', plays about restoration. But by the time his sonnets appeared in print, his reputation as poet had been eclipsed by his renown as a playwright.

Why then did Shakespeare, in 1594, choose a new patron? Not plays over poetry but one Henry over another. Henry Lord Hunsdon over Henry Earl of Southampton? In doing so he made a significant turn from one path to another. It's not as though there was no precedent for the life of the cosseted poet. He could have looked to the model of a contemporary from the same area of England, Samuel Daniel, who took the road that Shakespeare rejected. Who is Samuel Daniel you ask? *Exactly*. That's unfair, since Samuel Daniel, with his rhyming name, seemed fated for poetry and authored several landmark poems. But still.

Ever prudent, Shakespeare could have looked at those playwrights around him as a cautionary tale. Many had come to dismal ends: Marlowe, Nashe, Greene, Kyd. Even Ben Jonson – alive and kicking anyone within range – was not exactly cleaning up. In other words, there was not a good model for the path that Shakespeare pursued at this point, which is why he trailblazed a new one. He would not be a jobbing playwright, a freelancer, footing it from one company to another, living from hand to mouth. What he did, quintessentially, characteristically, typically, was *invest*. This turning point may have had to do with real estate not literature, and so the choice was not for plays over poetry but property over both. Sometimes we don't make choices, but the choices make us. Whether deliberate or not, the choice Shakespeare made at this point made him a company man.

10

Shakespeare's Company

It is possible – just – that Southampton hosted Shakespeare at Titchfield, the massive abbey refitted as a private home by his grandfather in the days of Henry VIII. He had John Florio in his train as an Italian tutor, renowned for his translations of Boccaccio and Montaigne into English. You do not have to meet a writer to enjoy or even employ his works, but Southampton attracted a bevy of writers and intellectuals and Shakespeare moved in their circle, if he had not moved in with them.

While Shakespeare may have been living the dream at Southampton's estate, his once and future colleagues were knocking gravel from their pumps out in the provinces. When the plague shut the theatres in 1593, Shakespeare may have hunkered down, but the Lord Strange's Servants took to the road. They could be found in Chelmsford, Bristol, York and elsewhere. Strange's lead actor, Edward Alleyn, wrote letters home to his wife Joan, his 'good sweetheart and loving mouse', which give us a glimpse of life on the road.[1] In addition to the detail that Alleyn called his wife by the pet name 'Mouse' – which is adorable – we learn something of the marvels of Elizabethan communication. In his letter of 1 August 1593 from Bristol, Alleyn asks Joan to send further letters to West Chester or York, calculating the trajectory that will ensure they meet him there. The engineers at NASA had nothing on Ned Alleyn.

For Shakespeare's part, if he had resided with Southampton, it will have served as a kind of writer's retreat and he will have come out of it richer both in mind and purse. Along with the cash, Southampton will then have given Shakespeare the four things every Elizabethan writer needed: ink, paper, light and time. Make that five things, since he probably also gave him access to books, not least Ovid's *Amores* and *Metamorphoses*. Whole handfuls of each appear in the narrative poems and in *Titus Andronicus*.

Shakespeare may also have met John Florio in Titchfield. Florio was Southampton's tutor, and the marvellous mind who rendered Montaigne's *Essays* into English. Montaigne's searching and companionable essays had a powerful impact on Shakespeare's thinking. And when a piece of writing really landed with Shakespeare, it stuck. Even in his late play *The Tempest*, he's still reckoning with Marlowe, Ovid and Montaigne.

Above all, Shakespeare brought to his plays from his time writing poetry the idea that every line counts. In his earliest history plays, there is some hack work, though hack work most writers would be proud to call their own. Still, there are lines that halt. But in the plays to come Shakespeare tries a new approach, in which every line is better than the one that came before it.

The mid-1590s were Shakespeare's Midas moment, when everything he touched turned to gold. *Romeo and Juliet*, *A Midsummer Night's Dream*, *Richard II* .... These plays read like narrative poems with speech prefixes dancing down the left-hand margin. They are also solo acts as far as we can tell, which does not alone account for their greatness but does help explain their concentration of energy.

It is also the period of Hal and Falstaff, who appear in a series of history plays tracing the death of Henry IV, the miseducation of his son Prince Hal and Hal's later emergence as Henry V. These history plays are starkly different from the sequence of Henry VI plays. For starters they feature some much needed laughs in the tavern antics of Falstaff, Pistol,

Poins and Hal. In the evolving character of Hal we see a character reckoning with ambition, the allure of fame and the horrors of responsibility. We also, in the second part of *Henry IV*, see Shakespeare meditating on old age. Old-fashioned well before he was old, Shakespeare writes powerfully about the autumn of life when still in its spring.

This was a period when even Shakespeare's 'bad' plays were good. Take *Comedy of Errors*, a perennially popular play today but not often ranked among Shakespeare's best. Still, *Comedy* is not like the early Henry plays or *Titus*. First, Shakespeare seems to have written it alone. Second, it's a comedy. Third, it's a masterpiece, if you ignore the writing. That is, the jokes are good but the plotting is *superb*. Modelled closely on Plautus' *Menaechmi*, Shakespeare created a cunning little drama machine, misfiring on all cylinders. The play is like a coiled spring with a flaw in it. Well before Newton had figured it out, Shakespeare discovered that velocity can be extremely stabilizing. The faster the play goes the smoother it rides. Furthermore, Shakespeare one-upped the Roman masterpiece he 'cured', adding a set of twins to the *Menaechmi*'s pair, doubling the confusion and quadrupling the fun.

Once Shakespeare had tossed all the characters in the air, there's no real reason he couldn't keep them aloft forever, juggling with their fates. Except that, in the end, Shakespeare out-Plautuses Plautus. He redeems the farce with a moment of revelation. Farce is fuelled by dramatic irony. Once the exposition is out of the way – accomplished in *Comedy* by Egeus' excruciatingly long opening monologue – we know more than all the characters for the duration of the play. This is enjoyable to the extent that being God must be enjoyable (though tedious in precisely the same way). But Shakespeare had an ace up his sleeve all along, or a lead pipe. The abbess we meet late in the play reveals herself to be Egeus' long-lost wife. We didn't know that, and when we meet her late in Act Five, our laughter *at* the characters catches in our throats, replaced by laughter *with* the characters.

In the next year or so the company also performed *Love's Labour's Lost*, a play whose purse of wit never quite pays for its lack of heart. But it too takes a late and unexpected turn by delaying the weddings it's been planning for five acts. This is a recurring trick of Shakespeare's: throw in a wrinkle just as he's wrapping up. Take the death of Cordelia at the end of *Lear*. Neither in his chronicle sources or the earlier *King Leir* does Cordelia die. One of the things that made Shakespeare's *Lear* shocking at the time is that he kills her off. Anyone who knew the story would have been taken unawares. It'd be like going to see a remake of *My Fair Lady* today in which Eliza Doolittle chokes to death on a crumpet.

So the writing at this time was exceptional, virtually unparalleled. We want then to understand something of the conditions that enabled it. Emerging from the perfumed rooms of Titchfield – if only figuratively – Shakespeare returned to the company of players. The plague had begun to abate near the end of 1593, but the long (and prudent) closure of London's playhouses had shaken the theatre industry. Around 1594, a new order emerged, with two stable companies securing residencies to the south and north of the City proper, at The Rose on the Southbank and The Theatre in Shoreditch (neighbourhoods whose names inscribe their marginality). They were not the only companies at the time but they proved to be the most durable, bringing some post-plague order to the theatre industry.

The two companies were arranged and licensed by the Court and, like most things in that rarified clime, they were a tangled family affair. (If the theatre world was tight knit, the aristocratic one was a knot.) Henry Carey, Lord Hunsdon and Lord Chamberlain formed a company. So did his son-in-law, Charles Howard, the previous Lord Chamberlain and now Lord Admiral. The two companies – the Lord Chamberlain's Men and the Lord Admiral's Men – first appeared together at a playhouse about a mile south of the city at Newington Butts on 3 June 1594, and played on alternating afternoons for about ten days. The owner of The Rose playhouse, Philip Henslowe, wrote upon that date, 'In the name of god Amen beginning at newington my lord Admiral men & my lord chamberlain men

As follows.'[2] This is the first surviving mention of the Lord Chamberlain's Men, the company Shakespeare would keep, and that would keep him, for the rest of his writing career.

This was a brief and rare run of two companies sharing a single playhouse. A list of their plays gives a quick glimpse of their 'starter repertories', assembled from the playbooks of the companies out of whose remnants they emerged. *Titus* and *Shrew* are there, along with the original *Hamlet* that Shakespeare would re-write, but also *Hester and Ahasuerus* (lost), Marlowe's *The Jew of Malta*, *Cutlack* (lost) and *Bellendon* (lost). Did the Lord Chamberlain's Men play one day and show up the next to stand in the pit to crack nuts and jokes at the Admiral's Men's expense? And vice versa? We can hope so. Once the plague finally quieted, the companies roosted in their respective nests at The Rose and The Theatre.

So in 1594 Shakespeare joined the Lord Chamberlain's Men, a group formed from the remains of Pembroke's and Derby's (formerly Strange's) companies, and they settled at The Theatre to the north-east of the city. This was the company he provided with plays and that, in return, provided him a steady income until late in his life. More importantly (from the perspective of posterity) the company provided the form and pressure that shaped his subsequent work. For however transcendent the plays, they flexed around the personnel and playhouses that Shakespeare had to hand. To understand the men he worked with and the playhouses he worked in is to understand the ways his art always answered both to his insistent muse *and* to the grubby materiality of playmaking. From 1594 onward, Shakespeare's company was the single greatest shaping factor upon the plays he produced. Shakespeare's plays are the plays that they are because of the players who first played them.

The first thing to say about 'Shakespeare's company' is that they were not Shakespeare's company. He was at best a co-owner since he bought a share in 1594. The share would fluctuate across his career, but he would not cash out until nearly fifteen years later. (Andrew Gurr has estimated that a share was worth fifty pounds in 1597 and so the price of entry was substantial.[3] Shakespeare may have used some of his plays as collateral or some of Southampton's cash.) So this aggregation of actors (a better collective noun would be a 'gripe') was not 'Shakespeare's company', it was the 'Lord Chamberlain's Men'. Except it wasn't that either, regardless of what Henslowe called them. Shakespeare and fellows were the 'Lord Chamberlain's Servants'.

This is more than just hair splitting. Calling Shakespeare and Co. the Lord Chamberlain's 'Men' sets Henry Lord Hunsdon up as a Robin Hood figure with a merry band of actors clinking tankards under the greenwood tree. Shakespeare and his fellow actors – Burbage, Heminges, Condell, Lowin, Kempe and the others – may have enjoyed being in Hunsdon's company, but that does not mean they enjoyed his company. Calling them his 'servants' reminds us that for all our romantic sense of company bonhomie, they were still a vertically integrated affair. In Elizabethan England, to paraphrase Bob Dylan, you had to serve somebody, and Shakespeare served the Lord Chamberlain until 1603, when James I became the company's patron.

In the years that follow 1594, across cast lists, warrants and wills, a core of men reappear around Shakespeare and give us a good sense of the confederates who made up his daily company, the men who shared his jokes, his meals and the million tedious tasks of putting on plays for money. Who was Shakespeare's best friend, though? After all, Shakespeare writes a lot about male friendship in his plays, and it is always a two-man show: Hamlet and Horatio, Brutus and Cassius, Palemon and Arcite. Was it Hemings and Condell – joined at the hip by history since they co-produced the 1623 folio – who gave Shakespeare the idea? Did Shakespeare have a particular friend, with whom he shared more than just worries over third-act problems or whether the new hand could pull his weight?

It is tempting to think that Richard Burbage, the Lord Chamberlain's principal tragedian, was Shakespeare's closest comrade, but there is no evidence for that. In his will of 1605, Augustine Phillips left Shakespeare 'a thirty shilling piece in gold',

while other actors like Robert Armin and Alexander Cooke
only got twenty. (Phillips's 'fellow Henry Condell' also received
thirty shillings in gold as did his 'servant Christopher Beeston'.[4])
Speaking of wills, Shakespeare left money for memorial rings
to both Heminges and Condell, who each had sons named
William (though that hardly makes them unusual at the time).
In his *Essay on the Genius and Writings of Shakespeare* of
1712, English critic John Dennis outlines the 'Inconveniences'
that stymied Shakespeare, citing the lack of friends with whom
to consult. He allows that Shakespeare might turn to 'two or
three of his Fellow-Actors' for consultation, but these friends
'were not qualified to advise him'.[5] In the end, there is not
much evidence for whom Shakespeare's bosom buddy might
have been. Perhaps his treatment of male friendship suggests
that such companionship was an ideal and an idyll.

There is, by contrast, evidence that while Shakespeare was
a company man he was not a company keeper. John Aubrey,
who cast the butcher's boy as Shakespeare's shadow, records
an interview with William Beeston, whose father, Christopher,
had worked with Shakespeare. He left a handwritten note that
reads, 'The more to be admired q[uia] he was not a company
keeper / lived in Shoreditch, would n[o]t be debauched, &
if invited to gout: he was in pain.'[6] The note is sketchy in a
number of ways. Christopher Matusiak has argued that it may
be about Beeston not Shakespeare.[7] It has also been variously
transcribed across the years ('gout'? 'court'? 'writ'?), but it has
consistently been cited by scholars to mean that Shakespeare
was a private man, who feigned physical discomfort to avoid
carousing or sexual exploits.

Aubrey's account contradicts another handwritten
testimony from the 1640s, this one by an unknown antiquarian
wandering London's suburbs. He visits Southwark's Tabard
Inn, renowned as the tavern in which Chaucer's pilgrims gather
in the *Canterbury Tales*. Of the Tabard he writes,

The Tabard I find to have been the resort Master Will
Shakspear Sir Sander Duncombe Lawrence Fletcher

Richard Burbage Ben Jonson and the rest of their roistering associates in King James's time as in the large room they have cut their names on the Pannels.[8]

The antiquarian pulls back the curtain and there they are! 'Shakspear' (authentically missing the medial 'e'), Burbage, Jonson, their fellow actor Lawrence Fletcher, and then – problematically – Sir Sander Duncombe, the Justice of the Peace for Middlesex, much younger than the others and who moved in different circles (he may well have added his name at another point). This trace about an act of historical vandalism – they 'cut their names on the Panels' – shows Shakespeare 'roistering' with the rest. The word practically reeks of clinking cans and filthy jokes. Shak[e]speare was a company keeper after all.

As so often with Shakespeare we are left with ambidextrous interpretations, with equally strong evidence on both hands. Was he a roisterer? Or not a company keeper? The two positions only conflict if we believe that human beings observe the behavioural stability that fictional characters do. Maybe Shakespeare sometimes liked to roister. Other times he did not. On one hand he enjoyed the company of co-workers. On the other hand, he did not.

Whether Shakespeare liked his co-workers or not – or vice versa – one thing is clear: they were hilarious. And so he wrote a string of gang comedies between 1594 and 1599: *Comedy of Errors* and *Love's Labour's Lost* but also *Much Ado about Nothing*, *A Midsummer Night's Dream*, *The Merry Wives of Windsor* and *As You Like It*. One man among them was the funniest of all. In fact he was the funniest man in England: William Kempe. His fame far surpassed his peers, and so securing him for the company was a major coup. The Lord Chamberlain's players look remarkable to us since they owned the plays of William Shakespeare and the talents of Richard Burbage. At the time, however, the most famous member of the company was also its clown. It was likely Kempe, not Shakespeare or Burbage, who was the company's ace in the hole, or joker up the sleeve. We see his imprint in *Much Ado*'s Dogberry, in *RJ*'s Peter, in *Dream*'s Bottom. He was a riot, and probably incited as much when he stepped out on stage after the final bows to perform a closing jig.

Shakespeare's romantic comedies dry up around the turn of the century with *Twelfth Night*. It is easy to conclude that when Shakespeare lost his son in 1596 he also lost all his mirth. But he also lost his clown. William Kempe left the company to pursue solo ventures early in 1599. This included a stunt where he morris-danced every bit of the 120 miles from London to Norwich in nine days, which doesn't sound funny. It sounds like a pain. In Kempe's picaresque but unfunny written account of the stunt at least one thing is clear. You kind of had to be there.

Kempe was replaced by Robert Armin, also funny but a different kind of funny. Snarky and sardonic where Kempe was rude and boisterous. The difference between Kempe and Armin is the difference between *Dream*'s Bottom and *Lear*'s fool. They are both 'wise fools' in their own ways. Lear's fool wears his wisdom on the sleeve where Bottom's comes from the bottom of his heart.

If Shakespeare was lucky to work with Kempe, he hit the jackpot with Richard Burbage. Not only was Burbage a great actor, he had his own playhouse. (Talent is silver; real estate is gold.) Burbage came from the most important theatre family in England, rivalled only by the Dutton brothers at the core of Queen Elizabeth's Company in the 1580s. James Burbage & Sons 'dominated the theatrical enterprise in London for three-quarters of a century', according to the great theatre historian John H. Astington.[9] Keeping company with Richard Burbage meant an affiliation with his father James and brother Cuthbert, whose connections and holdings were powerful and deep.

Unlike Shakespeare, Richard Burbage was a Londoner born and bred, and so he knew the turf in a way that Shakespeare didn't. His family lived in Shoreditch quite close to The Theatre, built by the joiner, player and family patriarch

James in 1576. If the Lord Chamberlain's Servants looked like a good bet to Shakespeare in 1594, the talents of Kempe and Burbage were part of the allure but so was the chance to join a tested theatre family with their own playhouse. Always attracted to property, Shakespeare's professional decision in 1594 was a prudent business move.

It was for, or with, Richard Burbage that Shakespeare wrote Hamlet, Othello, Macbeth, Lear and many many others. Not a bad run, but one that might have made friendship awkward, with William forever putting words in Richard's mouth. With William looking at Richard and seeing a murderer, a dotard, a lunatic, a magus. We know too little about Burbage's style of acting, but we can hear his cadences in these characters as surely as Shakespeare heard his voice in his head when he wrote them. Burbage was not just Shakespeare's colleague, he was his co-conspirator.

We occasionally hear Shakespeare riff on Burbage's roles, which we only surmise were always serious ones. *Twelfth Night* may be a *Hamlet* parody,[10] or at least a companion piece. Written just after the century turned, both plays open with a young person mourning the loss of a loved one. Both are determined to mourn far longer than others think fit. And both are visited by an unusual spectre, be it the ghost of their father or a cross-dressed woman. If Burbage played Malvolio, he could have paused after 'To be ...' when he came on stage alone at the outset of Act Two, Scene Five. Did the young law students of Middle Temple who watched *Twelfth Night* on 2 February 1602 titter before Burbage completed the line, '... *Count* Malvolio'? The 'wiser sort' who knew their *Hamlet* recalled a more famous ending to that line and let out the kind of chuckle that in-the-know audiences give to signal their membership in a coterie. What you will, Will.

Aubrey's note about Shakespeare's position on debauchery also runs headlong into an anecdote about Burbage and Shakespeare that circulated around 1602, and just because it did not happen does not mean it is not true. At the very least, it glances at the pair's celebrity. It appeared in the diary of

John Manningham – who was at the production of *Twelfth Night* at Middle Temple – and if ever an anecdote was reverse-engineered from its punch line, surely this is it.

> Upon a time when Burbage played Richard the Third there was a citizen grew so far in liking with him, that before she went from the play she appointed him to come that night unto her by the name of Richard the Third. Shakespeare, overhearing their conclusion, went before, was entertained and at his game ere Burbage came. Then, message being brought that Richard the Third was at the door, Shakespeare caused return to be made that William the Conqueror was before Richard the Third.[11]

This is absurd, of course. Groupies never sleep with the writer.

It took roughly four hundred years but Burbage finally came up with a snappy comeback. Antony Sher relates in his diary that when he played *Richard III* in 1984 his director, Terry Hands, warned him about sustaining a crippled position all evening. He urged him to alternate legs and hump from night to night and said, 'It's a little known historical fact, but apparently after the original production Burbage said to Shakespeare, "If you ever do that to me again, mate I'll kill you".'[12] That *is* a little known historical fact. But what nags these anecdotes into life is rivalry, and in particular the rivalry between the writer and the player. Shakespeare's and Burbage's working relationship may have been so close that it forbad friendship.

So the men Shakespeare wrote for left their mark upon his work. Through the veil of print we see their shadowy forms. There's the thin (the lean and hungry Cassius; the bull's pizzle Hal); the fat (the tun of bombast Falstaff); the long (painted maypole Helena) and the short (that minimus of knot grass Hermia). Or even Rosalind and Celia in *As You Like It*, who are alternatively and then simultaneously taller than one another according to the Folio text. Today, producers of these plays cast around typographical characters, shaping one kind of body to another. Originally, these characters took their shape from the bodies cast in these roles. Rosalind is not tall because the text says so, the text says so because Rosalind is tall – at least the boy playing her was. The plays have gone on to transcend the bodies that gave them first flesh, but something of the men and boys who first performed them haunt these characters even today.

Around 1594, then, Shakespeare shifted patrons from Henry Wriothesley to Henry Carey, and shifted his company from courtiers to comedians, as actors in the period were often called, whether funny as Kempe or sober as Shakespeare. He also exchanged the library at Titchfield for the boards of a Shoreditch playhouse. As noted above, 'The Theatre' was built around 1576 by James Burbage (and John Brayne), so when Shakespeare and the others took up occupancy there in 1594, Richard Burbage was coming home.

To us, 'The Theatre' may seem like the least imaginative name possible for a playhouse – it would be like calling this book 'The Book' – but consider this list:

The Red Lion
The Red Bull
The Curtain
The Rose
The Globe
The Hope
The Swan
The Fortune
The Theatre

One of these names is not like the others. They all share a definite article and they all name early modern playhouses, but only one of them is not named after a pub. To be more precise, these playhouses – all but one – are named like early modern inns and are, in that respect, perfectly conventional. The kind of name that perfectly conventional people might give to a playhouse. This is a banal observation but banality was exactly what these names had in mind.

And the banal end these names served was to identify their location. These names were also functional. It was not until 1762 that London began to number its buildings, to impose some order on London's teeming rebus of signs and symbols, an ancient and allusive network of images linked to occupations. For years, a London perfumer would traffic under the sign of a civet cat, whose flux forms an element of his work.

Since there were no numbered street addresses in London at the time, public buildings hung out signs to mark their locations. You can see this on the title pages of books from the period, advertising where you might buy them: at the sign of the gun on Threadneedle Street, at the sign of the little eagle on Butter Lane, etc. Calling a playhouse the 'Swan' or the 'Hope' inscribed it upon the surface of London's open page. It was a bid for normalcy, a bid to make these weird-looking buildings seem as common as an inn – as ordinary as, well, an ordinary. All but one: 'The Theatre'.

So what might seem to us like the least imaginative name on this list is the most imaginative name on the list. What James Burbage and John Brayne had in mind when they called their theatre 'The Theatre' was not the corner pub but classical antiquity, and the Latinate name they assigned their playhouse broadcast their ambitions (or their pretensions). The word 'theatre' means a place to see, and for Burbage and his partner Brayne, what they saw was the past, and – to some degree – their own role in the English Renaissance, a re-nascent interest in the drama of classical antiquity and an attempt to revive its spirit in a seedy London suburb.

The preacher John Stockwood knew just what James Burbage was up to. In a sermon preached at St Paul's Cross in 1578, he gripes about those 'gorgeous playing palaces erected in the field' (there are those fields again) and notes the players 'please to have it called a Theatre after the manner of the old heathenish Theatre at Rome'.[13] It didn't catch on. The

Theatre would be the only playhouse in the period to market itself explicitly as a bid for theatrical revivalism. When it was dismantled and re-mantled around 1599, it received a new name, one that might strike us as pretty ambitious but was in fact entirely normal: 'The Globe'.

*

From 1594 on Shakespeare's fortunes were tied to this company, the Lord Chamberlain's and then the King's Servants from 1603 through to around 1613 when he stepped back from the biz. Let's entertain a brief counterfactual for the sake of clarity. Following the run at Newington Butts, Shakespeare's career goes south, though only literally. He joins the Admiral's Servants on the Southbank at The Rose, where his plays mingle with those of Marlowe to form a killer repertory. He would have linked his fortunes to another powerful theatrical family, the entrepreneur, financier, and theatre owner Philip Henslowe and his son-in-law Edward Alleyn, an actor every bit the equal of Burbage.

Would things have turned out differently? Yes, if the argument of this chapter holds, that players and playhouses shaped Shakespeare's plays as much as his pen. What plays would he have bent around the talents of Alleyn and the rest of the Admiral's Servants (the 'Lord Admiral his servants')? Would he have a written a comedy about a beggar, since the Admiral's seemed to like such things? Or added a scene to Marlowe's *Faustus* for a late 1590s revival (Hamlet and Faustus passing each other in the dining hall of Wittenberg U.)? Who knows?

One thing is sure: had Shakespeare joined the Admiral's Men, his biographies would be even longer, because Henslowe and Alleyn possessed one thing that the Burbages did not, an archival impulse. Henslowe wrote things down and Alleyn saved them. We would know precisely when Shakespeare's plays were performed, what costumes they required and how much money they made. We would know how popular they were with audiences, something we now can only guess at through the uncertain metrics of print and contemporary allusion. We would know more precisely the chronology of the composition of Shakespeare's plays. And on and on. We would know, in short, far more about the commerce of Shakespeare's craft. We might even be able to answer with more precision the central questions of 1594: Why plays over poetry? Why the company of clowns not courtiers? Why popular audiences over private readers?

The choice of the one over the other, if it was a choice, is too starkly outlined here, since Shakespeare made a move at this time that suggests that the circles he moved in during the plague had not entirely lost their appeal. He may have left Titchfield for Finsbury Fields, but he was still haunted, or at least impressed, by what he'd witnessed there. For Shakespeare was chasing more than just money in these years. He was chasing status.

11

William Shakespeare, Gent.

Shakespeare's bid for gentle status was the one big buy he made in his life that did not promise a financial return. The purchase of New Place, a share in the Lord Chamberlain's, the acquisition of Stratford tithes, all these splashes were *investments*, promising, if not guaranteeing, capital returns. But the purchase of a coat of arms, the acquisition of the word 'gentleman' that he could stick on the back-end of his name, well, there was nothing in it. You could not bargain with it, live in it, buy sheep with it, or use it as dowry for one of your daughters. We need to shift the question, then, and ask not what was the *value* of the word 'gentleman' to Shakespeare, but what was it *worth*.

It was apparently worth a lot to him, since he pursued it despite the weakness of his claim, a weakness he was too wise not to recognize. (This is a man who wrote a parodic passage of over sixty lines in *Henry V* outlining Henry's claim to France based on a genealogical chain of ancestors that grows weaker with each link.) In his dedicatory epistle to *Lucrece*, Shakespeare wrote, 'were my worth greater, my duty would show greater. ...' This plaintive non-sequitur tells us something of the writer's insecurity, even as we allow that dedications are governed by convention, as predictable as the blues. And if Shakespeare had the blues in the 1590s it was because he was on the outside looking in. Actually, it was worse than that. Having performed at court, having possibly lived at Titchfield with Wriothesley, he was on the inside looking in. Not to the manor born, only a guest there.

Shakespeare's desire for his duty to 'show greater' draws our attention to what kind of show his newly acquired status, if he could acquire it, would allow him to make. What was in it for him that made it worth the time and money? According to the letter of the patent, holders of coats of arms were free to emblazon it just about anywhere they liked, on their luggage, on their house, on their rings, on their clothing. There's no evidence Shakespeare ever did so, which suggests that he acquired a coat of arms that he was reluctant to wear, expressing a tension between reticence and display, an agony that informs his sonnets and possibly drew him to and repulsed him from a life on the stage.

*

Social climbing ran in his family since it was Shakespeare's father, John, who initiated the claim in the 1570s, when Will was just a boy. The claim evidently went nowhere, and while there's no surviving documentation about who re-opened it in 1596 it was likely William of London, not John of Stratford. The easy reading is a lightly Oedipal one, without the unfortunate Jocasta stuff. Shakespeare acquires a coat of arms in John's name as a way to redeem his father's fallen financial stature, or remind him of it. But that version of things might overstate his father's penury while clearing Shakespeare of status anxiety.

It also might exaggerate William Shakespeare's role in what was, after all, a coat of arms awarded to his father. The application and approval of John Shakespeare's appeal for a coat of arms was typical of the time. By the standards that governed the entire heraldic racket, the claim was slightly spurious. An unnamed ancestor – a grandfather in one draft, great-grandfather in another – performed some service for Henry VII, who rewarded him with land and revenue. Besides, the application goes on, John Shakespeare wed Mary Arden, heir to Robert Arden of Wilmcote, esquire. And that's it. Not exactly knights-of-the-roundtable stuff.

The grant was approved but Shakespeare, father or son, added a defensive motto to their coat of arms – a shield of yellow bisected by a spear against a black stripe with a silver falcon clutching a gold spear (the visual pun on the family name appears twice in case you miss it the first time). With hindsight, the falcon's silver-tipped spear looks a lot like a fancy fountain pen.

Mottos were not requisite, and it's not included with the coat of arms on Shakespeare's bust above his tomb in Holy Trinity. But bearers could compose a Latin motto to accompany their coat and Shakespeare's was *'non sans droict'*, or 'not without right'. The nervous double negative tells us all we need to know, but, reliably, Ben Jonson is on hand with a sardonic gloss. In his *Every Man out of his Humour* (1599) Puntarvolo mocks Sogliardo, a country rube, saying that his motto should be 'Not without mustard' (3.1.244). This likely refers to Shakespeare's motto and, possibly, the yellow colour of his arms. Shakespeare probably appeared in this play and might have winced at the gag, or at least regretted ever getting involved in the business.

If he felt that way in 1599, he had more reason to do so in the coming years because Shakespeare got caught in the crossfire between William Dethick, Garter King of Arms, and Ralph Brooke, a York herald. The 'Garter King of Arms' was the highest ranking herald in the land, chief among the thirteen others who formed the College of Arms. Brooke hated Dethick and his enmity produced a fortunately long paper trail.

Fortunate for us, that is, since we know what we know about Shakespeare's coat of arms because Brooke challenged the claim. Essentially, the York herald snitched on Dethick to any noble who would listen – all the way up to Elizabeth I. His beef was that Dethick was granting arms not for the protection of the realm but for personal profit (the application fee was steep, between five and ten pounds). As bad, the crests were derivative from more established families. In few, Shakespeare shows up on a list of twenty-three names whose claims were both dubious and derivative and, Brooke alleges, evidence of a crass cash grab by William Dethick.

From a modern perspective, the entire enterprise looks absurd – the fancy crests, the tangled lineages, the obvious profiteering. Shakespeare's Edmund in *King Lear* dismantles the flimsy apparatus of gentility in his casual deconstruction of the word 'legitimate' as he stands up for bastards. Still, early modern England had a lot invested in upholding a class, or caste, system, which is just one more way in which it did not differ from modern England. The granting of arms at the time was an institutional fiction, an agreement whereby arms could be had for ready money, and pedigrees purchased for a price. Arms were part right, part racket.

If one thing is clear from the affair, it is that you did not want to get caught in the middle of a tiff between two heralds. This was not a slap fight between two ink-stained antiquarians. Dethick was a violent and hot-tempered man, and Brooke was every bit his equal. He took his complaints right to the top, and claimed to have submitted his grievances to Queen Elizabeth in late 1601. If she looked at it, she might have seen the name of a player known to her, if not by name then by sight, since Shakespeare had performed for her at court many times. According to anecdote, she'd even asked him to write *The Merry Wives of Windsor*, a play about a 'knight', Sir John Falstaff, whose behaviour belies his status. However much she liked Shakespeare's plays, she might have wondered what he was doing claiming gentle status.

In the hurly burly between Brooke and Dethick, there is some slipperiness between the names of John and William Shakespeare, father and son. As the affair dragged on, William replaces John in the complaint since John had died by 1602. Dethick's defence – and it was as detailed as it was spirited – came to rest not on John Shakespeare but on his fortunate son. It is slightly unclear, but when Dethick defends the Shakespeare claim and notes that he has 'lands and tenements of good wealth and substance, 500 pounds', he seems to refer to 'Shakespeare the player' not John the glover. Noble or not, William Shakespeare was well off, at least in the expedient argument of Dethick's defence.

Countering Dethick, Brooke described Shakespeare as a 'player'. He didn't mean it as a compliment. In fact, it was part of Brooke's strategy to demean the status of the holders of these arms by accurately describing them. Elsewhere, he calls William Sanderson a 'fishmonger' and William Norton a 'bookbinder'. Both were important merchants or artisans and held high offices within their guilds. It would be like calling Spinoza a 'lens grinder' or Jesus a 'woodworker'. Strictly true, but not exactly the point. But Brooke is hewing to the definition of a 'gentleman', as one who, in Sir Thomas Smith's definition, 'can live idly and without manual labour'. Whatever you could say about Shakespeare, you could not call him idle.

When the smoke finally cleared it may have been Shakespeare who felt burned. Or at least emerged with his wings singed. The subsequent records give us a figurative fix on the sorry affair. For like stamp collecting and train spotting, heraldic records attracted amateur interest, and enthusiasts compiled 'alphabets and ordinaries', lists of the blazons and arms of noble families. There is then fairly ample documentation of the Shakespeare coat of arms into the early seventeenth century.

One oddity of these records is that they do not agree about what the falcon perched on the top of Shakespeare's shield is doing. In some, the falcon is 'mantling', spreading its wings in a show of strength, or simply to warm them in the sun. In roughly half of the records, however, the falcon's wings are tucked demurely into its body, one side of its face turned away from the world. In the language of heraldry, in one version the falcon's wings are 'displayed'. In the other, they are 'addorsed'. Was Shakespeare a bold falcon or a retiring one?

Through an accident of record keeping we have an image of a tension in Shakespeare's temperament, a tendency to preen on one hand and cover up on the other. There is something in Shakespeare of that familiar oxymoron, the shy actor, as retiring in his private life as he is revealing in his public one.

In fact the figure is so familiar that a 'shy actor' is not an oxymoron. It is an explanation. Shakespeare the player, the playwright, the poet, the public figure and the private man, was neither entirely displayed or addorsed. He was both.

Whether displayed or addorsed, Shakespeare is first identified as a 'gentleman' in a deed of trust from 7 October 1601 when the owner of the land upon which The Globe was built mortgaged it to his stepbrother.[1] If he was hesitant to emblazon his coat of arms on all of his belongings – what would Ben Jonson have said had Shakespeare turned up at rehearsal with his coat of arms emblazoned on his hand bag? – he was willing to prefix 'Mr', for 'master', to the front of his name and suffix 'gent' to the end. We can draw one conclusion from this affair of arms. Shakespeare had come a long way in his first thirty-four years. From Stratford schoolboy to London gent. We can also conclude that Shakespeare was one of those rare individuals whose wealth and status increased not diminished when he turned his back on the family trade and took up writing instead.

*

Where did the money come from? Shakespeare's first biographer thought that Southampton gave him a thousand pounds. To give you a sense of how much money a thousand pounds was in 1594, today it would be *a thousand pounds*. Still not a sum to scoff at. (It would actually be worth nearly 400,000 pounds in twenty-first-century currency.[2])

A more meaningful comparison is that a thousand pounds is a greater sum than all the real-estate investments Shakespeare made in his lifetime. With a thousand pounds Shakespeare could have purchased New Place, a coat of arms, a share in a playing company and have had enough left over to pay Francis Meres to say nice things about him.

Whatever the amount, it is a near certainty that the poetic shakedown worked, and Southampton gave William some heavy bank. What exactly he did with it is unclear, though he made three major investments at this time. Or, rather, one major investment and two substantial purchases. He invested in the Lord Chamberlain's company, and he purchased New Place and a coat of arms.

From here, the grant of arms looks like a slightly sweaty, reverse-engineered gentility. It was no doubt a nice thing for Shakespeare to do for his dad, but one stipulation of the grant was that 'it shall be lawful for his [John's] children issue and posterity (lawfully begotten) to bear use and quarter and show for the arms'. The coat of arms was a gift that kept on gilding, made by a son to his father which had the added benefit of profiting the giver. Like the Clown in *Winter's Tale*, Shakespeare was preposterously 'a gentleman born before my father' (5.2.149–50). More importantly, the coat made William Shakespeare second-generation gentility, clearing the air of the smell of fresh paint that clung to the coat itself.

Until his father's death, William was entitled to bear these arms 'with a difference', an added mark that indicated that he was the holder's son. His father died in September of 1601, after which Shakespeare could bear the arms 'without difference'. The phrase echoes faintly in *Hamlet*, when Ophelia tells Gertrude she should wear her rue 'with a difference' (4.5.180–1). The rue emblematizes both sorrow and repentance – Hamlet and Ophelia believe Gertrude lacks both – but the language of heraldry draws our attention elsewhere. It is not Gertrude's but Ophelia's father who has died. It is Ophelia not Gertrude who can now wear her coat without a difference. As so often, if Shakespeare's personal preoccupations leak into his plays, they do so obliquely.

For instance, *Hamlet* is a play about a son mourning a father, not the other way around, although by the early seventeenth century Shakespeare had cause to do both. The coat of arms was granted in October of 1596, but the sweetness of it might have tasted of ashes. Two months earlier, on 11 August 1596, Shakespeare's only son, Hamnet, had been buried in Stratford. Cause of death – and location of grave site – unknown. The irony is cruel, even vicious, even Shakespearean. Shakespeare now had a coat of arms and no one to pass it on to, a mundane version of the 'barren sceptre' that nags Macbeth to death.

What was the coat of arms worth to William Shakespeare without a father to appreciate it and a son to inherit it? He was not shy about using the title of 'gentleman' throughout the rest of his life, at least in legal matters, where the status could attain better terms of credit for the holder (Shakespeare was also not shy about finding the best angle in his various transactions). When reliable Ben Jonson refers to 'gentle Shakespeare' in his commendatory folio poem, it is worth remembering that it refers both to Shakespeare's natural temperament but also a position dearly bought. Perhaps guaranteeing that you will be remembered as 'gentle' was worth it in the end.

12

Shakespeare at Court

It is a little-known historical fact today that Shakespeare shared the stage with Elizabeth I. The Victorians knew it, however, since back in the early nineteenth century:

> It is well known that queen Elizabeth was a great admirer of the immortal Shakespeare, and used frequently (as was the custom with people of great rank in those days) to appear upon the stage before the audience and to sit delighted behind the scenes while the plays of the bard were performed. One evening Shakspeare performed the part of the king (probably *Henry the Fourth*) the audience knew of her majesty being in the house. She crossed the stage while Shakspeare was performing his part, and on receiving the accustomed greeting from the audience, moved politely to the poet, but he did not notice it! – when behind the scenes, she caught his eye and moved again but still he would not throw off his character to notice her; this made her majesty think of some means to know *whether he would or would not depart from the dignity of his character while on the stage.* Accordingly, as he was about to make his exit, she stepped before him, dropped her glove, and recrossed the stage; which Shakspeare noticing, took up with these words, so immediately after finishing his speech, that they seemed as belonging to it, 'And though now bent on this high embassy, / Yet stoop we to take up our cousin's glove.'

He then walked off the stage, and presented the glove to the queen, who was highly pleased with his behaviour and complimented him on its propriety.[1]

The idea that Shakespeare handled Elizabeth's glove and called her his 'cousin' is even more implausible than the Richard III anecdote. At least the story doesn't conclude with Shakespeare reminding Elizabeth I that William the Conqueror came before her as well.

The anecdote is from the early 1800s and who knows where it came from (it shows up 'first' in the *Dramatic Table Talk* of Richard Ryan in 1825). It exaggerates Shakespeare's familiarity with the Queen, but he *was* a familiar face at court. In fact, the first mention of him as a member of the 'Lord Chamberlain's Servants' comes on 15 March 1595 when he, Richard Burbage and William Kempe collected twenty pounds for performing 'Comedies or Enterludes' the previous Christmas before Elizabeth. (The payment was late. Seems Shakespeare and the Queen both belonged to the order of the tight fist.) It does not take three men to collect twenty pounds, suggesting a formality to the occasion or at least some fun. A chance to fluff your ruff and natter with the nobs.

Shakespeare, Burbage and Kempe were not alone. Edward Alleyn, Richard Jones and John Singer of the Lord Admiral's Servants were there as well to collect payment for *their* Christmas entertainments. In fact, the Lord Admiral's Men had outpaced the Chamberlain players the previous Christmas, giving three plays to the Chamberlain's two. Could they have resisted the chance to needle Shakespeare and crew about outperforming them? Still, these men were more even than at odds. They were members of a small fraternity of players who crossed paths in provinces and palaces throughout their working lives.

Christmas 1594 might have been Shakespeare's first visit to court as a servant of the Lord Chamberlain, but he probably had played there before and would often again. There are records of one hundred and seventy performances at court by the Lord Chamberlain's/King's Men between the formation of the company in 1594 and Shakespeare's 'retirement' around 1611.[2] In 1611/12 alone the King's Men appeared at court on over twenty separate occasions. Given the plague closures that shut the playhouses over and over again under James, in the mid-1610s the company was almost exclusively a court company.

This is worth keeping in mind. We tend to associate Shakespeare with The Globe, whose trademark Tudor timber-and-lath registers Shakespeare's popular touch. He is the playwright of the common sort, who thronged to the outdoor playhouse to roar at Kempe's antics and weep at Burbage's tears. And of course he did write for the outdoor playhouse, but he also wrote for court. We need to temper our image of *al fresco* Shakespeare with the fact that his plays were designed to please the royals.

In fact, they were licensed to please. It may have been a mere legal nicety, but playing companies were permitted to play in public to keep them in readiness to come up to court and amuse the monarch. When King James patented Shakespeare and his fellow players in 1603, they were licensed to delight James' 'loving subjects' but charged 'for our solace and pleasure when we shall think good to see them during our pleasure'.[3] Shakespeare wrote to amaze the common crowd but he also wrote to appease an audience of one, one who wore the crown.

The opening anecdote also depicts Shakespeare as utterly sure footed. And yet, in the mid-1590s, he stepped in it, stumbling into a minor 'crisis' he could easily have avoided. The anecdote identifies *Henry IV* as the play in question (with Shakespeare playing the king), and it was this play that tripped Shakespeare up. It all started when he got the bright idea that central to his dramatic treatment of Henry IV and his interesting son Hal would be a voluble and drunken knight named Sir John Falstaff. Except that, at least at first, Sir John Falstaff wasn't named 'Falstaff'. He was named 'Oldcastle'.

Shakespeare was neither stupid nor lazy, but naming a fat buffoon 'Oldcastle' seems like both. 'Oldcastle' was an ancestor of William Lord Cobham, who was, at the time of the play's composition, the Lord Chamberlain. Confusingly, he was *not* the Lord Chamberlain whom Shakespeare and co. worked for. In 1596, just two years after the company formed, their patron, the Lord Chamberlain, Henry Lord Hunsdon, died, and William Lord Cobham assumed his office. Cobham was not particularly hostile to the theatre, but his ascension may have rankled the players who thought their new patron, Sir George Carey, the weak-chinned son of Henry Lord Hunsdon, should assume the office of Lord Chamberlain upon his father's death. They soon got their wish, since Cobham caught an 'ague' in the winter of 1596–7, made his will on 24 February 1597 and died at Blackfriars on 6 March. In the interim between Shakespeare's patrons serving as Lord Chamberlain, however, Cobham was the man literally in charge of playing at Court, and Shakespeare's 'Oldcastle' was an unmistakable allusion to Cobham's honoured ancestor.

There is another alternative, that Shakespeare misunderstood his source or trusted it too much. He lifted 'Oldcastle' from the *Famous Victories of Henry the V*, a very good play that is often maligned for not being as good as the one it engendered. *The Famous Victories* opens with England in a panic about Protestantism – no man may speak of it, none shall leave the parish, people are starving (far from Falstaff's gourmandizing, Oldcastle distributes food to the hungry) – a religious conflict largely stripped from Shakespeare's *Henry IV* and of little account to his treatment of Oldcastle. In fact, the historical Oldcastle died a Protestant martyr and was honoured in John Foxe's *Acts and Monuments*, a chronicle of England's persecuted protestants. Shakespeare's treatment diverges widely from this history, to put it mildly. But if he misunderstood his sources in converting Oldcastle into a buffoon, why didn't anyone gently clear their throat and point it out to him?

In addition to being neither stupid nor lazy, Shakespeare was not a poor reader of literary fiction. Let us extend him some credit then (he's good for it; he's got property still gathering interest in Stratford). Let us consider that Shakespeare knew exactly what he was doing. Maybe Cobham just got up his nose. After all, as Shakespeare wrote in *Merchant of Venice*, some men piss themselves at the sound of a bagpipe. Maybe Cobham was a windbag Shakespeare could not stomach. Or perhaps he was demonstrating his loyalty to the Hunsdon clan, who expected George Carey to assume the position of Lord Chamberlain upon his father's death. Perhaps Cobham called Southampton a girl. Who knows, but the evidence is as good if not better that Shakespeare satirized Oldcastle than that he tripped over his own feet and landed in hot water. On balance, the evidence suggests that he converted Oldcastle from a Protestant martyr into an avaricious lout to needle William Cobham.

Whatever the reason, it was a misstep, and he was forced to backtrack. And since he overstepped, he overcorrected. In the epilogue to *Henry IV Part 2*, Shakespeare (or someone) goes out of his way to point out that 'Oldcastle died a martyr, and this is not the man' (Epi. 31–2). It's a clunker of a line and not the sort of thing you usually get in an epilogue. It sounds like an errata slip at the end of a book, a fault that escaped. It doesn't particularly sound like Shakespeare, and not because he was incapable of writing clunkers ('Bring hither Harry Hertford', wrote Shakespeare in *Richard II*). It doesn't sound like Shakespeare because it's so forced. It sounds like a line written by a man with a gun at his head.

The more famous anecdote about Shakespeare and Queen Elizabeth finds her asking him to write another play about Falstaff: 'the queen being so pleased with the character of Falstaff that she "commanded him to continue it for one Play more, and to shew him in Love"',[4] according to Nicholas Rowe, whose biography launched a number of what Bob Dylan calls 'traditional facts'. If true, the play turned out to be an act of mild insurrection, since the play shows Falstaff in a buck basket, in a mire, in a pickle, but not in love. In fact, it shows him chasing women out of economic as much as erotic desire, a theme Elizabeth was all too familiar with.

In *Merry Wives* Shakespeare tried on the fashion for contemporary drama like a modish coat. It did not fit. He shrugged it off and went on to write plays set in Venice, in Denmark, in Rome, in Athens. Everywhere but England. But the play has half-a-dozen comic set pieces that more than earn their keep and offers a rich look at life among the middle-class English at the time. As Friedrich Engel wrote to his pal Karl Marx in 1873, 'There is more life and reality in the first act of the *Merry Wives* alone than in all German literature.' Whether you consider this high praise or the faint kind depends on whether you are German.

The Elizabeth anecdote is a typically misogynist way to excuse Shakespeare's most feminist play – a woman made him write it, against his will. *Merry Wives* was probably not composed upon command, but it did enjoy a command performance. It was almost certainly played to celebrate the induction of several knights into the Order of the Garter (which is not even remotely what it sounds like). The play finds Shakespeare yet again pillorying Cobham. Disguised in an attempt to catch his wife philandering, Master Ford assumes the name 'Brook' in the play's 1602 quarto. 'Brook' was Lord Cobham's surname and the name appears as 'Broom' in the 1623 folio. Perhaps a revision was made after the first performance to sweep Shakespeare's cheek under the rug.

Among those inducted into the Order of the Garter in May 1597 was Shakespeare and company's new patron, Sir George Carey, now Lord Hunsdon, and now Lord Chamberlain. This may have been what Shakespeare wanted all along. He may have lost the battle, but he won the war. And yet the 'Oldcastle' incident is an unusual episode for the reticent Shakespeare, who didn't stick his neck out very often. There's not much in his plays that smacks of anti-this or anti-that. No scathing satire of Protestants or biting take-downs of Catholics (you can hear Shakespeare murmur across the years, 'Catholics buy tickets too …'). The Oldcastle incident may have alerted Shakespeare to the opalescent uncertainties of political favouritism. It may also have made Shakespeare long for the relative security of writing smutty Ovidian fan fiction for well-heeled young courtiers.

Both Elizabeth anecdotes indulge a fantasy that Shakespeare was her pocket poet. The Queen probably knew who he was, but these anecdotes are fuelled by a desire to link the two greatest celebrities of the age. Queen Elizabeth had bigger fish to fry at the time than the fate of Sir John Falstaff.

Shakespeare and Elizabeth had one more rendezvous with history, or with a history play. The Oldcastle incident was an unforced error. But the King's Men scored an own goal with a performance of *Richard II* in 1601. For that year the Earl of Essex made a play for the crown. Formerly one of the Queen's pets, the Earl of Essex had fallen out of favour by the turn of the century. Possessed of a certain glamour, he inspired both idolatry and idiocy (the former often leads to the latter). He and his followers marched on the court on 8 February but were rebuffed. They returned to the city to rally support but Londoners were literate enough to read the writing on the wall. Essex holed up in a house on the Strand, but he and his followers soon surrendered and were executed over the next two months.

Southampton was of Essex's party, but his charm and good hair came in handy once again (so did Mary Wriothesley, his powerful mother). His sentence was commuted and he spent two years in the Tower, accompanied by his books and – legend has it – his black and white cat who crawled down the chimney to join him. Let us imagine he named it 'William'.

Shakespeare's company was drawn into this miserable farce by one of the plotters, Sir Gelly Meyrick, who paid them to perform *Richard II* on the eve of the coup. Meyrick imagined that *Richard II* would be topical since it features the deposition of an unpopular king by a charismatic bully (as with the Elizabeth and Essex affair, there was no legal pretext for the usurpation. Richard is deposed because nobody likes him).

One of the Chamberlain players, Augustine Phillips, testified to the court who made the inquiries that *Richard II* was 'so old and so long out of use' that the company feared that no-one would come. Meyrick gave them forty reasons (or forty shillings) to do the play anyway. It speaks to the political acumen of Essex and his followers that they thought one good way to overthrow a monarch was to perform a 3,000-line, talky blank-verse drama about a medieval king to really rile the people up.

The attempt to find in this episode a charged centrality of Shakespeare and company in the era's political affairs founders on the fact that no one really *cared* that a group of players had staged *Richard II*. They *noticed*, of course, and the Privy Council summoned them to explain themselves. But while the Privy Council noticed, they *still* didn't really care. The Lord Chamberlain's Servants were let off with a slap on the wrists and were back at court later that year performing for the Queen in their borrowed robes. In fact, they performed for the Queen on the very eve of Essex's execution. This was either a 'no harm done' gesture or a reminder of just who paid the piper.

Shakespeareans like to cite this episode to demonstrate the vital importance of Elizabethan drama at the time. But there are several readings of this scene that do the company little credit. The lack of punishment may reveal that they were viewed as patsies, or pawns of more powerful men. Ready for hire but none the wiser about the affairs they had been paid to participate in.

The other conclusion is that Essex was an idiot. The only judgement he seems to have possessed was the bad kind. Perhaps he was the kind of man who surfaces now and then, possessed of a certain kind of charisma that attracts followers despite (or because of) his ludicrously poor decisions.

Taking a longer view of Shakespeare's career, it is possible to conclude that these scrapes with the law put him off history plays for good. He would not write another until much later in his life when Elizabeth was good and dead and her distant cousin James sat upon the throne.

It is also possible, in fact likely, that James' accession was very good for the company for which Shakespeare worked, ensuring their stability, longevity and profitability when he became their patron in 1603. But the passing of Elizabeth may have marked a turning point in Shakespeare's popularity, which seemed to be at a height around the turn of the century. He had, without question, magnificent work ahead of him. Some of his best, so that the passing of the sixteenth century saw no diminution of his theatrical powers, quite the opposite. But of sweet, honey-dripping Shakespeare, beloved of the younger sort for his sugared sonnets? He had gone sour.

Indeed, Shakespeare's plays fit awkwardly with the Jacobean enthusiasm for masques, satires and learned encomiums. In keeping with his lifelong reticence, Shakespeare did not contribute to the coronation masques and speeches celebrating James' ascension, despite being in the official employ of the new king. That honour went to Dekker and Jonson. Nor did Shakespeare write a stand-alone court masque, as far as we know, and his own version of a masque, inserted into his late play, *The Tempest*, is beautiful but breaks off before it can conclude.

It may be unrelated but Shakespeare's print output dried up. Though his early plays continued to sell well in reprint, after 1603 only three Shakespeare titles appeared during his lifetime, *Lear* in 1608, *Troilus and Cressida* in 1609 and *Pericles* that same year. It may be that Shakespeare seemed, in a very real way, a strictly Elizabethan playwright. His time, like his Queen's, was past. It is fitting then that one of his last plays, *Henry VIII*, looks back to Elizabeth, in fact looks back beyond her. Her birth ends his last play as perhaps her death marked the height of Shakespeare's popularity.

Lois Potter coined the phrase 'Elizabethan Merry/Jacobean Decadent' to characterize the difference in the cultural moments that Shakespeare's career straddled.[5] Plays need not fall strictly under one monarch or the other to 'count' as Elizabethan or Jacobean – there are plays from Elizabeth's reign, like Marlowe's, that 'feel' Jacobean, and vice versa – rather it's the way that plays palpate certain cultural fixations or anxieties.

We could choose two plays from Shakespeare's works to signify this difference, *The Merry Wives of Windsor* (1597) and *Troilus and Cressida* (1602). The former is a merry suburban romp, the latter a piece of sordid classical drag. The former ends with a group of children dressed as fairies dancing a rondel around Falstaff under Herne the Hunter's oak. The latter ends with a pimp bequeathing his diseases to the audience. The two plays are separated by about five years but they are worlds apart. The one antic, the other attic. The one merry, the other decadent. Shakespeare lived, worked and thrived in both ages, but if James was the monarch he died under, it was during the Elizabethan reign that he came to life.

Whoever sat on the throne, court was the crucible in which his plays were proved. However much the groundlings mattered to Shakespeare – particularly the pennies they parted with to under-stand his plays – it was the hothouse of court that might make or mar his fortunes. The court was the Chamberlain's Men's steadiest gig since the commercial theatre was hostage to a thousand contingencies – bad weather, ill actors and, above all, the plague. Theatre is also plagued by real estate, and in the late 1590s, just as the company was finding its stride, they were losing their lease.

13

Shakespeare's Globe?

The Globe was an afterthought. In 1597 the Chamberlain players faced eviction from their Shoreditch Theatre. No matter. They had something bigger in mind. Or smaller, rather, but warmer and drier. For in the last of his bold moves, James Burbage had purchased the large upper rooms of a defunct monastery in the exclusive Blackfriars neighbourhood in the south-west corner of the City of London. A children's company had played elsewhere in the compound in previous decades, but Burbage's big idea was to house a company of adult actors in a customized indoor theatre where they could perform daily all year round at a prestige ticket price.

It was a terrific idea, ahead of its time, but Burbage neglected one thing. He should have asked the neighbours if they'd mind a bunch of grown men putting on plays in their backyard. He didn't, and they did.

The neighbours petitioned the Privy Council, who scuppered Burbage's plans. He got out of this jam by dying, but he left his sons in a pickle. They now had two playhouses – inside and out – but could not perform in either. It was only then that Shakespeare and his co-workers built The Globe. And so the Western world's most famous theatre was a stop-gap, a second thought, a last-ditch effort to salvage the professional fortunes of Shakespeare's company.

The story of how The Globe came to be is too good to be true. Except that it is true. The Lord Chamberlain's Servants stole their own playhouse from under the nose of their landlord. As legend has it, Shakespeare and his intrepid fellows, in the dead of a dark and snowy night, dismantled The Theatre and transported the timbers through the City to the Thames, which had fortuitously frozen, enabling them to drag the material across the river and avoid the fee to pass over London Bridge. They then re-mantled The Theatre and called it 'The Globe'.

Like Shakespeare's *Henry V*, which turns the 'accomplishments of many years' into a couple of hours, this story compresses a labour of many months into a single night. It adds the fancy of a frozen river for a dash of local colour. The Thames *did* freeze from time to time, allowing for the occasional 'Frost Fair', in which the iced-over river was picturesquely dotted with pop-up pubs, football pitches, shoemakers, barbers and more. The first fair wasn't until 1607, however. Still, Shakespeare could have got his hair cut on ice, if he had any left by then.

While legend has applied its usual lacquer, the unvarnished facts shimmer with intrigue. The problem was this: the Chamberlain's Servants owned The Theatre but not the land it stood on. James Burbage had originally negotiated a lease of the land for twenty-one years with the property owner, Giles Allen. As their lease neared termination in 1597, their landlord did what landlords do, hiked the rent, and the company would not meet his terms.

Cuthbert and Richard Burbage inherited more than just their father's debts. They got his daring as well. They hatched a plan to pick up their playhouse and move it to the Southbank to a plot of land they leased in December 1598. Just after Christmas, when Giles Allen was at his home in Hadleigh, Essex (*not* enjoying the holiday since his leanings were Puritan), the builder Peter Street and crew demolished The Theatre and took the timbers south, stored them for the winter, and in the spring 'The Globe on the Bank Side' took root and bloomed.

Giles Allen did what Giles Allens do. He sued. In the lawsuit Allen charges that on 28 December 1598 Richard Burbage and a scrum of eleven armed themselves with diverse and many unlawful and offensive weapons, as namely, swords daggers bills axes and such like And so armed did then repair unto the said Theatre And then and there armed as aforesaid in very riotous outrageous and forcible manner and contrary to the laws of your highness Realm attempted to pull down the said Theatre.[1]

The Burbages countersued, and the court found in their favour on 18 October 1599. Allen was left with a vacant plot in a down-market neighbourhood. Shakespeare and his fellow actors met the new century with a spruced-up playhouse south of the river, where The Rose had drawn audiences for over a decade. Every play Shakespeare wrote from this time on would appear at The Globe, and his fortune and fame are tied to this playhouse.

There was an interim between the end of the lease on The Theatre and the building of The Globe. During that period, the Chamberlain's Men moved next door to The Curtain, a Shoreditch theatre dug up in 2012 during construction. (Groundbreaking discoveries are an occupational hazard for London builders. They can't set a spade in the earth without turning up a bit of Roman terracotta or an Elizabethan playhouse.) Intriguingly, The Curtain seems to have been rectangular, not polygonal. As was The Red Lion, discovered in 2019. These finds tell us that there was no such thing as a 'typical' London playhouse. All plays at the time were elastically constructed, in any event, built to flex to fit a wide range of places, inside and out, upscale and down-market.

Shakespeare was probably not among the wrecking crew that took down The Theatre in 1598, but the move to the Southbank set him packing. He relocated south of the river, to the Clink parish in Surrey, an easy walk to The Globe, where he'd work for the rest of his writing career. He can be found there on the Southbank not paying his taxes in 1597 and 1598.

Shakespeare likely moved to Southwark to be closer to work, but also to avoid the hassle of crossing the Thames every day. The Southbank was accessible by bridge from the

City, but it required money and a passport to cross and enter Southwark. It was easier to go by water but that required a penny fare. (Maps from the era show the Thames full of ferries scurrying like water bugs from bank to bank and capsizing now and then.) London's watermen depended upon the playhouse traffic for their livelihood. In 1593 they petitioned the Lord Admiral to re-open Henslowe's Rose after the plague since they missed the traffic. After 1598, however, they would not be getting any of William Shakespeare's pennies.

The move to the Southbank eased Shakespeare's daily commute, but it added an hour to his trip home to Stratford. (He still didn't purchase property in London, continuing his bachelor's habit of living in rented digs.) In moving from the north of the City to its southern suburb, he found himself in a different sort of neighbourhood. The Southbank of legend is a licentious place, full of brothels and bear-baiting pits, and so fit for poets and players. It was also the home of hospitals and holy houses, palaces and prisons – the Clink, Counter, Marshalsea, White Lion and the King's Bench. If it was a place of liberty, it was also a place of restraint.

But those are just facts. In the popular imagination the places of playing – Southbank and Shoreditch – were playgrounds. One rhymester wrote,

> Speake Gentlemen, what shall we do today?
> Drink some brave health upon the Dutch carouse
> Or shall we to the *Globe* and see a Play?
> Or visit *Shorditch* for a bawdy house?
> Lets call for Cards or Dice, and have a Game,
> To sit thus idle, is both sin and shame.[2]

Playhouse, whorehouse and then a drink at the tavern. If you're going to pay the ferryman, might as well make a day of it.

But what impact did The Globe have on Shakespeare, other than shortening his walk to work? Would he have written the plays that followed had the Burbages and Allen come to terms? Hamlet refers to 'this distracted Globe' and notes a roof 'fretted with golden fire', likely describing the underside of the stage canopy, star-spangled with zodiacal figures. Rosencrantz winks at The Globe's flag as well, which depicted 'Hercules and his load too', or an image of Hercules toting the world on his back. The references are incidental, though. They do not really register a full-scale change to Shakespeare's plays when his company shifted ground. Shakespeare probably would have written the same plays for The Curtain, The Theatre, or for any theatre for that matter. After all, The Globe was not materially much different from The Theatre. In fact The Globe was materially the *same* as The Theatre.

The Globe was simply The Theatre 2.0, then, though now under new management. For it was a new management model rather than the new venue that made the most difference for Shakespeare. If The Globe didn't alter his plays, it altered his prosperity (and his posterity, treated below). Because The Globe was financed not by a daring entrepreneur like James Burbage or Philip Henslowe, who laid out the capital and pocketed the profit. The Globe was financed by a collective, a joint-stock company who pooled their resources to capitalize the project. Shakespeare was among a small group of players who bought shares in The Globe to finance its construction. He was now a sharer in the company, a householder of The Globe, a player, and a playwright in the Lord Chamberlain's service. If in the mid-1590s he had ever contemplated life as a patronized poet, he was now all in as a man of the theatre.

The funding model bound him even closer to a small group of figures, a company within the company who owned The Globe. One of those figure's sons, William Heminges, claimed in the 1630s that playing could yield decent profits 'when the playhouses are imployed and the players take paines and have good plays and live quietly together without wrangling'.[3] This last factor may be the rarest. It could be that the secret sauce to the Lord Chamberlain's Servants' success was that they actually liked each other.

However chummy, Elizabethans arranged their business affairs in the most complicated way possible, and the

Chamberlain's Servants were no exception. They drew up an agreement on 21 February 1599, a 'tripartite lease' among the Burbage brothers, Nicholas Brend (who owned the land) and five other members of the playing company: John Heminges, Augustine Phillips, Thomas Pope, William Kempe and William Shakespeare. Shakespeare initially owned a 10 per cent share of The Globe, or one-fifth of the half interest not owned by the Burbage brothers. His percentage would fluctuate across the years as players sold out or died, for the joint tenancy was initially a tenancy 'in common': when one man died his shares passed to the other sharers, not to his heirs. (The joint tenancy was later converted to a tenancy in common, which allowed shares to be sold or bequeathed to heirs.) We can wonder if, in 1599, Shakespeare agreed to these terms with a wince since by this time he had no male heir. In one sense, his fellow players were now his family and the company his heirs, though this likely romanticizes the relations. Shakespeare may have sold his share of The Globe to his fellows before his death.

*

Why 'The Globe'? It was made of the same stuff as 'The Theatre' and could have shared the name. But the change in location meant a change in name. Did the company turn to Shakespeare to christen it? Or, since it was owned by five players, did they take a straw-poll to choose the name? History draws a blank here. All we know is that when the playhouse opened in 1599, it was known then and forever after as 'The Globe' and flew a flag from its pitched roof showing Hercules carrying the world. The easy answer here is that 'The Globe' took its inspiration from the image though that doesn't tell us what inspired it.

As treated earlier, the 'Globe' was more in line with other playhouses of the time: The Rose, The Fortune, The Swan, The Red Lion. All of these playhouses could have been inns or ale-houses, public houses or book stalls, sailing ships or taverns. They are colourful but common London names, underscoring the sign or flag that hung out front or fluttered overhead.

From 1599 forward, Shakespeare's printed plays often advertise that they were performed at 'the Globe on the Bankside', as though to distinguish between this Globe and that one. *Not* the Globe in Clerkenwell where you can get some supper. *Or* the Globe on the Fleet where you buy an astrolabe. *But* The Globe on Bankside where you can empty your pockets but enrich your soul. As the years went by, and more new quartos and old reprints of *Lear*, *Mucedorus*, *Philaster* and others emerged, the title-pages begin to drop the 'on the Bankside' bit, as though the name became proprietary. By 1610 or so there is only one Globe.

Still, however common the name, there are no identifiable inns, ordinaries, public houses or taverns in London called 'The Globe' before 1599. There was a book-stall in St Paul's Churchyard called 'The Crown and Globe', but they were not in business when Shakespeare was. So 'the Globe' did not appear among the colourful names given to the bookstalls that rimmed St Paul's Churchyard – 'the Sun', 'the Little Gun', the 'Spread Eagle' – names Shakespeare noted while browsing to see how his plays and poems were selling. (Or possibly checking in to see what he had written, since by the mid-1590s things he had not were piling up, such as *The Lamentable Tragedy of Locrine*, 1595, written by 'W.S'.)

Maybe Shakespeare, Burbage, Kempe and the others encountered a 'Globe' on tour. Maybe it was the name of a favoured inn they always stayed at on the road, and the name stuck in their heads as a good one. It is not likely, in any event, that 'The Globe' was the first building so named in all of England. After playing at the strangely named 'Theatre' for a number of years, the Lord Chamberlain now had a new but familiar playhouse with a new but familiar name.

Whatever its origin, the name was apt. It riffed on a cliché, the *theatrum mundi* notion of life, what Walter Raleigh called this 'stage-play world'. The idea was a familiar, even weary one in seventeenth-century London. The induction to John Marston's *Antonio and Mellida* (1599–1600) speaks of 'this world's stage'. John Donne writes that God 'made this world his theatre'. John Webster's Duchess sighs to Bosola, 'I account this world a tedious theatre, / For I do play a part in't 'gainst my will' (4.1.99–100), and so forth.[4] When Jacques steps forward in *As You Like It* to proclaim that, 'All the world's a stage' just as though he was the first one to think of it, the audience might have muttered, not marvelled. The speech does not distinguish Jacques as a profound thinker. It marks him as a peddler of clichés. Unlike Donne's God, the Lord Chamberlain's Servants made their theatre their world. If life was a stage-play world, why not spend it at The Globe?

*

There's a kind of literary parlour game about which Shakespeare play opened The Globe. *Henry V* with its humble brag about 'this unworthy scaffold'. *As You Like It*, which glosses the name of The Globe via Jacques' set piece. *Julius Caesar*, which opens by ordering its audience to leave. (The opening lines of *JC* – 'Hence! home, you idle creatures, get you home!' [1.1.1] – sound like the result of a writers' bet made over late-night drinks. Ben Jonson to Shakespeare: I dare you to open a play by ordering the audience out. Shakespeare to Jonson: I dare you to write a play without a single sympathetic character. They both won.)

Whether it opened The Globe or not, *Julius Caesar* was definitely playing there during Shakespeare's first autumn at the new playhouse. On 21 September 1599, a Swiss traveller named Thomas Platter recorded his impressions of the play and the playhouse. (Platter is often referred to as a 'tourist' in biographies, as though he'd Eurostarred in from Zurich to visit Westminster Abbey and 'Shakespeare's Globe'.) Platter provides some intriguing details about what an afternoon at The Globe was like:

On September 21st after lunch, about two o'clock, I and my party crossed the water, and there in the house with the thatched roof witnessed an excellent performance of the tragedy of the first Emperor Julius Caesar, with a cast of some fifteen people; when the play was over they danced very marvellously and gracefully together as is their wont, two dressed as men and two as women …[5]

Platter does not mention the name of the playhouse but he does describe the thatched roof, which Peter Street added so The Globe could catch fire fourteen years later and fulfil the destiny of every theatre by burning to the ground. He also notes that after they performed *Julius Caesar* the company danced a four-in-hand with two men dressed as women and two men dressed as men – the latter detail a curious feature, as though masculinity is a game of dress up, which perhaps it is.

The question of which of Shakespeare's plays opened The Globe does not often entertain the idea that any one of the Chamberlain's plays might have done the trick. Judging by print – an uncertain measure of theatrical success – the anonymous *Mucedorus* was the hottest property in their repertory. Or the company might have opened The Globe with Ben Jonson's hit, *Every Man In His Humour*, a savagely topical play in which we know Shakespeare appeared. Or *Every Man Out of his Humour*, with a self-conscious opening in which Asper interrupts his tantrum to address the audience, 'I not observed this thronged round til now! / Gracious and kind spectators you are welcome' (1.1.54–5). Nor is there evidence of any hoopla around the first play staged at The Globe – a red-carpet launch with the mayor smashing a bottle of champagne against its timber frame. Given that 'The Globe' was just 'The Theatre' in a different spot with a different name, the opening of the place may not have seemed like a gala affair.

The question of which play opened The Globe also obscures the more important point that Shakespeare was on fire in 1599. His three plays that year – *Henry V*, *As You Like It* and *Julius Caesar* – showcase his talent in three wildly different genres. From the fields of France to the forest of Arden to the Roman senate, the plays gave posterity Henry V, Rosalind, Brutus and more. It's almost like Shakespeare was just showing off.

As You Like It might not be the best of these three plays, but it is the weirdest. *Henry V* is a classic piece of English chronicle history. *Julius Caesar* is straight-up Roman tragedy. *As You Like It* is ... a fantasia on pastoral themes? It is almost anything you want it to be, as its title suggests. You could, in fact, exchange the names of *As You Like It*, *Much Ado about Nothing* and *All's Well That Ends Well* and do no real harm. Or all three plays could traffic under the alternate title of a fourth play a year later, *What You Will* (a subtitle to *Twelfth Night*). The interchangeable titles of the four comedies deliberately do not tell us much, like American sitcoms whose titles give nothing away – *All in the Family*, *Too Close for Comfort*, *The Facts of Life*. Or, the most Shakespearean of them all, *It's Like, You Know* .... These names invite us to take it or leave it. You could not, by contrast, exchange the names of *Henry V* and *Julius Caesar*. For that matter, you would not want to call *Othello* a *Comedy of Errors*.

It may have an impersonal title, but *As You Like It* feels personal. A play about escaping to the woods from a suffocating court, with its obsessions over dynastic marriages and squabbles over who inherits what. *As You Like It* could have been titled *Anything Goes*, since everything, or everyone, eventually goes to the forest of Arden where just about anything can happen, or nothing at all. The forest offers an alternative court, where exiles kill time fretting about the feelings of the animals they shoot. The immediate source of that worry, Jacques, is one of Shakespeare's most interesting characters. He is a gentleman who has liquidated his land to become a traveller who comments upon the ways and means of mortals. Observing the hunt, he occupies the point of view of the *deer*, a radical empathy breathtaking in its originality. At the end of the play, with marriages being clapped up with alarming efficiency, he decides the best course of action is to become a hermit. If he blows a raspberry as he walks off the stage, the text does not record it.

The play is a fantasy of escape and features a country bumpkin named William. No playwright has ever given a character their own name without having a second thought about it. There may be something wistful in the play, then, as 36-year-old William Shakespeare reflects on a decade of social climbing, urban living, plague dodging and theatrical hustling and longs for the fields and forest of Warwickshire, where – as the next chapter details – he was setting up a comfortable sylvan retreat.

If *As You Like It* feels personal, *Henry V* is the most topical, the most 'of the moment', though it tells the story of a medieval king. In one of the choruses, Shakespeare tries his hand at some political prognostication, which did not turn out so well. (He might have learned his lesson from the Oldcastle debacle.) In a late chorus, he parallels the homecoming of the victorious Henry with the Earl of Essex – or his successor Lord Mountjoy – triumphally returning from Ireland with 'rebellion broached upon his sword' (5.0.32). But Essex returned from Ireland with egg on his face not rebellion on his sword. And mud on his boots, which he didn't bother to wipe off before storming in to see the Queen to crave her forgiveness for his failures to put down the Irish uprising. If Essex had not had bad judgement he wouldn't have had any judgement at all. The Queen was unhappy, Essex sulked off, and not long after he tried again to storm the Queen's redoubt, as treated in the previous chapter. This time, his poor judgement cost him his life.

The parallel between Essex and Henry didn't age well. Shakespeare was on safer ground with Julius Caesar, who also captured Shakespeare's attention at the time. A broken-back tragedy, it pivots upon the point of Brutus's dagger, which delivers the fatal blow. Just after killing Caesar, Cassius marvels, 'How many ages hence / Shall this our lofty scene be acted over / In states unborn and accents yet unknown' (3.1.122–4). Scholars call such moments 'meta-theatrical', meaning the play acknowledges that it is a play. Consider meta-theatricality the blush a play gives off when it gets too full of itself.

Thomas Platter would have heard the line but could not have known how prescient it was. If Shakespeare blew the Essex prediction, he got this one just right. Now, every actor who steps forward to proclaim that this 'scene' of Caesar's murder will play again and again in unborn states and unknown accents becomes a self-fulfilling prophecy. Every actor who says it is sampling an actor who said it before. And *that's* the main reason the line sticks like glue. Every time you say it, it becomes more true. The line inoculates the play against oblivion, guarantees its repetition, while gambling on its fame. Here, smack dab in the middle of the play, Shakespeare's audacious move is to wager that the singers will change but the song remains the same. And he was right. Over 400 years later we're still singing along.

*

The back-up plan worked. The Globe thrived. It stood until 1644 when it was pulled down to make way for tenements (it did burn down in 1613 but was swiftly rebuilt, as treated below). But on a soggy summer afternoon, flogging away at a sub-Seneca tragedy, or trying to wring one more laugh from *The Merry Devil of Edmonton* on a freezing February dusk to a half-filled house of chattering apprentices, it might have galled the Chamberlain players that they owned an indoor playhouse just across the river that they weren't allowed to use. The Globe was probably a terrific playhouse, but you wouldn't want to live there.

The Blackfriars was not just sitting empty, however. Burbage leased it to Henry Evans, who ran a company of boys there – the Children of Her Majesty's Chapel – for the first decade of the seventeenth century. (The boys performed just once a week, which the neighbours apparently did not mind so much.) So when Hamlet gossips with the First Player about the popularity of the children companies, it is not a complaint, it is a cross-promotion. Though he could not perform there, Richard Burbage was at least pocketing some rent from The Blackfriars.

Still, something doesn't quite add up about The Blackfriars. As with the Oldcastle debacle, when smart people do stupid things we must be missing a trick. While James Burbage was bold, he was not reckless. Why would he invest a princely sum to build an indoor playhouse without checking with the neighbours?

If he felt secure in his venture it is likely that he had the go-ahead from the company's patron, the Lord Chamberlain, Henry Carey. But, as treated in the previous chapter, Carey died on 22 July 1596 while construction was under way. Carey was immediately succeeded by Lord Cobham, who had no reason to look favourably upon the company due to the Oldcastle affair. Though *he* soon died and Carey's son George became the company's patron, Burbage's bad luck held out. George Carey's house was literally next door to the playhouse, and he was among the signatories to a petition of November 1596 that asked the Privy Council to bar Burbage from opening a playhouse there. The company's own *boss* in effect told them they could not use their new playhouse.

George Carey's signature is the second on the list of complainants, and the fourth was Shakespeare's schoolmate Richard Field, who had printed his *Venus and Adonis* and *The Rape of Lucrece* just a few years previously. The gist of the complaint is that a playhouse is a nuisance. It will bring a 'great resort and gathering together of all manner of vagrant and lewd persons'. Furthermore, 'the same Playhouse is so near the Church that the noise of the Drums and Trumpets will greatly disturb and hinder both the Ministers and the Parishioners in time of divine service and Sermons'.[6] The petitioners were powerful and their complaint plausible. In sum, it seems James Burbage's luck and life ran out just around the same time.

It would not be until over a decade later that the Chamberlain's Servants – by then the King's Servants – got access to their own playhouse. All this might be a triviality of theatre history except it sets up a counter-factual more plausible than most. Might Shakespeare's life have taken a different turn had he and his company started to play at The Blackfriars in 1596? The company might have planned The Blackfriars as a winter house to complement their summer lodgings at The Globe. But it is just as likely they were planning on playing inside all-year long.

Had they been successful, Shakespeare's career would look quite different. Not that the plays he wrote would necessarily have altered, but his image would have. As it turned out, William Shakespeare's character arc runs from the inside out: from a courtly maker of conceited verse to the full-throated Bard of the popular boards. Shakespeare is virtually synonymous with The Globe, the name of which underscores his universal touch.

Had the Chamberlain's Servants moved into The Blackfriars in 1596/7, however, Shakespeare would look like a playwright to the monied sort, his plays out-of-reach of The Globe's penny groundlings. This might have put a dent in our faith in Shakespeare's accessibility, the faith that his plays were both plain and fancy, gags for groundlings and poetry for princes.

The wooden O of the 'Globe' shaped Shakespeare's reputation more than his plays, then. We can ask how things might have played out had Giles Allen been a theatre fan. Or had James Burbage's plan paid off and Shakespeare spent the second half of his career writing indoor drama. It is doubtful that his pace would have slackened or that the plays would have turned out differently. Again, plays in the period were tailored to the frame of just one playhouse. They were designed to play on a market scaffold in Chester, in a Guildhall in Stratford, in a private house on the Fleet, and – most important of all – at the banqueting house at Whitehall or the royal residence at Greenwich. And yes, they were written for The Theatre, The Curtain, and then finally The Blackfriars. Nevertheless, the judgement of history is that Shakespeare was most at home at The Globe.

*

'Shakespeare's Globe' was rebuilt in 1999. The name is savvy, though it would surprise Shakespeare's co-sharers of 1599 to discover that The Globe belonged solely to him. ('Brend's, Burbages', Kempe's, Heminge's, Pope's, Phillips' and

Shakespeare's Globe' wouldn't fit on the brochure.) Today, The Globe is dwarfed by buildings that stretch their necks across London's skyline. Compared to buildings like 30 St Mary Axe – once memorably called the 'erotic gherkin' – The Globe looks detumescent. Walking across Millennium Bridge, it can be hard to spot at first, a squat, lumpen building notable for its finish of plaster and lath not its shape or stature. Today, The Globe has shrunk.

But in 1599 The Globe would have stood out, not just by its size but by its shape. As already detailed, title pages in the period often note the Lord Chamberlain's/King's Men can be found 'playing usually at the Globe on Bank-side'. However usually they played there, the playhouse was *un*usual, a polygonal structure in a city of squares and rectangles. As also noted above, recently discovered playhouses like The Curtain and Red Lion seem to have been rectangular. And Edward Alleyn and the Admiral's Servants – who decamped from the Southbank just before Shakespeare and co. arrived – traded in their polygonal, and faded, Rose for a sturdy, square, brick playhouse in St Giles-without-Cripplegate called The Fortune. The Globe was, and is, a strange theatre.

The Globe featured a stage often called a 'thrust' but if so it's an unenthusiastic one. It's far broader than deep – and in that sense not so different from the stages of West End and Broadway theatres. The difference is that proscenium theatres frame the stage and provide a narrow aperture on the picture within, an aspect ratio familiar from landscape paintings and movie screens. The Globe gives the audience a wide angle view, blurring at the edges into the audience ranged about it.

But despite its name, The Globe was not a theatre in the round, and most audiences looked the actors in the eyes, not at the sides or the backs of their heads. In any event, Shakespeare's plays appeared for many more years on the proscenium stage than they did (and do) on thrusty ones. Today, Shakespeare's plays have 'returned' to stages like those of the Royal Shakespeare Company's main stage that protrude more rudely into the audience than The Globe's.

What the 'Globe' does that the 'Theatre' does not is return us to the circularity of Shakespeare's life, just as though there *was* a special providence that shaped his ends, as Hamlet suggests. The 'Globe' seems a perfect emblem for the roundness that Shakespeare's life achieved. It also emblematizes the near universality of his plays – if not universally loved, they are universally available, universally known, ubiquitously quoted and relentlessly performed. They have become as liturgical as they are dramatic.

There are a thousand and more instances of the name of the 'Globe' standing in for Shakespeare's global influence. Consider just for one the popular 'Globe Edition' of Shakespeare's plays, released between 1863 and 1866. This edition attempted to provide a 'good edition' of Shakespeare's works 'at a price which brings it within the reach of even the working classes'.[7] This laudable attempt requires some historicizing. The release of the Globe Edition was an expression of Victorian Nationalism – like the development of the telegraph, a national railway system or its robust foreign policy. And the dissemination of Shakespeare in affordable print editions was part and parcel of that national programme.

The 'Globe' in the edition's title was not, or not just, a reference to one of the theatres in which the enclosed plays appeared. It was a reference to the Global ambition of the edition, which it largely achieved. After all, Master William Shakespeare, an English gentleman, was revered as the greatest poet of all time, whose plays contained timeless characters and universal values which defined humanity. Matthew Arnold placed Shakespeare in unquestioning pre-eminence in his introduction to *The English Poets*, published in 1880. The Victorians believed that exposure to high culture like Shakespeare made you a better person. In the post-enlightenment age, art became a humanist surrogate for religion, with Shakespeare as high priest.

What is undeniable is that The Globe marks another significant turn in Shakespeare's fortunes, in which an accident of history looks, in hindsight, like a prophetic event. This is a central dynamic of Shakespeare's biography; every turn he took ends up looking like fate itself was at the wheel.

More mundanely, Shakespeare's shares in The Globe stabilized his income and the company he kept. And while he rented rooms (and avoided taxes) on the Bankside, he sent a steady flow of cash north to Stratford. However frugally he lived in London, he was laying up something lavish in Warwickshire, establishing his capital there.

14

Shakespeare's Properties

By 1599 the Lord Chamberlain's Servants were playing at their new place on the Southbank, but Shakespeare had a new place as well. While the Burbages were quarrelling with Giles Allen over The Theatre, Shakespeare's mind – if not his body – was in Stratford, conducting some real-estate wrangling of his own. In May 1597 Shakespeare bought New Place, a great big house across the street from the Guild Chapel and the school where he was lettered. As he aged and started a family it probably looked like an appealing upgrade from the crowded house on Henley Street.

'New Place' was already called 'New Place' when Shakespeare bought it. The name first appears in a document of 1532.[1] It's not one of those names, then – Bard, Birthplace, Shakespeare's Globe – fastened to Shakespeare long after his death that have subsequently stuck. 'New Place' was New Place even when it was old, and it's what the townfolk of Stratford called it. Still, there was a time when New Place was new, when it was built in the 1480s. It was torn down in 1759 by the Reverend Francis Gastrell who'd grown sick of people asking to see where Shakespeare had lived. 'New Place' is now no place, the only place among Shakespeare's Stratford properties that's no longer there.

'New Place' was the second largest house in Stratford (five gables, ten fireplaces), smack in the middle of town, with gardens and orchards stretching out back, a fine place to sit on a long summer evening and write *Timon of Athens*. It was plenty big enough for his family, who were likely thrilled. Anne and the children had remained in the house on Henley Street with his parents after Shakespeare left for London. New Place, with its many rooms and ample yard, was lavish by comparison. When we think of Shakespeare's bachelor's life in London and wonder about the care he took for his family, the purchase of New Place might tell us that he wanted them to live in comfort. New Place might have been Shakespeare's 'retirement home', but he showed no sign of giving up on London in 1597. The new home on Chapel Lane was for Anne and the children, and his occasional return to Stratford.

The house was grand, but it might have been a fixer upper. In January 1598, the borough chamberlain notes in his accounts that he paid 'Mr Shaxpere' 10 pence for 'on load of stone' to help repair the bridge over the River Avon (Shakespeare *always* had an exit strategy).[2] He had just purchased New Place, and so perhaps had stone left over from some wall patching or fence mending. It is otherwise odd to find Shakespeare peddling rocks in Stratford when his career in London was at a dicey stage, with his company also looking for a new place. This curious archival entry may reveal Shakespeare's investment in home improvement. If so, New Place constitutes another of Shakespeare's creative projects, into which he poured his money and his imagination.

By the time he bought New Place, Shakespeare had been lining his pockets in London for nearly a decade. If he checked them at the turn of the century, how full were they? Let's do a rough count of his returns. First, there was the share he'd purchased in the Lord Chamberlains' Servants. There's almost no evidence of how much it cost him and what it returned. Based on the price of shares in other companies at the time, however, scholars have estimated that the initial cost would have been between £50 and £80 and offered an annual payout of £50. At this point, biographers usually point out that this was a handsome sum, 'twice the annual salary of Stratford's schoolmaster or vicar'.[3] We don't normally look to teachers and preachers as indexes of fathomless wealth. As the mathematicians teach us, twice of a little is still not a lot.

The company's returns were not the all of it, however. By the turn of the century this fifty pounds per annum was supplemented with the cream he skimmed off The Globe. As with his share in the company, it is not clear how much his corner of The Globe cost. In any event, it would have taken a few years to pay off, but in a year when the theatre was not closed by the plague he could have taken in as much as £80 per annum. By 1605 these two revenue streams – from the company and the playhouse – produced a relative torrent of cash, in a good year as much as two hundred pounds.[4]

That's two hundred pounds in a good year (or eight times the annual salary of Stratford's schoolmaster or vicar). But the years were rarely good. The playhouses were often closed due to plague. Between May 1604 and April 1605 alone the playhouses were closed entirely, and the torrent of cash may have slowed to a trickle, the company relying on touring and court performances. If there's one transhistorical truth about the theatre, it's that it's a boom-and-bust business, hostage to a thousand accidents of weather, disease, hostile landlords, unsympathetic mayors, sniffy critics and the fickleness of audience taste.

The uncertain returns of his trade taught Shakespeare what to do when the years *were* good. When he got money he didn't keep it long. He turned it into property in his hometown. In May 1602 he came to terms with John Combe for the purchase of 107 acres of land in Old Stratford for £320, the rent on which produced a modest return each year. In September 1602 he acquired a cottage in Chapel Lane, probably to augment his land at New Place. In 1605 he bought a share of the parish tithes, which also threw off an annual return. In the eight years alone between 1597 and 1605 he spent around £900 on Stratford properties. Over and over we see Shakespeare turning cash into land, money into more money. The Globe may have been closed for months on end, but his handsome house on Chapel Lane was open to him any time he wanted to make the long trip home.

Shakespeare's financial pattern is clear. He never sat on money for long. He invested it to ensure a steady return. Ultimately, one of the most modern things about Shakespeare is his life-long preoccupation with property. Save for the Blackfriars Gatehouse in London, that property was always in Stratford. His mind and body were at work in London, but his heart and his purse were in his hometown.

*

Shakespeare bought property throughout his life – houses, land or tithes on other people's land. Perhaps it was the natural result of spending so much time in an imaginative world. Who needs 'real' estate more than a poet, whose estates are so fanciful? Theatre may – as Prospero says – 'Leave not a wrack behind' but it will buy you a few hectares in Warwickshire. All the worlds Shakespeare gave away eventually came back to him.

Iago is an unreliable biographer, but he is also a terrible financial consultant. In *Othello* he tells Roderigo to sell his land and 'put money in thy purse' and tells him so roughly seventeen times. Shakespeare took Iago's – which is to say his own – advice. He did not sell his land, but he made all the money he could. (Shakespeare wrote a long essay on the difference between cash and real estate called *The Merchant of Venice*.) Not to say that Shakespeare was a shark, skimming the bark off of every tree, looking for three halves in every whole. What he seems to have been is a plotter of both money and men, thinking at least several scenes ahead. And he did so until his dying day. What is a will but a script, one that plots the behaviour of both parts and properties even after death?

Alexander Pope gibed that Shakespeare wrote for 'gain not glory', and many have followed him in concluding that Shakespeare cared more about cash than art. It is possible to care for both. To quote Micky Bergman from David Mamet's

Heist, 'everybody needs money. That's why they call it "money".' Turns out a surprisingly large range of people need money. Even writers.

It is not the taste for cash that tells us much about Shakespeare. It is his approach to it. Not how much he got but what he did with it. Consider the Stratford tithes that he purchased on 24 July 1605. In a financial move of fiendish complexity, Shakespeare bought the lease of half of a share of the 'great tithes of Old Stratford, Welcombe and Bishopton ...'. This document contains six 'Whereasses' and seventeen 'aforesaids' just to establish the lineage of the purchase. The gist of the matter was this. Shakespeare invested 440 pounds to purchase a portion of annual tithes on land in and around Stratford. This would return him about 40 pounds a year, so the investment would pay off in a decade. For the twenty-four years remaining on the lease, Shakespeare would clear 40 pounds a year pure profit.

Consider this: in 1605 Shakespeare was forty-one. His company was riding high, but the plague played havoc with his profession. The tithes were a kind of pension. They guaranteed that – come what may – in Shakespeare's later years he'd have a reliable income. With the Stratford tithes he was laying up a winter harvest. Something to come home to after his London days were done.

His investments in *properties* are also revealing. Shakespeare evidently never bought into any of the period's wilder schemes – voyages to discover an eastern route to China or to plunder the mines of the new world. There were fortunes to be made that way, but Shakespeare was no Antonio of *The Merchant of Venice* whose fortunes are all at sea. Maybe there is something of Shakespeare in Shylock's scepticism towards merchant venturers. And of *course* there is something of Shakespeare in Shylock, just as there's something of him in all his characters, even Bassanio. His savvy financial plan is that, when he loses money on a venture, he will 'shoot another arrow that same way' in hopes of recouping his losses. Bassanio sounds a lot like a gambling addict, whose hopes always hang on the next roll of the dice. On balance, Shakespeare was neither a lender nor a gambler, though he probably did a bit of both. His investments were as conservative as his imagination was wild.

Shakespeare's commitment to real estate aligns with his purchase of a coat of arms. For there is something old-fashioned about Shakespeare – not for him the flashy lifestyle of London's merchant adventurers whose money was quicksilver. Shakespeare wanted a big house in the middle of the town he grew up in and a coat of arms to hang over his front door to announce to the world that he was *somebody*, maybe because his line of work required him to be almost anybody from day to given day. He was 'William Shakespeare of Stratford-upon-Avon, gentleman' as he's called in the conveyance of the land he bought in 1602.

The Marxist art critic John Berger wrote that, 'Property … is opposed to all other values.'[5] He was exaggerating to make a point, but there is no reason to see the value Shakespeare placed in property as the opposite to the value he placed in his art. It is easy to hold them apart, as though he led two lives – Shakespeare the plump burgher of Stratford versus Shakespeare the sublime artist of London, intimate of aristocrats and maker of plays. (Was Shakespeare ever tempted, while quarrelling over tithes with his Stratford neighbours, to say, 'Do you know who I *am*?') These two men were one and the same and to understand how they were at home with one another is to understand something of his singular life.

We could think of the 'two Shakespeares' in terms of the title of his narrative poem of 1600, 'The Phoenix and the Turtle'. By 'turtle' Shakespeare meant a 'turtle dove', not a tortoise. But to the modern eye the two creatures convey the immortal writer aloft on fancy's flight and the slow and steady crawler preoccupied by real estate. This Aesop's version of Shakespeare's life suggests an incompatibility between the two creatures, but consider the third word of the title. Shakespeare was not a phoenix *or* a turtle, he was both: *and*. Perhaps we need to revert to the Elizabethan meaning of 'turtle'. If Shakespeare was a turtle, he was a turtle that could fly.

A revisionist account of his life could retail Shakespeare as a business man with a side hustle in playwriting. An early modern T.S. Eliot, a banker with a line in poetry. It should not surprise us, though, that a man who can plot an intricately structured 3,000-line verse drama should be able to knock up the purchase of a pile of real estate. Both pursuits – the business of drama and the drama of business – involve the careful investment of resources. Both require deliberate planning and creative daring. Both, it is almost too obvious to say, involve plots, be they dramatic ones or parcels of land.

It would actually be *more* surprising had such a skilled dramatist as Shakespeare been inept at business. In short, the opposing personas of practical business man and impassioned poet are not actually opposing. Fictional artistry and financial acumen may often seem contradictory, even incompatible, but they obviously aren't since Shakespeare (and many others) enjoyed both. There is more incompatibility in the fact that the man who wrote *Venus and Adonis* also wrote *Timon of Athens* than in the notion that the writer who could plot *Cymbeline* could manage the purchase of a London gatehouse. There is in Shakespeare's life no friction between artistic creativity and economic savvy. If Shakespeare made one perfect marriage in his life, it was between art and commerce.

*

By the turn of the sixteenth century, Shakespeare had made a name for himself. Both one that he paid for and one that he earned. The first was apparently worth a lot to him, but the second was evidently worth something too since publishers began to print it on the books they peddled. To take full stock of Shakespeare's properties at the turn of the century, we have to count the literary ones as well. There were the early quartos of *Rape of Lucrece* and *Venus and Adonis*, still selling like hot cakes in St Paul's Churchyard in 1600. In that year alone, *2 Henry IV*, *Henry V*, *The Merchant of Venice*, *A Midsummer Night's Dream* and *Much Ado about Nothing* all appear in print. Some even featured his name on the title-page, far from standard practice at the time. The wryest joke in *Shakespeare in Love* occurs when the moneyman asks Philip Henslowe who Shakespeare is. He replies, 'nobody, he's the author'. But by 1600, Shakespeare was a somebody.

His literary properties probably didn't earn him much – other than the patronized poetry he wrote early in his career. His plays were company property, not his, and when a stationer purchased one to print, the money probably went into the company coffers, not William Shakespeare's pockets. (The plays may have fetched a couple of pounds apiece, far from a princely sum.) As an investor in the company, he got his piece of the pie but no more than his share. If Shakespeare cut a deal with the company – collecting, say, the whole profit from the sale of a play – there is no evidence of it.

But the printed plays and poems gave Shakespeare something he apparently cared about as much as money, which is a name. Quotable and notable by the turn of the century, Shakespeare shows up in commonplace books – diaries of handwritten quotations – in other plays, and in works of literary appreciation that catalogue his accomplishment across his first decade of work. Francis Meres' *Paladis Tamia*, *Wits Treasury* of 1598 credits Shakespeare with an even dozen plays, calling him 'the most excellent in both kinds' – tragedy and comedy – 'among the English'.[6] Poetic miscellanies from around the time include whole heaps of Shakespeare. *The Garden of Muses* from 1600 includes over two hundred passages from Shakespeare, the bulk from *Venus and Adonis* and *The Rape of Lucrece*, reminding us, again, that his reputation at the turn of the century was every bit a poet as a playwright.

The same is true of *England's Parnassus, or, The choicest flowers of our modern poets*, compiled by Robert Allot in 1600 just shortly after John Bodenham cultivated his own *Garden of Muses*. When Allot went picking, he plucked nearly a hundred quotes from Shakespeare (who, it's hard to remember, was a 'modern poet' at the time). The vast majority are again from *Lucrece* and *Venus and Adonis*. In fact, Allot selected thirty-nine quotes from *Lucrece* alone, surpassing all the flowers culled from the fourteen plays then in print by Shakespeare.

He was a hit among the younger set in particular. Recall Gabriel Harvey's comment in 1601 that, 'The younger sort takes much delight in Shakespeares Venus, & Adonis.' And he had made a splash with the critical set of tastemakers at England's elite universities. In the Christmas season between 1598 and 1601, the students of St John's, Cambridge produced a couple of plays that lampoon a character who speaks 'nothing but pure Shakspeare', and who sleeps with a copy of *Venus and Adonis* under his pillow.[7] Shakespeare's reputation, then, was of the rarest kind. As his popular reputation rose, so did his critical regard. More often, the one comes at the expense of the other.

Had the plague carried Shakespeare off in 1600, his catalogue would still rank him among the elite poet-playwrights of the English Renaissance. But as we contemplate what Shakespeare would not have written had he succumbed to illness without seeing the seventeenth century, we can take stock of what he *did* write in the first decade of his scribbling life. Plays and poems by the handful. Sonnets of heartbreak, envy and praise. Long poems of erotic disaster. Plays about doomed lovers, brawling kings and randy fairies.

By the numbers, Shakespeare had written around a dozen plays or so, a few long narrative poems and a bunch of sonnets by 1600. These were his 'literary properties', then, but what were the properties of that literature? What is Shakespeare's continuous subject, his enduring theme be it a pastoral play in a sylvan setting, a chronicle history on the battlefields of France or a fourteen-line sonnet? The answer is harder to spot than with some of his fellow writers. Ben Jonson's continuous subject is the human fantasy of change in all its folly. In the words of Katharine Eisaman Maus, Jonson ultimately concludes that, 'you are you, unfortunately'.[8] Or Shakespeare's immediate contemporary Christopher Marlowe, who was always writing about over-achievers who end up achieving their own demise.

But Shakespeare invested his energies across poetry, tragedies, histories and comedies over the first half of his writing life. This is a playwright hopping like a restless bird from one style to another. Given the volume of output – a couple of plays and one lawsuit per year – this bespeaks a restless impatience. Not a creative writer drawn to one style in particular because he was unable to do otherwise but a canny artist trying various styles on for size to see what fit best.

Restless and reticent, as a solo act or as a collaborator, if there is an enduring theme or continuous subject here it is language. Words, in other words. Art is an intensification of what is dispersed in nature. Shakespeare fantasized a world where everything everybody ever said was *interesting*. And he found a congenial home on the Elizabethan stage since the big idea of the drama of the time was that no one should ever say anything uninteresting.

Later English dramatists would find poetry in the hems and haws of inarticulate speech. Eloquence would come to seem suspect – loquacity frosting half-baked ideas – and the purest expression of passion would be mute wonder. Perhaps the most typical line in twentieth-century English drama comes from Noël Coward's *Peace in our Time* from 1947. A married couple bids farewell to dear friends:

NORA
Good luck to you both – always. (*She dabs her eyes.*)
FRED
Now then, Nora – none of that.

All of that and then some, said Shakespeare and his contemporaries. Words for Shakespeare were what colour was for Matisse, an expression of pure pleasure. And he coloured the last decade of the sixteenth century with them.

*

Given the glories of Shakespeare's output up to 1600, it is rude to mention what is missing from the catalogue. But masques,

Lord Mayor's shows, public encomia, funeral eulogies or civic verse? If Shakespeare produced anything of this kind, posterity forgot it. And there was ready money in such work. Many of his contemporaries turned their hands to it, writing speeches of lavish praise for a new mayor or a poem to mourn the death of a noble. It seems unlikely that no-one ever asked Shakespeare to turn out a speech to mark a notable civic event. If they did so, he demurred. (Except for a later career 'impressa' treated later.) In fact, in 1603, Henry Chettle takes a shot at Shakespeare for not writing a poem to mourn the death of Elizabeth, noting, elliptically, the silence of 'Melicert' on the matter ('mel' means 'honey', Shakespeare's code name).

Perhaps it is just as well. A number of funeral elegies and headstone epitaphs have been ascribed to Shakespeare across the years, all of them terrible. And that includes the verse inscribed on his own tomb. If he wrote it, among the crueller, or funnier, ironies of history is that Shakespeare is buried under the worst thing he ever wrote.

Among the funeral elegies Shakespeare did not write was one for his only son. Hamnet Shakespeare died on 9 August 1596. Unless Hamnet had been ill for some time and Shakespeare saw it coming, he likely missed the funeral. Burials happened within two days of death. It took at least that long for news to travel from Stratford to London and for a Londoner to make a return visit. In any event, Shakespeare and company may have been on tour in Kent that summer. Even if he made it home in time, the only mark the death left was in the parish registry. There's no headstone for Hamnet outside Holy Trinity (or at least not one that survived). No surviving poem to sound the depths of a father's feeling. Shakespeare's sonnets are full of grievances, but no grief.

It's hard to spin this episode to Shakespeare's advantage. At the least, it takes some special pleading to make it look good. We can always cite those 'thoughts that do often lie too deep for tears', but Ben Jonson wrote feelingly on the death of his children, and we do not call his grief shallow for being able to put words to it. Graham Holderness has written about Shakespeare's silence at Hamnet's death and wryly concluded that Ben Jonson's moving poem on the death of *his* only son is the poem that Shakespeare would have written had he gotten around to it.[9]

Sometimes scholars cite Constance's moving expression of grief for her son in *King John*:

Grief fills the room up of my absent child,
Lies in his bed, walks up and down with me,
Puts on his pretty looks, repeats his words,
Remembers me of all his gracious parts,
Stuffs out his vacant garments with his form.

(3.3.94–8)

No parent can get through it. The play may precede the death of Hamnet, however. If we hear in it an 'echo' of Shakespeare's feeling for his son, it is a pre-echo, an eerie premonition.

Of course, circa 1600, Shakespeare re-wrote an old play called *Hamlet,* which might be a delayed response to the death of his son, though 'Hamlet' was *not* the name of his son and a father would have noticed that. Besides, *Hamlet* would be a peculiar play to write as, what, a tribute, a memorial, an homage to mark the death of a young boy? A Senecan tragedy about the thwarted ambition of a Danish prince is not the first thing that comes to mind when a poor child of sixteenth-century Warwickshire succumbs to accident or illness.

If eulogy was not Shakespeare's style, neither was encomium. He wrote a couple of sycophantic dedications early in his life, but when his verse turns to flattery it is for his loves not his lords. Nor did he, as far as we know, ever write a court masque to entertain the monarch. (Masques did not really become modish until James came to the throne, but no one asked Shakespeare to write one then, either, and he worked for King James, as the next chapter details.) Maybe Shakespeare avoided the topical since every time he tried it he botched the job – as with Essex – or got his hand smacked – as with Oldcastle.

For the main, Shakespeare avoided 'current events'. Did he ever get his nose out of a book long enough to see what was going on around him? Shakespeare was obviously interested in England, particularly its past. He wrote ten history plays after all. But was he interested in England's present? Of his own life and times, of the city around him, of the grandees of court, of the emerging imperial nation whose capital he lived in, on those topics Shakespeare was fairly reticent. On balance we might conclude that though Shakespeare was from a small town, his mind was not parochial. His artistic vision was an eccentric one, fired by other plays, by stories out of novella and fable, by the classical past and England's pre-Christian era, not the events that eddied around him every day.

Shakespeare's reluctance to be timely helped him to become timeless. His works are not tethered to his time, which allowed them to achieve escape velocity from his age. Shakespeare was a modern artist but not a contemporary one, in that modern art is always about the future. Today, plays more contemporary to Shakespeare's contemporaries – say, *The Fair Maid of the Exchange* – now seem antiquated, while *The Tempest* reads like science fiction.

The adjective that Meres and many others reached for when they thought of Shakespeare's early work was 'sweet'. Shakespeare is 'honey-tongued', the writer of 'sugared sonnets'. Chettle calls him 'Melicert'. Milton would later call him 'sweetest' Shakespeare. There was a change coming, however, a change of monarchs, a change in season, a change in taste, and a narrowing – though a deepening – of Shakespeare's focus. Sweet Shakespeare was about to turn sour. As the seventeenth century dawned and a new monarch emerged, Shakespeare began to write like he couldn't help himself.

15

The King's Man

On 24 March 1603 Queen Elizabeth died and nothing happened. Her courtiers wept, a nation mourned and the theatres were closed the next day. But John Manningham – a lawyer responsible for some early glimpses of Shakespeare – noted that there was 'no tumult, no contradiction, no disorder in the city; every man went about his business as readily, as peaceably, as securely, as though there had been no change, nor any news ever heard of competitors'.[1] This is a surprising reaction to the death of a Queen who had reigned for nearly fifty years. The Elizabethans – who were no longer Elizabethans – probably saw it coming. Elizabeth had been in decline for some time and spent her final years as a zombie Queen, every cough kicking up a cloud of concern about her successor.

Londoners, at least, had been tipped off. The theatres were shut on 19 March. The ports were closed. And the usual suspects – vagrants and Catholics – were rounded up. Courtiers later apologized for being uncourteous to their correspondents, since letters were forbidden to control the spread of rumour. The lack of furore about her death was a symptom of Elizabeth fatigue, the sign of a nation ready for a change they had long seen coming.

Shakespeare might have seen it coming too. In the first three years of the seventeenth century, he had been thinking a lot about succession, about the responsibility of the living to the dead, about the ghosts of the departed who haunted his waking days. In both *Hamlet* (1600) and *Twelfth Night* (1601) Shakespeare features a young person mourning the loss of a father and, in Olivia's case, a brother too. Both are liable to Claudius' charge that they indulge, even luxuriate, in 'obstinate grief'. Why 'seems it so particular with thee?' Gertrude asks Hamlet. 'Now then, Hamlet, none of that', had Noël Coward written *Hamlet*.

If death seemed particular to Shakespeare, he had his reasons. In the years leading up to Elizabeth's death he lost his son Hamnet in 1596 and his father John in 1601. This left Shakespeare adrift between generations, without a father to live up to or a son to leave a name for. Orphaned and heirless we might call him, except that his mother was living and his daughters as well. His Stratford household was a world of women in contrast to matey London.

The particularities of patriarchy might have left him feeling barren, however, a man who made a name for himself but only for himself. His dearly purchased coat of arms might even have mocked him, since he alone could enjoy it – and coats of arms are not designed to be enjoyed alone. He could not know it, but with the death of his granddaughter, the childless Elizabeth Hall, in February 1670, the Shakespeare line was out.

Public calm followed Elizabeth I's death in 1603, but James' accession brought a storm of ink. Over fifty publications on the subject date from the time – and that's just what has survived. Some of these works appeared with suspicious speed, such as Richard Fletcher's judiciously titled elegy on Elizabeth and encomia for James, 'Our Present Sorrow, and Our Present Joy'. The poem appears in a book called *A Brief and Familiar Epistle Showing His Majesty's Most Lawful, Honourable, and Just Title to All His Kingdoms*, published on 23 April 1603, St George's Day and Shakespeare's thirty-ninth birthday. This is just a month after the queen's death and suggests that – like a modern obituarist with files full of stuff on aged ex-presidents and faded film stars – Fletcher and others had material in the can just biding its time.

In keeping with his official reticence, Shakespeare did not contribute to the literature on Elizabeth's death. As noted in the previous chapter, Chettle scorched him for not speaking publicly about the queen under whom he had thrived. Neither did Shakespeare, as far as we know, contribute to James' accession celebrations, while Jonson, Dekker and others were hired by the City to write speeches of lavish praise for James' London premiere.

This is all the odder since Shakespeare worked for the new king. For one of the first things James did was get himself a playing company, as though he had nothing better to do. Newly arrived in London, on 17 May James adopted the Lord Chamberlain's Men as his own. The company got a new name, and each player received four-and-half yards of red fabric, the official livery of James' household. They may have rendered that cloth into clothing to make a good showing for James' entry into London. For Shakespeare, writing a speech for ready cash might have seemed beneath him now that he was part of the royal retinue.

For Shakespeare and company the new name might have felt a bit like a coronation too, some borrowed majesty for aspirational Shakespeare and his ambitious peers. It was the last name change the company would go through. If Shakespeare started his working life as a Queen's Man, he would end it as a King's Man.

From history's perch, it makes perfect sense. The promotion of the Lord Chamberlain's Servants to the King's looks inevitable, a fitting title for the finest band in all the land. But it is not likely that James – 500 kilometres north in Edinburgh – kept close tabs on the relative qualities of England's playing companies. The upgrade more likely reflects some back-room jockeying among courtiers eager to prove their mettle to the new monarch. (Some scholars believe that one of James' new favourites – he had a few – the Earl of Pembroke might have been behind the move.) The company's promotion could have been the fruition of a well-laid plan by a shrewd noble.

What is striking is the speed of this transaction. Shakespeare's friends and rivals the Lord Admiral's Servants were named 'Servants of Prince Henry', James' son, but not until the following February. The 'Servants of the Queen' did not get their licence until 15 April 1609 – five years later. The former Lord Chamberlain's Servants had their patent in hand *less than a week* after the king arrived in London.

The paperwork gives us a clue to their promotion. The 'letters patent' allow the company to play 'Comedies Tragedies histories Enterludes morals pastorals Stageplays and Such others like as these have already studied or hereafter shall use or study'. (The list suggests that Polonius was understated when he described the range of the tragedians who stop in at Elsinore.) But the first name on the licence is not Shakespeare, Burbage, Hemings or Condell. It is the newcomer Lawrence Fletcher who had played before James in Scotland. Fletcher does not appear twenty years later in the first folio's list of 'principal players'. Was he drafted by the company to curry the king's favour or foisted on them by James, the price of preferment?

Whether welcomed gladly or grudgingly, Lawrence Fletcher was now one of the King's players and so joined the company at Somerset House from 9–26 August 1604. They were there to dance attendance on the Constable of Castile and his retinue, who had come to London to negotiate the 'Treaty of London', which finally halted hostilities between England and Spain, which had stretched for several decades. The visitors' large retinue occupied two great London houses, and the King's Men were drafted to swell the ranks of the English attendants. If they put on a play to entertain the visitors – *The Spanish Tragedy* comes to mind – no one mentioned it.

Did these two weeks irritate or fascinate Shakespeare? He might have chafed at the time it robbed from his writing. Or might he have been intrigued by the drama before him? If nothing else, it let him know where he stood, which was among those men silently watching high-level statecraft accompanied by – and accomplished via – lavish hospitality. A couple of weeks of good feeding probably went down well, since the company was hard up at the time from the restraint of playing.

Shakespeare had been around grandees before, so a brush with greatness was nothing new. (How unlikely it would have seemed to *any* of the visiting delegates that the immortal in the room was the quiet balding man watching from the corner.) At the very least it gave him and his co-workers – the newly christened servants of the King – some insight into the new monarch's style, which would prove vitally important in the coming years. With their new name came a new responsibility: they were licensed to please one man alone, King James I of England, Scotland and Wales.

*

Newly named and royal endowed, the King's Men were primed to play. And yet they couldn't. The plague that raged while Elizabeth died lasted for nearly a whole year. The King's Men performed often at court during that year, but The Globe stood idle from 19 May 1603 to 9 April 1604. Thomas Dekker, in *The Wonderful Year* (i.e., full of wonder; i.e., not wonderful), imagined the plague as Christopher Marlowe's 'stalking Tamburlane' who 'hath pitched his tents ... in the sinfully polluted suburbs', where The Globe stood empty.[2] In fact, the theatres were open for business for only two of the first six-and-a half years of James' English reign. For much of the first decade of the seventeenth century Shakespeare was a court playwright.

The numbers speak for themselves. During Shakespeare's years as a King's Man – 1603–1612 – the company appeared a total of 125 times at the court of James. We can identify sixty-two plays across those appearances (including repetitions): twenty-two of them are by Shakespeare, or more than a third of the total. All the new plays he wrote in the period showed up at court, as well as many of the old ones. Richard Dutton concludes that it is 'highly likely' that everything Shakespeare ever wrote – except his poetry and his will – was performed at court at least once.³ It's a bracing corrective to our image of Shakespeare as the laureate of the public playhouse.

One of his first plays for his new patron stinks of Dekker's polluted suburbs. *Measure for Measure* played at court on 26 December 1604 and marks a departure from Shakespeare's earlier comedies. Set in the seedy suburbs of Vienna, love is transactional, leadership rotten, marriage punitive. It features a ruler who, unlike James, does not enter the city in triumph but departs it in silence. The Duke has let things slip and so steals away so he can stage a triumphant comeback, where, like a god winched down on a creaking trapeze, he returns to save the day.

You can learn a lot about a playwright by the lengths they go to. What is the most implausible thing they will try in service of a story? For Shakespeare under Elizabeth, it was cross-dressing. Portia in *Merchant of Venice*. Viola in *Twelfth Night*. Rosalind in *It's Like, You Know* ... (aka *As You Like It*). Even Malvolio's cross-garters in *Twelfth Night* are a form of cross-dressing, the kill-joy steward trying to pass as a figure of fun. (The comic Ken Dodd once described Malvolio as a man who stands up during a strip tease to ask when the jugglers come on.)

Under James, Shakespeare gave up on cross-dressing (at least in his plays) and turned to bed-tricks he imported from Italian novella. Bertram of *All's Well* and Angelo of *Measure* go darkly to bed with subjects of their lust only to end up with women for whom they're objects of desire. Bertram and Angelo are thoroughly bad news. As a critic drily pointed out of Angelo in 1790, '*Angelo* affords very few opportunities for an actor to obtain applause'.⁴ Compare larkish cross-dressing with the seedy bed-trick and you get a crude register of Shakespeare's shifting outlook. Cross-dressing cheekily suggests that all gender is performance. Bed-tricks cynically suggest that all cats are grey in the dark.

The play joins others that do not strike the reader today as the most obvious form of flattery for a new monarch. During the Christmas of 1604, *Measure* was followed the very next day by the now-lost masque *Juno and Hymenaeus*. *Juno* probably struck a more celebratory mood than *Measure for Measure*, though that's a low bar. Shakespeare was the King's servant, but his plays are never servile, even in these years when the primary audience he wrote for was James and his extended court, not a sea of surging groundlings.

Measure was not Shakespeare's first play at court that season. That honour went to *Othello*, also not the first play you might wish to watch by the flickering light of the yule log. But the play lets us think seriously about the role Black men and women played in Shakespeare's life and art. In addition to families from the African continent whom Shakespeare might have met, there were Black entertainers in and around the court of James. Buried in a stage direction of *Love's Labour's Lost* in the 1623 folio is a call for 'moors' to accompany the four male lovers who disguise themselves as Muscovites to present a masque (it's complicated). Matthieu Chapman has argued that there is no reason to assume that these 'moors' were white men in blackface.[5] When the King's Men presented *Labour's* for Elizabeth at the Inns of Court in the mid-1590s, it may have been with an integrated cast. Shakespeare met Black men and women in his life. He may even have worked with them.

That Shakespeare took note of what we, but not he, would call 'racial' difference is evident in plays like *Othello*, of course, but also in *Titus Andronicus* and *The Merchant of Venice* – the former features Aaron the Moor, the latter a cameo for the Prince of Morocco along with Shylock. But it is *Othello*'s early performance and textual history that tells us that Shakespeare, or somebody, knew *exactly* how toxic the play was. There are two surviving texts of Shakespeare's *Othello*, both of which were printed after his death. There is a quarto – a single-play edition – from 1622, and the play then appears the following year in the collected works of Shakespeare's plays. The texts are different. Not as different as black and white, but different nonetheless.

To simplify something that's not simple, the folio text of *Othello* contains 160 lines not present in the quarto, and those lines ratchet up the play's racial toxicity. Or, the quarto vacuums the play of its most racist language. Whichever way the vector runs, somebody – Shakespeare or another – added to the manuscript behind the 1623 folio text to amplify the depiction of Othello's racial otherness. Or, Shakespeare or another excised from the manuscript behind the quarto text the play's most potently inflammatory language.

Either way, Shakespeare or somebody demonstrated an acute sensitivity to the play's depiction of the way white men think about Black men. This is to conclude something that probably shouldn't surprise us, which is that the charged language of racial and sexual representation in *Othello* struck its original makers in much the same way it strikes us: as potentially inflammatory, possibly offensive and to be handled with extreme care.

*

James' ascension was a net positive for the company for which Shakespeare worked. But the passing of Elizabeth marked the passing of Shakespeare's peak popularity, in the strictest sense of a writer with a touch for the popular marketplace. The darling of the younger sort who slept with his poems under their pillows.

He had magnificent works ahead, of course. The first decade of the seventeenth century saw no diminution of his theatrical powers. Quite the opposite. But Shakespeare's merry métier, his giddy word feasts and heroic history plays did not suit the Jacobean taste for cryptic masques, cynical satires and pointed topicality. Was Shakespeare ill at ease under James, out of step with the times? Hard to know, but his plays got tougher, more sinewy, more gristle and less sugar from the outset of the seventeenth century.

It might be unrelated, but Shakespeare's print output also ebbed. After 1604 there would be only a few Shakespeare titles printed in his lifetime. You were out of luck if you wanted to read *Measure for Measure*, *All's Well* or *Othello* while their author was still living. If you wanted to read *Macbeth*, *Antony and Cleopatra* or *Coriolanus*, you would have to wait until 1623 when they all appeared – for the first time – in Shakespeare's posthumous folio. It is possible, however, that when it came to popularity, by 1605 Shakespeare was an Elizabethan writer in a Jacobean court.

In the final years of the 1610s, Shakespeare got hitched to a younger playwright, John Fletcher, with a knack for tragi-comedies, which were the temper of the time. Fletcher was a generation younger. Maybe Shakespeare's fellows thought he had lost his touch and could use some help from a modish newcomer with his finger on the pulse. After Elizabeth's death, Shakespeare like Hamlet may have lost all his mirth. He never wrote another funny play.

16

The Plague Years

It is a wonder he could write at all over the sound of the bells. Like a modern writer tuning out the wail of sirens, Shakespeare worked with an earful of racket, if he hadn't stuck wadding in them to shut out the din. For bells were the soundtrack of London life, pealing from the spires of its hundred churches. Bells on the hour and on the half. Bells to summon Londoners to service or call them to a meeting. Bells to celebrate an apprentice who had served his turn or to alert them to the fires that plagued London – when it wasn't the plague that was plaguing London, which it did throughout the first decade of the seventeenth century. In the early years of James' reign, Shakespeare wrote to the sound of bells tolling the score of plague deaths.

And yet Shakespeare did not write about the plague. Not directly at least. It shows up as an expression of incredulity – 'What a plague means my niece to take my drinking so?' – or a way to talk about hard times: 'Tis the time's plague when madmen lead the blind.' Or as a grim plot point in *Romeo and Juliet*, where it stops the Friar's letter from reaching Romeo in Mantua. There is no one play that is 'about the plague', but all the plays of this period are 'plague plays'. All were written under a cloud of pestilence.

The disease devastated London in the early years of James' reign – stubborn, insistent, persistent. In the summer that followed Elizabeth's death, more than a thousand deaths a week. This in a city of only 200,000. The plague hung over the last half of Shakespeare's working life. It touched him personally – he knew plague victims both intimately and incidentally – but it also upset his profession. The theatres were closed more often than they were opened during these years. As the previous chapter claimed, the plague turned Shakespeare into a court playwright, the only sure market for his work at the time.

It also turned him into a touring actor. The new King's official entry into London was delayed for a year due to widespread illness. James had taken his time getting to London in the first place, allowing a respectful period of grieving for Elizabeth. Once he finally arrived in London in the late spring of 1603, he turned around and left. His players did the same. Initially, the King's household went south while Shakespeare and crew went north. James sought a safe harbour to ride out the plague while his company of players chased profits in the provinces. The King tried Woodstock and Oxford first, but those sites turned out to be infected, and he and his long train decamped to Winchester, where they spent the autumn.

Shakespeare and company caught up with the court from time to time. They pocketed twenty shillings for playing in Oxford, likely when the King was there. Throughout the autumn they could be spotted on a midland tour of Coventry, Bridgnorth and Bath before they joined the King in Wiltshire and then played at Hampton Court during the Christmas season.

Maybe the irony was lost on Shakespeare. Probably it was not. The 'promotion' to King's Men might have been cold comfort to Shakespeare who – now middle-aged – was once again a 'strolling player', a name that hides the hardships of travel, with its uneven roads and uncertain lodging ('travel' and 'travail' are cognates for a reason). Four-and-a-half yards of red fabric do not help when you're three to a bed in a Coventry inn listening to Condell mumble iambs in his sleep.

If there was one silver lining to the plague that sent him packing, the tour brought Shakespeare within reach of

Stratford, where he could check on his properties and chuck his daughters under the chin. Susanna and Judith still lived at home with Anne in the big house on Chapel Lane. It was in 1605 – in the midst of these tours – that Shakespeare leased the tithes that provided him a pension.

Was he at all tempted to lay down his pen and pick up his pipe? To rest his head in his second best bed after a day picking pippins in his orchard? He had plays and poetry by the pound to his name and a handsome house to settle down in. What did he have left to prove? But he did not stay home. Not yet. But any notion of Shakespeare the King's Man riding high on cresting fortune in the early seventeenth century has to be tempered by the time's plague. Even the sound of his greatest plays could not drown out the toll of the bells.

*

Maybe because the theatres were opened so seldom – The Globe sat empty for months on end – Shakespeare moved from the Southbank to the City around 1604. Why worry over your commute when the office is always closed? He may have stopped acting in these years as well and turned to full-time writing. Whatever the reason, Shakespeare took a room on Silver Street in Cripplegate in the north-west corner of the City. Always the London bachelor, he rented a room with the family of Christopher Mountjoy, a Huguenot 'tiremaker' of ornamental headgear for fancy ladies.

The Mountjoys lived and worked in a large, twin-gabled house at the corner of Monkwell and Silver Street. It was a middle-class neighbourhood of silversmiths and wigmakers. Captain Otter in Ben Jonson's *Epicene* quips of a woman that her 'teeth were made in the Blackfriars ... and her hair in Silver street' (4.2.64). In one of his earliest plays, *Comedy of Errors*, Shakespeare riffs on bald men who 'recover the lost hair' of other men (2.2.74–5). By 1604 the line may have come back to haunt – or taunt – balding Shakespeare, who now lived among the means for his own recovery.

Shakespeare got more than he bargained for when he moved to Silver Street. He just wanted a room with eastern exposure to let in morning light. That was likely when he wrote since theatre business consumed his afternoons. He might have written late at night as well, of course, burning the midnight wax. Still, theatre is *not* a morning business. This is an industry that calls a show at 2 pm a 'matinee' after 'matin', or morning. Theatre folk think the sun comes up at noon.

Shakespeare may have gotten his well-lit room, but he also got tangled in a Huguenot drama that didn't even rise to the level of French farce. The Mountjoys wanted their only child, daughter Mary, to wed one of their apprentices, Stephen Bellot. Bellot had his eyes peeled for a fortunate marriage, and Mary was apparently not the likeliest lass. Enter Shakespeare the go-between once more, playing Pandarus to a reluctant Troilus. As noted earlier, there was something about Shakespeare – a level head, a smooth tongue – that made parents turn to him to persuade young people to marry.

We know this because a decade later Stephen Bellot was still trying to collect the promised dowry from his father-in-law. Turns out the 'Mountjoys' were ill-named, since Christopher was a miser who never came across with the promised dowry. (Christopher Mountjoy was the only person who ever lived whose first question about Shakespeare was *not* 'did he really write those plays' but 'will he pay his rent on time?')

Bellot was counting on sixty pounds in hand at the time of the wedding and two hundred more when Mountjoy died. One scholar estimates the current value of sixty pounds at about £12,000 in today's money; not a king's ransom but nothing to sneeze at. Bellot never got even a whiff of it. Mountjoy gave the newlyweds ten pounds and a bunch of junk lying about the house. A feather bolster, an old bobbin box and two pairs of scissors. There's something particularly petty about that second pair of scissors. A single pair might be something special, but the second is just snippy.

Years later, Shakespeare was summoned in the late spring of 1612 by the Court of Requests to testify in the suit of Bellot vs. Mountjoy. He'd made the trip many times, but never for so petty an action. We can imagine how irritating this might have been, but he dutifully appeared at court to give his testimony.

The incident is interesting because it is here – not in his narrative poems, not in his plays and not even in his sonnets – that we hear the voice of Shakespeare himself, set down by the recording secretary. It is not a verbatim 'recording' but paraphrased through a transcript. Still, this is what Shakespeare had to say about his part in the affair:

> The deponent [i.e., Shakespeare] sayeth that the said defftes [the defendant, Christopher Mountjoy] wife did solicit and entreat this deponent to move and persuade the said Complainant to effect the said Marriage and accordingly this deponent did move and persuade the complainant therunto: And more to this Interrogatory he cannot depose.[1]

Well it's not exactly 'To be or not to be' part two, but it is the sound of Shakespeare from across the years, the only transcript of his voice. Ever the reticent, he does not expand upon the bald facts of the matter. The rest of the deposition is just as thin. He reports that Stephen Bellot was a 'very good industrious servant' but that he could not remember the exact amount of money promised nor what 'necessaries of household stuff the defendant gave the plaintiff in Marriage with his daughter Marye'. If Stephen and Mary had been counting on Shakespeare to come through for them, they were disappointed. He came all the way from Stratford for that? Maybe he muttered that he got paid to write. If you want me to really unwind, pay me by the word.

*

Stephen Bellot and Mary Mountjoy wed at St Olave's of Silver Street on 19 November 1604. Maybe they asked Shakespeare to read something. Maybe this was the very first wedding to feature, 'Let me not to the marriage of true minds admit impediment ...'. In any event, the new couple soon moved out of the house on Silver Street, and things quickly soured between Stephen and Christopher. Bellot's squabbles with his father-in-law provided – along with the bells – the backdrop to Shakespeare's work in 1605.

Shakespeare escaped the racket by immersing himself in a light comic soufflé he whipped up called *Macbeth*. The 'Scottish play' is assumed to have been written to please the new Scottish monarch. Again, a play about a Scottish regicide does not seem like the *first* thing you'd write to please your Scottish boss, but Shakespeare always worked by indirection. Banquo, who does not make it out of act two, was James' distant ancestor. But he's brutally murdered. This might have chilled James, whose family history was a horror show of bloody daggers and backroom murders. Banquo's son Fleance scampers off from the crime scene while his father covers his retreat. He is never heard of again, one of the loose strings that Shakespeare does not tie up. But Fleance gets out of the play alive, and in his escape James could have seen his own destiny.

King James was interested in witches even if Jonson and Shakespeare were not. He had written a long work on witchcraft called *Demonology* (1597), which takes seriously the idea that the world is haunted. James was not a credulous man. He had a forensic interest in the difference between real and fake possession. He pulled the curtain back on phonies more than once during his reign. Yet his witch hunting did not shake his belief in the supernatural. It only confirmed it.

There is a superstition that *Macbeth* is an unlucky play. Citations of the superstition endow it with a deep tradition, stretching back to 'Hal Berridge', a boy actor who died just prior to his premiere as Lady Macbeth in 1606.[2] *Macbeth* was performed around 1606, and Lady Macbeth was played by a boy who died at some point, though not, of course, as a result of his appearance in *Macbeth*. In fact the 'curse' that lies over the play is not even mentioned until the twentieth century, though it is always called 'ancient'. Whatever the fate of this unlucky play – a play so cursed it's still being performed over four hundred years later – it does not seem to have done Shakespeare any harm.

The play's anecdotal afterlife is prompted by its interest in witchcraft. One Victorian commentator asked if Shakespeare was 'an Actual Believer in Witches' and answered in the affirmative: 'It is known that Ben Johnson, literary contemporary and close friend of Shakespeare, was a victim of hallucinations, and he and Shakespeare may have talked over the phenomenon of the ghostly visitors in the flickering candle light of the Mermaid tavern.'³ Anytime somebody says, 'it is known', it means they are making it up. There is no evidence that Jonson and Shakespeare talked about witches by candle light at the Mermaid or elsewhere. It is known that they talked about what playwrights still talk about: bad reviews, irritating actors and theatres that have been shuttered by public health crises.

Macbeth is a later play than *Julius Caesar*, but Shakespeare is still thinking about Caesar, still ruminating upon the horror of regicide. And no wonder, since between the writing of *Julius Caesar* in 1599 and *Macbeth* in 1606, Guy Fawkes had tried to take out King James by planting thirty-six barrels of gunpowder underneath his parliamentary throne.

The Gunpowder Plot, still remembered on the fifth of November even today, brought an end to James' honeymoon. In the spring of 1604, not long after he made his delayed entrance to the City of London, he gave a long speech to parliament in which he described his idea of monarchy. He did so in marital terms, concluding that, 'What God has conjoined, then, let no man separate. I am the husband, and all the whole isle is my lawful wife.'⁴ Guy Fawkes and his followers wanted a divorce.

The plot failed and James reigned for another twenty years. Shakespeare glances obliquely at the plot through a word – 'equivocate' – put into the mouth of the hung-over porter who muses in a monologue about 'an equivocator that could swear in both the scales against either scale, who committed treason enough for God's sake, yet could not equivocate to heaven' (2.3.8–11). Shakespeare has Father Henry Garnet in mind, one of the principal Jesuits of England who was executed for his part in the Gunpowder Plot, though his role was unclear. He knew of it but claimed the privilege of confession, which obliged him to secrecy. His trial hung upon the practice of 'equivocation', a fancy term for what Macbeth calls the 'lies like truth' the witches tell.

The prosecution complained about Garnet's 'equivocation' – a practice that allowed Catholics to lie under oath while remaining truthful to God. Even on the stand, a Catholic might answer 'truthfully' out loud while qualifying the statement silently in his head, satisfying both God and man. The authorities saw this as Jesuitical casuistry, an affront to both language and meaning. While Shakespeare probably did not sympathize with the plotters, he might have admired their tactical equivocation. Playwrights also lie like truth.

*

On 12 August 1607, Shakespeare's nephew died. The Register of St Giles, Cripplegate records the burial: 'B. [buried] Edward son of Edward [sic] Shack-speere, player: base-born'.[5] The 'base-born' refers to the baby, not to Shakespeare's brother. The entry gets one thing wrong and two things right: William Shakespeare's younger brother was named 'Edmond' not 'Edward'; he was an actor; and Shakespeare's nephew was a bastard.

Edmond was born on 3 May 1580, Shakespeare's youngest sibling. He was only three years old when William and Anne had their own first child, and so Susanna Shakespeare's naughty uncle Edmond was just a few years older than she was. Shakespeare's brother is called 'Edmond' in the records of Holy Trinity, Stratford: 'C. [christened] Edmond Son to Mr John Shakespere'. He is also called 'Edmond' in the burial record from the last day of December in the year his son died: 'B. [buried] Edmond Shakespeare, a player: in the church'. A fee-book adds 'with a forenoon knell of the great bell, xx [shillings]'.[6]

William Shakespeare died in 1616. Anne or Agnes Shakespeare died in August 1623, a few months before the London publishers Edward Blount and Isaac Jaggard registered their intent to print the 'first folio' with the Stationers Company, the guild that controlled the English book trade. (This is fitting since it's the year the name of 'Shakespeare' began to detach itself from the body and become a book.) As noted, with the death of Shakespeare's granddaughter, the childless Elizabeth Hall, in February 1670, the Shakespeare line was out.

There is nothing to it beyond an accident of genetics, but the curious fact is that in the 1560s when Shakespeare was born, there were loads of Shakespeares. By the 1660s there were none. Unless we conjecture that something in the Shakespeare strain raged against reproduction, there is little to make of this. Except for the fact that by the middle of the seventeenth century, Shakespeare was a name from out of the past. When he is referred to in the 1700s, the adjective attached to his name is not 'sweet' but 'old'. Shakespeare's line barely survived him by fifty years. His end-stopped line contributes to a tendency to see him as a freak. Singular, one of a kind, without heirs to argue over his legacy and fail to live up to it.

It might have been William Shakespeare who paid twenty shillings to ring the bell for his little brother, the brother who followed in his footsteps to London, walked the stage, met a woman he liked, and probably died of the plague. Among the clamour of 1607 was a bell that tolled for Shakespeare's brother.

*

Times got bad and the plays got weird. That's a facile way to put it, but Shakespeare followed *Macbeth* with, among other things, *Timon of Athens* and *Coriolanus*. These plays take the novel dramatic strategy of featuring totally unlikeable title characters. Coriolanus is the only protagonist in all of Shakespeare's plays who refuses to act. Allergic to dissembling, he refuses to politic before the crowd, who are willing to confer leadership upon him for his military genius. All he has to do is lie.

It is a peculiar fact of this play – and perhaps a revealing one – that many writers have tried to rewrite it. Nahum Tate, Bertolt Brecht, Günter Grass, John Osborne. It emerged, bizarrely, in 2020 that the fascist politico Steve Bannon wrote an unreadable hip hop adaptation of the play. Many admire *Coriolanus*. Few love it. George Bernard Shaw called it 'Shakespeare's greatest comedy', deliberately getting the genre wrong to wrap his head around this peculiar play.

Admired but unloved is precisely the ambition of the protagonist of *Timon*, co-written with or by Thomas Middleton. Timon does Coriolanus and Shakespeare one better. He leaves his hometown and never looks back. Indeed, both Coriolanus and Timon try to escape the plays named after them. Coriolanus turns his back on Rome, claiming that there is a 'world elsewhere', and Timon flees Athens for a life in the wilderness after a farewell banquet of rocks and lukewarm water for his enemies. These are plays of disenchantment, above all else.

Unlike Timon and Coriolanus, the protagonists of *Antony and Cleopatra* are lovable, all too lovable. (Though Kenneth Tynan called *Antony and Cleopatra* England's most characteristic love story since it contains no scenes of love.[7]) With *Coriolanus* and *Antony and Cleopatra* Shakespeare was struck by what Cleopatra calls a 'Roman thought', though he never really stopped thinking about Rome. From the early *Titus Andronicus* through *Julius Caesar* and onto *Coriolanus* and *Antony and Cleopatra* Shakespeare never shook his zeal for Roman history. Even the late *Cymbeline*, set mainly in ancient Britain, finds Shakespeare still reckoning with Rome.

Unlike his English histories, which cluster in the first half of his writing career, Shakespeare's Roman plays were produced across the span of his writing life. Rome seems, however, to have lost some of its lustre in Shakespeare's later treatments. Like Coriolanus, the aging Antony gives over Rome, preferring the banks of the Nile to the shores of Tiber. In fact, Coriolanus, Timon and Antony all abandon city life. These plays are not pastorals, of course. They do not romanticize the shepherds' life or the hermit's remove. They are not pro-rural, they are anti-urban. Antony flees Rome for Cleopatra's upholstered boudoir, but both Timon and Coriolanus prefer a hermetic life in the wilderness or turn their back on the town. You might even say they avoid the city like the plague.

*

It is not clear how much James liked plays himself, but his court's appetite for entertainment quickly consumed the King's Men's stock. Turns out the naming of Shakespeare and his fellows as the King's Men was more than an honorific. They were expected to sing for their supper, and they did so until their throats ran dry. They played over and over again for the court in the early days of James' reign. However well stocked, their cupboard was soon bare. By January 1605 Burbage tells a court official that, 'there was no new play the queen [James' wife Anne] has not seen'.[8] They fobbed her off with *Love's Labour's Lost* – the most Elizabethan play Shakespeare ever wrote, or the least Jacobean one – but the court wanted something new. Faced with the call for a new play for a new monarch, Shakespeare gave them an old one about an old man named Lear.

17

Shakespeare's Daughters

Some things are so obvious they bear repeating. 'Never, never, never, never, never.' And yet one measure of Shakespeare's talent is that it took him a long time to start repeating himself. He was nearly always able to make it new, even when he revisited familiar ground. But with *Lear* he repeated himself. 'No cause, no cause.' 'Look there, look there!' 'Howl, Howl, Howl.' And, awfully, as Lear hovers over the lifeless body of his youngest daughter, 'Thou'lt come no more. / Never, never, never, never, never' (5.3.306–7). A line that only ends because the metre runs out.

King Lear is an old play about an old man. How old? 'Fourscore and upward, not an hour more nor less' (4.7.61). So both vaguely and precisely over eighty. Why an old play for a new king? In one of Shakespeare's savvier nods to the national mood – or, what's more important, the monarch's – *King Lear* scratched James' itch to unify England and Scotland, if not Ireland and France and Wales. But as with *Macbeth*, the play is not a sop to the sovereign. It is an appeal to his interests. Both plays are, in their own ways, cautionary tales. The 'Scottish Play' features a backroom murder too familiar to James from his upbringing. And *Lear* opens with an impolitic division of the kingdom and shows the calamity that comes from it. It ends – *they* end, since the 1608 and 1623 texts of *Lear* end differently – with the country at an uneasy peace as the younger generation picks up the pieces of a broken nation.

James Shapiro reckons that Shakespeare bought a copy of the anonymous play of *King Leir* in 1605 at John Wright's bookshop at 'Christs Church door, next Newgate-Market', not far from Shakespeare's lodging on Silver Street.[1] Maybe Shakespeare read it on the road during the plague tours of the 1600s.

But Shakespeare knew the play without book. It was an old Queen's Men play, and he'd raided their rep before. Shakespeare's *Henry V*, *King John* and *Richard III* all dust off plays that once belonged to the Queen's Men. If he had toured with the company in the early years he likely appeared in all these plays, so they lived in his body as well as his brain. If he was not a Queen's Man, he had seen *King Leir* along with these other plays. We imagine Shakespeare's sources as books stacked high upon his desk, but many of them ran in his blood and rang in his ears.

There was a time in Shakespeare's life that his complete works would not have included *King Lear*. Had he chosen – like Ben Jonson – to put together a collection in mid-career, say at the end of Elizabeth's reign, it would be a winning one of zesty comedies, rousing histories and juvenile tragedies. But it wouldn't have included *Othello*. It wouldn't have included *Macbeth*. And it wouldn't have included *King Lear*.

It is *Lear* that provides some defining, even definitive shape to Shakespeare's complete works. As Algernon Charles Swinburne wrote in 1902, 'If nothing were left of Shakespeare but the single tragedy of *King Lear*, it would still be as plain as it is now that he was the greatest man that ever lived.'[2] Swinburne contemplates not a collection of Shakespeare's works that does not include *King Lear* but one that includes only *King Lear*. For this play alone, Swinburne would crown Shakespeare the nonpareil. It is, in itself, a complete work.

*

Whether it was the plague, the death of coworkers and of his brother, or his entry into his fifth decade of life, Shakespeare's late plays turn from the younger sort to the older kind. In the early comedies and tragedies, youngsters chase after love and either catch it or die trying ('So quickly may one catch the plague', one heartsick victim in *Twelfth Night* calls falling in love). In the history plays, young men seek 'the sweet fruition of an earthly crown' as Christopher Marlowe calls it in *Tamburlaine*. Even the two plays about *Henry IV* are not about Henry IV, they are about his son Hal. Hamlet and Olivia are also children. Not that they are childish but that their problems are the problems of children newly bereft of a parent. Under Elizabeth, Shakespeare's plays are about young people, on the make or on the mend.

After James, Shakespeare turns to greyer beards and graver ends. Lear and Macbeth are fathers troubled by their children or by their childlessness. (Macbeth's third-act problem is that he doesn't have an heir.) Prospero is a single father, Leontes a dead-beat dad. Shakespeare's seventeenth-century characters are 'wrinkled deep in time', as Cleopatra calls herself. This is not a matter of Shakespeare 'identifying' with one character over another – he's everybody and nobody in his plays – it's a matter of where the centre of gravity sits in his plays. Increasingly, he's drawn to characters looking back to see who's gaining on them, since the only thing they have to look forward to is death.

The generational shift was matched, if it wasn't caused, by the company Shakespeare kept. The Lord Chamberlain's Servants had been laddish when they formed in 1594, but they were daddish by 1603, a group of middle-aged men griping about their creaking knees and needy kids. Shakespeare was the oldest of them all – forty-one in 1605 – but none of them were spring chickens by the standards of the time (though they weren't autumn fowl, by ours). Richard Burbage was in his late thirties when he played Lear, Macbeth, Othello and Ben Jonson's aged Volpone. Always, Shakespeare had an eye out for his greatest resource after his own imagination, which were the men who put flesh on the bones of his plays. By 1605 that flesh was sagging.

Shakespeare also turns his back on the fathers and sons of the history plays, all those Henries *père et fils* fretting about succession. Or Hamlet the younger grieving for Hamlet the elder. Beginning with *King Lear* of 1605, Shakespeare writes a run of plays about fathers and daughters: *Lear, The Winter's Tale, The Tempest, Pericles, Cymbeline*, and the most important father and daughter of them all – for the English at least – Henry VIII and his daughter Elizabeth. After *Hamlet* – after Hamnet – Shakespeare stops writing about disappointed sons and starts to write about redemptive daughters.

These daughters all redeem their dads by listening to them talk. *Lear, Cymbeline, The Winter's Tale* and *Pericles* all end with an old man who hopes to spend his latter days catching up with his daughter. (*The Tempest* starts with a father talking with his daughter, though he bores her so thoroughly she falls asleep.) Imprisoned with Cordelia, Lear hopes to 'tell old tales' and laugh with her at the 'gilded butterflies' of court. Leontes leads his long-lost daughter Perdita from the stage to talk at leisure about what they have been up to 'in the wide gap of time' since they were last together. Pericles reunites with his left-for-dead Marina (who could distil the entirety of Shakespeare's encyclopedic learning into a simple piece of advice: 'Never get on a boat'). Cymbeline closes the play by peppering his daughter Imogen with a series of who, what, where, when and why questions:

> Where? How liv'd you?
> And when came you to serve our Roman captive?
> How parted with your brothers? How first met them?
> Why fled you from the court? And whither?

> (5.5.385–8)

These plays end with an old man exiting the stage – or in Lear's case being carried from it – with the simple wish to talk with his daughter. 'Truth is the daughter of time', according to Shakespeare's contemporary, Francis Bacon, translating from the Latin. Daughters are the truth.

In all these instances, daughters answer an old man's ache for home, hearth and hospitality. Lear's main outrage at Regan and Goneril is not that they won't put up with him but that they won't put him up. He saves his 'dragon's wrath' for their inhospitality, which always comes in for a hard time in Shakespeare's plays. At the point of having his eyes gouged out by Regan and Cornwall, Gloucester objects that 'you are my guests' (3.7.30)! As though they had soiled his best linen.

If Shakespeare came home in the summer of 1607 and asked his daughters 'how lived you?' Susanna at least had some news for him. She married in June 1607 but also had a scrape with the law to confess to her dad. Apparently not particularly religious about religion, she was cited by Stratford in 1606 for not taking communion at Easter that year. Her timing was bad since just a few months earlier Guy Fawkes and crew had failed, explosively, to blow up parliament. The nation was on edge and on the look-out for Catholic sympathizers and their Catholic sympathies. The charges were dropped once she eventually showed up in court.

She cleared her name by marrying a stalwart Protestant, John Hall, who was, in Maria's terms from *Twelfth Night*, 'a kind of puritan' (2.3.138). He was also a very good physician, remarkable for the time in that his remedies did not kill his patients. After 1607 Anne (Agnes?) Shakespeare could boast to her neighbours that while her husband might be a playwright, her son-in-law was a doctor.

Perhaps learning from Lear (if not Christopher Mountjoy), Shakespeare gave the couple 107 acres of his land in Old Stratford (with no division of this little kingdom). In fact, Shakespeare settled decent dowries on both of his daughters, setting them up in comfort. Always alert to the ebb and flow of money, Shakespeare looked after his own.

But what kind of dad was he? An absentee one, mostly. He provided his girls the means to live, but his time, his attention, his care, his love? It's impossible to quantify love ('There's beggary in the love that can be reckoned', Cleopatra says), but he was obviously stingy with his time. He became a grandfather in February 1608, when Susanna and John welcomed daughter Elizabeth. No sonnets about that Elizabeth either.

However often he made it back to Stratford, he lived largely in London during his daughters' development. He may have made it home now and then, with ribbons for his daughters purchased at the Royal Exchange or feathers for their finery from the Blackfriars district. Still, the gift of his time he gave to his work. 'I gave you all', Lear lies to his daughters. Shakespeare could not truthfully say the same.

*

While his daughters grew and wed in Stratford, Shakespeare was still living on Silver Street, though the house was quieter by this time. Six months after they wed, Stephen and Mary Bellott went to live with a shady character named George Wilkins. He ran a tavern and a brothel and was a left-handed playwright. He was also a thug. One of his many criminal charges was that he kicked a pregnant woman in the belly. It speaks to the atmosphere on Silver Street that Wilkins' house was apparently an upgrade.

Shakespeare may have met Wilkins through Stephen and Mary – or the other way around. He knew him through literary circles or patronized his tavern or brothel. However they met, they collaborated on *Pericles* around 1607, the story of an abandoned daughter and her errant father. Wilkins and Shakespeare worked together despite the language barrier. Wilkins' English was poor, Shakespeare's was perfect. In fact, Wilkins may be responsible for the single worst line in all of Shakespeare: 'He, doing so, put forth to seas, / Where when men been, there's seldom ease' (2.ch.27–8). It's almost unspeakably bad.

Like *Pericles*, *Timon of Athens* was also a collaboration, though with a sensational writer named Thomas Middleton – a playwright nearly the equal of Shakespeare in range and scope and imaginative power. *Measure for Measure* and *Macbeth* bear his touch, since the plays as we have them in the folio of 1623 were brushed up by Middleton in the years that followed Shakespeare's 'retirement' or death. Middleton was both Shakespeare's writing partner and his reviser, and his imprint upon the second half of Shakespeare's writing career is immense. Scholars are still trying to weigh it.

The tale of the tape tells the real story. As noted earlier, late in his career Shakespeare is coupled with a younger writer: Thomas Middleton (b. 1580), George Wilkins (b. unknown) and John Fletcher (b. 1579). It might have been a savvy marketing move by Shakespeare and company – an effort to marry the Elizabethan Shakespeare with a Jacobean playwright, one with a finer touch for the time.

Still, Shakespeare was only in his early forties at the dawn of the seventeenth century. Forty-one when he wrote *Lear* (so two-score year and upward, not an hour more nor less). While the pace of his writing might have slightly slowed, that was probably due to the closure of the theatres, not the flagging of his energy. The plays themselves show no signs of slowing down. The writing still flames with intensity – language operating at the limits of expression. *King Lear* is not the work of a burned-out playwright. It throbs with a dark energy. If we call these plays 'mature', it is what happens when an artist assimilates his experience to his form.

However fit, Shakespeare was nearer the finish line than the starting blocks in the mid-1600s, and even he must have known it. There are signs of nostalgia in Shakespeare's last plays. In keeping with his orbital life, he finished what he started in the late 1580s since his last play, like his first ones, was a history. *Henry VIII* is much different from the *Henry VI* plays because of course it is. It is written by a man in his late forties with dozens of plays behind him rather than one in his late twenties with it all ahead of him. Like those first history plays, it is a collaboration (with Fletcher) and, like those plays, tends to the glory of the Tudor dynasty. Even well into the Jacobean years, Shakespeare is still thinking like an Elizabethan.

In this last play, the word 'England' shows up again and again. This is unusual, since after James, Shakespeare substituted 'British' for 'English' as the new king with his zeal for a great union preferred (James was the original Union Jac). The word

'England' appears 224 times in his Elizabethan plays, and 'English' 132 times.[3] Shakespeare never used the word 'British' before James came to the throne, and it first appears in his *King Lear* (and then twenty-nine more times in his Jacobean plays).

In his final play Shakespeare's Elizabethan roots show. It ends with the birth of a daughter, the future Elizabeth the first, in whose reign Shakespeare was born, reared and thrived. He would end his writing career as he began it, an Elizabethan playwright. He would also end it where he began, in Stratford-upon-Avon, where he lived out the last season of his life with his wife, and with his daughters.

18

The Returning Point

John Osborne once observed that, 'nobody ever wrote a great play after forty'. Like most blanket statements, it is easy to refute. Even Osborne wrote some great plays after forty, or at least some very good ones. But Osborne is getting after something here. The idea that playwrights flame out fast and spend their last years banking their fires.

Osborne's observation might suit Ben Jonson, who went on writing well into his fifties, though his greatest plays – *The Alchemist*, *Volpone*, *Every Man in His Humour* and *Epicene* – were all produced before he turned forty. He wrote so long and so late that when his last play, *The Magnetic Lady*, appeared it was greeted with surprise. His friends all thought he was dead.

Osborne knew his Shakespeare but left him out when he mused about playwrights after forty (two score years and upward). Shakespeare turned forty in 1606. *Lear*, *Macbeth* and *Antony and Cleopatra* all hover around that date, with *The Winter's Tale* and *The Tempest* still to come. Shakespeare's output might have dropped after forty, but the quality did not suffer. Shakespeare in his forties was not a playwright in decline.

Age is just a number and the better measure of Shakespeare's output are those few playwrights who measure up to him: Marlowe and Jonson, Fletcher and Ford, Webster and Middleton. The lives of Marlowe and Jonson and Shakespeare would all seem like unbearable clichés if they had not been the first to live them. Marlowe, a scholarship boy, a blazing talent, coming and going like a storm in summer. Ben Jonson, a mordant bricklayer, always on the make and unhappiest when he made it. And then there was Shakespeare, steady, productive, reliable as a clock, which also always ends up right back where it started.

They set the mould for how to live the life of an English writer. Marlowe established the Icarus model, a promise so great it can only be broken. Jonson, the mason, who built a wall of work so tall it finally enclosed him. Shakespeare traced the orbital life, in which a writer comes home again, life and work right back where they began.

It is not hard to find their followers – Marlowe has his Keats, his Shelley. Jonson his Waugh, his Shaw. But who has had a writing life quite like William Shakespeare's? Charles Dickens? Anthony Powell? James Joyce? Agatha Christie? Tom Stoppard, also writing Romances, like the *Coast of Utopia*, in his later years? Perhaps the closest model might seem far-fetched. P.G. Wodehouse wrote for nearly as long as he lived – ninety-three novels in ninety-plus years. He was a commercial as well as a critical success. And in addition to filling his buckets with money, he was also a political naïf. The only dust up in his life came when – having been a POW in a Nazi camp – he tried to make light of it during England's darkest hour. His personal biography is almost as boring as Shakespeare's. All he did was write.

(Alexander Cockburn compares the atmosphere of Wodehouse's Wooster stories to Shakespeare's comedies, with their 'reversal of hierarchies': 'Jeeves is in every way – except socially – Bertie's superior.'[1] Wodehouse inherited Shakespeare's treatment of master–servant relations, itself inherited from Roman comedy, where the servants are superior to those they serve, which does not subvert, it only sustains, the conservation of social relations.)

The analogy is strained. Part of Shakespeare's exceptionalism is that his artistic life conformed neither to Marlowe's or Jonson's or any of his contemporaries – or followers really if truth be told. Shakespeare neither burned out early nor faded away. Like a champion marathon runner, he started fast, picked it up in the middle and finished strong. He was a tortoise, not a hare, though a tortoise capable of astonishing bursts of speed.

As the decade dwindled, he might have sensed the end, which was back where he began, in Stratford-upon-Avon. 'Shakespeare's death, like his works, left nothing unfinished, no broken fragment of time to reckon up; it completed a circle', the *London Times* wrote in 1861. The circle is such an alluring form since it includes itself, but excludes all others. Shakespeare was a member of a circle of writers of which he was the only one.

*

By 1609 Shakespeare was in his later years, though he did not know they were his later years. He knew he was aging. He had known it for some time. In sonnet 73 he writes, 'That time of year thou mayst in me behold / When yellow leaves, or none, or few, do hang ...' (ll. 1–2). We do not know exactly when he wrote this gorgeous poem, which meditates upon the autumn of life. Scholars have recently dated it to the mid-1590s, when Shakespeare was in his late twenties or just turned thirty. Not a child, of course, but not exactly Father Time.

We can quote this sonnet because it was printed in 1609 along with 153 others. By that point Shakespeare had been on London's literary scene for two decades. It is unlikely that the sonnets were pirated, then – compiled, printed and sold without his consent. He knew the world too well and was too well connected to be taken by surprise by a bootleg version of his private poems.

Thomas Heywood suggested in 1612 that Shakespeare's irritation with the earlier, unauthorized publication of some of his sonnets in *The Passionate Pilgrim* led him to take action: 'he to doe himself right, hath since published them in his own name'.[2] Whoever's decision it was to print them, the release of the sonnets in 1609 meant that Shakespeare would leave London the way he came in, as a published poet not a public playwright.

Stanley Wells argues that the sonnets can be read autobiographically, though with care and in part. The tricky bit is figuring out which part. After all, as Peter Holland has written, Shakespeare led a life of 'fissured opacity', one which lets in just enough light to read these poems as testaments to Shakespeare's preoccupations, grievances, desires and melancholy.[3]

The question of 'are they' or 'are they not' autobiographical is complicated by the fact that the sonnets are not one thing and one thing only. The question cannot be 'are the sonnets autobiographical' but 'is *this* sonnet autobiographical'. The answer to which is sometimes yes and sometimes no (Shakespeare ends sonnet 136 with 'my name is Will' so we're safe to assume the affirmative in that case). Some are achingly, searingly personal. Others are detached, even antiseptic. Five-finger exercises, a writer cracking his knuckles before getting down to work.

What 'they are', broadly speaking, are private poems, by contrast with his public plays. The sonnets are designed to be enjoyed in private and sometimes blush at the thought of it. In fact, the temerity of writing is something of a theme with Shakespeare. When he stages scenes of writing in his plays, the overriding fear is that your friends might catch you at it. From *Much Ado* to *As You Like It* to *Love's Labour's Lost*, poets are caught with their pants down and their pens out. These scenes are ripe with adolescent funk, in which red-faced boys are caught right-handed.

So poetry in Shakespeare is always written behind the backs of your closest friends. 'When will you see me write a thing in rhyme?' (4.3.178) Berowne asks in *Love's Labour's Lost*, fearing less that his friends see his writing than that his friends see him writing. Whatever else this scene is about, it blushes at its onanism, the anxiety that someone might see you do it. What's embarrassing about poetry in Shakespeare is not that it rhymes but that it's written. The sonnets in *Love's Labour's Lost* are produced by a series of jerks.

Released in 1609 near the end of Shakespeare's public career the sonnets can be read as a kind of emotional memoir. But just how telling are they? 'Presumably these poems would have been as puzzling to readers of Shakespeare's time as they are to us', Wells writes, 'a fact that supports the idea that the sonnets are private poems'.[4] We could draw the opposite conclusion: If the poems are so private why don't they name names? Why do they wrap their subjects in cyphers so intricate that critics still try to crack them? If Shakespeare sensed they might be read by others, he withheld names to protect the guilty, since the innocent need no defence.

A handful indulge in self-praise, boasting that the verse will survive the time and immortalize the subject more than marble monuments ever could. The sublime irony is that Shakespeare was right, but we don't know who he was talking about (we have *some* ideas, see Chapter 9, but nothing definite). The poems end up immortalizing the subject writing, not the subject being written about.

Read auto biographically, they are not an attractive set of poems. We learn nothing from them of his love for his family, his grief at the death of his son, or his queen, or his father. You would never know from these poems that Shakespeare had a wife. He was a married man but he did not write like one, i.e. not about his wife. (Or, more cynically, Shakespeare wrote exactly like a married man, i.e., not about his wife.) Instead they bemoan his reputation, his erotic failures, his envy of others' beauty, wealth and talent. However pretty, they are often petty, which is to say entirely human.

Personal or impersonal, Shakespeare's sonnets did not make the splash that his early poetry did. There's far more interest today in a 'memoir' of Shakespeare's emotional life than there was in the early seventeenth century. Not much evidence survives of people noting or quoting them. There are only twenty surviving manuscripts that include copies of Shakespeare's sonnets. By contrast, there are nearly 250 that cite John Donne's poetry.[5] (This may be because Shakespeare's sonnets are often complicated but not complex while Donne's are the opposite.)

If Shakespeare's sonnets did not seem newsworthy, it is because they were old news. Many had seen print before. Four show up in *Love's Labour's Lost*, still others in poetic miscellanies across the years. The collection has the feel of an aging rocker repackaging earlier work to squeeze some cash from his wheezing fan base. There is some startlingly original work here, but there are also some rarities and B-sides. If sonnet 145 – with its unusual iambic tetrameter and pun on Anne Hathaway's name – dates from their courting days, then the sonnet sequence spans over twenty-seven years and includes some of Shakespeare's first and last work, a retrospective of sorts.

Calling the sonnets a 'sequence' is deceptive, however, since the word reverse-engineers an intentional order to the collection. Shakespeare may have countenanced their release, but there is no evidence he arranged their order. Even less that he composed them in a deliberate sequence (though a good number of good commentators have argued that he did). In this respect the 1609 sonnets borrow an idea but not the execution of the deliberately plotted sonnet sequences of Philip Sidney, Edmund Spenser, Mary Wroth and others. In those sequences, the tension between each atomistic poem and the larger cycle rewards bi-focal reading. Shakespeare's 1609 collection is a batched and baggy group of poems in which some hang together but do not add up to a suspended narrative. There is not a sustained story here that runs from Shakespeare's courting days until his dying ones.

In fact Shakespeare doesn't even show up until sonnet 10. Or, what may be the same thing, the first-person pronoun 'I' does not appear until the tenth sonnet. As noted in Chapter 9, the first group of sonnets urge a young man to marry and reproduce. Far from being autobiographical, they may have been bespoke, tailored to the lineaments of the idle son of a fretful mother.

Other sonnets seem self-tailored, though, cut to his own lines. One will serve here, sonnet 110, which reflects ruefully upon both his work life and love life:

Alas, 'tis true I have gone here and there
And made myself a motley to the view,
Gored mine own thoughts, sold cheap what is most dear,
Made old offences of affections new.
Most true it is that I have looked on truth
Askance and strangely: but, by all above,
These blenches gave my heart another youth,
And worse essays proved thee my best of love.
Now all is done, have what shall have no end!
Mine appetite, I never more will grind
On newer proof, to try an older friend,
A god in love, to whom I am confined.
    Then give me welcome, next my heaven the best,
    Even to thy pure and most loving breast.

Like many of the sonnets, the meaning is obscured by twisty syntax and dated diction ('blenches', 'Gored'). It opens with Shakespeare confessing to a turn as a touring player, one who wandered 'here and there' to play the fool for a handful of coins. It's strange to think of Shakespeare degraded by the art that made him. But the clearest part of this shady poem is that he feels tarnished by his trade.

He analogizes his turn as a touring player with his errant career as a lover, one who has exposed himself to a wide range of onlookers. It's one of Shakespeare's 'special pleaders', a poem or passage in which the speaker excuses bad behaviour as a learning experience, making a virtue of a vice. Here, Shakespeare's wandering eye proves that his first love was his best love – a sort of erotic empiricism. Had he not been faithless, the argument goes, his fidelity would not be worth as much.

If the sonnets are autobiographical – even opaquely so – then one thing is crystal clear: Shakespeare cheated on his wife. He was apparently willing to pursue both physical and emotional infidelity. In fact, what troubles him in 110 is his infidelity to the lover with whom he's being unfaithful to his wife. However you run the numbers, this doesn't add up to an ethical position. Yet the biographical record is quiet on this count. No one ever mentions when rehearsing the William the Conqueror gag that Shakespeare was a married man. Even the Victorians, normally sniffy about these things, fail to mention that 'William Shakespeare, gentleman' was not. Just one more reason that history calls Shakespeare's wife 'Anne Hathaway' and not 'Anne Shakespeare' is to redeem him of the crime of betraying her. You can't cheat on your wife if you're unmarried.

*

'Now all is done ....' The release of the sonnets in 1609 could signal that Shakespeare was thinking of leaving London, chucking it in and going home for good. By 1609, he might have been tired of going 'here and there', and there was that big house on Chapel Lane for which he was paying but in which he was not living.

But New Place was not the only house Shakespeare owned but was not using. There was another one; this one in London. Even with the King as their boss, Shakespeare and co. still had not got use of their indoor playhouse. Denied access to The Blackfriars back in 1596, the Burbage brothers leased it to a group of boy players, who performed there for years until James got fed up with them for staging plays that mocked the Scots. It seems that then, as now, actors cannot resist showing off a Scottish accent. (This applies to Scottish actors as well.) The boys finally went too far in 1608 with George Chapman's *Conspiracy and Tragedy of Charles Duke of Biron*, which irritated the French ambassador so much that James shut the company down.

At this point, a group of the King's Servants drew up one of those early modern contracts designed to share risk among investors and give fits to theatre historians. Shakespeare and six others formed a syndicate of 'housekeepers' who committed to paying the annual forty pounds rent. The syndicate features some of the usual suspects – Richard and Cuthbert Burbage, John Heminges, William Condell and William Sly – and one unusual one, Thomas Evans. (Lucy Munro has discovered that Thomas Evans was the son of Henry Evans, former lessee of The Blackfriars. The share was assigned to son Thomas as compensation for his father's losses.[6]) William Sly died just a week after the deed was drawn, so Shakespeare's share rose to one-sixth. He now added a share in The Blackfriars to his holdings.

The Blackfriars offered one last frustration to the King's Servants. Even with the deal in place, the company could not move in, since the plague had kicked up once more. Finally, in the late autumn of 1609 the King's Servants had a roof over their head. From then until the theatres closed in the 1640s, the company had a winter haven, a warm room in which to ply their trade while The Globe offered a summer home.

What comes first, the play or the playhouse? Did Shakespeare write his last plays 'for' The Blackfriars? There are elements of *Cymbeline*, *Winter's Tale* and *The Tempest* that 'feel' like Blackfriars plays. Shaped for the smoky intimacy of an indoor playhouse, with a smaller but better heeled clientele than The Globe. You can picture Ariel dangling from The Blackfriars' windlass, entering 'like a harpy' from the heavens to admonish and astonish the audience below. Or Jupiter in *Cymbeline* entering in a thunderclap and exiting in a sulphurous fume. And you can feel the charge that *Henry VIII* would spark in the very room in which Henry's divorce proceedings with Catherine of Aragon had played out nearly a century before. Full of indoor fireworks, the late plays are Blackfriars plays, site-specific ones in the case of *Henry VIII*, or *All Is True*, as it was likely called at the time.

All of this *is* true: these final plays were written 'for' The Blackfriars. But the plays filled the stage at The Globe as well, still pulling them in across the Thames on summer afternoons. (There's a rich account of *Henry VIII* at The Globe detailing the extravagance of its staging.) And these plays entertained the court of James in Whitehall and at Greenwich. And they played in the provinces as well, during intermittent tours. Shakespeare's plays – all of them – were written for a range of spaces, including, after 1609, James Burbage's dream of an indoor playhouse.

The Blackfriars also signalled a sort of homecoming for Shakespeare. The indoor playhouse – with a screen or *frons* at one end of a rectangular room – resembled the guild halls and great houses in which drama was staged in Shakespeare's youth. He saw his first plays in the guild hall in Stratford, and he wrote his last ones for a swanky version of one in London.

Shakespeare *et al.* began to perform in The Blackfriars in late 1609, but no one much talks about what play may have 'opened' there. Sarah Dustagheer reckons it was *Coriolanus*.[7] Perhaps Shakespeare recalled another opening a decade earlier when his *Julius Caesar* may have opened The Globe. Both plays begin with patrician figures quelling a crowd, as though the opening of a new theatre reminded Shakespeare that the first job of a playwright is crowd control.

In any event, it is not clear if Shakespeare was still around in 1609. He's conventionally thought to have left London for Stratford around 1610 (alleged to have 'retired' as the next chapter examines). The evidence for his abandoning London for Stratford is pretty thin, but it seems, at least, that he was dividing his time and attention between the one and the other, though, to be fair, he had done so all his life. The last years of the first decade of the seventeenth century are, at any rate, full of homecomings. The late plays all feature reunions of fathers, wives and daughters, soldering what was sundered, joining what was severed.

*

If you are reading a physical copy of this book you will notice there's not much left. If this were a life of Ben Jonson or George Bernard Shaw, you'd be about an inch deep in Vol. 1. But as the rest of this book dwindles in your hand, so do Shakespeare's remaining years. You might temper your pleasure at nearly being done with the thought that so was Shakespeare, whose brief life was running out. The house he may have coveted from his youth, those investments he made against his later years, a reunion with his daughters that his late plays anticipate ... he did not get to enjoy them very long.

One last bit of good luck was that Shakespeare died when he did. He did not live long enough to fail to live up to himself. You can imagine an early connoisseur of English drama sniffing that he liked 'the early stuff' better, but you cannot seriously argue that the last plays do not rise to the standard of *Shrew* or *Two Gents*.

The inescapable conclusion about Shakespeare's life is that he stopped writing and then he died. This is not a claim of causation, but the effect is that his life is both brief and tidy. There is nearly no superfluous life after he stopped writing plays. No long decline, no embarrassing 'comeback', no descent into senescence. He did not die with his boots on, but they were still warm.

When and why did Shakespeare go back to Stratford for good? Sometimes questions contain their own answers. He went back to Stratford for the good of the story. The complete life of William Shakespeare requires that it end where it began, in the town he was born, in the house next door to the school that lettered him, and near the church that christened him. Once he left Stratford in the 1580s, it was clear that he would make his way back home again. (As Pablo Neruda writes, 'he who returns has never left'.) Shakespeare left Stratford so he could come back and end up in a grave about a mile from where he was born. You couldn't make it up.

Would Shakespeare's life be a tragedy if he had not come home again? No. But his life would look different, not tragic but incomplete, like a chord that did not resolve. The roundness of his life would be cut off, curtailed, and in its place a parabolic one. Up to London and on to success. Perhaps passing away from the plague after the heights – or depths – of *Lear*.

What then? Perhaps a nook in the Poets' Corner of Westminster Abbey and so a very different kind of afterlife: working-class boy makes good, and then made great. But the return to Stratford brings the story back home, grounds the life in the soil of its origins. Like many of Shakespeare's plays, the beginning contains the end.

E.K. Chambers marks 1610 as the year of Shakespeare's likely 'migration' to Stratford – as if he was a seasonal bird, an upstart crow winging it home to find repose in a sweet swan's life. The go-to verb that comes to mind is that, in his late forties, Shakespeare 'retired' to Stratford. Nicholas Rowe spoke of Shakespeare 'in ease, retirement, and the conversation of his friends', giving the first push to the idea that Shakespeare 'retired' in 1610 or so. Lewis Theobald describes Shakespeare's 'retirement from the stage' in the preface to *Double Falsehood* of 1727. Biographers have often followed suit.

When Nicholas Rowe used the word 'retirement' in 1709, it did not mean what it means now, a quasi-formal departure from a profession, where an aged employee leaves a firm with a gold watch, a pension and a hearty stock of resentment. But the word 'retirement' gives the sense that Shakespeare, like Prospero of *The Tempest*, was going home to die, where 'every third thought shall be my grave'. If so, what preoccupied the other two-thirds of his thoughts? Family, legacy, home improvement?

It troubles the country-retirement story to discover that, just a year before his death, Shakespeare was still wrangling over real estate in London, the Blackfriars gatehouse he purchased in 1613. It is an odd irony that Shakespeare did not purchase a house in London until he left. He was also still writing plays with young John Fletcher (*Henry VIII*, *The Two Noble Kinsmen*, the lost *Cardenio*). In fact the same year Shakespeare bought the gatehouse he embarked on one last project with Richard Burbage. Shakespeare wrote and Burbage painted an 'impressa', an emblem and motto, for Francis Manners, the sixth Earl of Rutland, to carry in a tilt on the King's Accession

Day, 24 March 1613. There may have been some other motive, but this looks like a commission since Shakespeare and Burbage were paid quite well (four pounds, eighteen shillings a piece). By this point in their lives the writer and actor had done well for themselves, but this may have been easy money. In any event, it might have been the last thing Shakespeare wrote for money, until he drew up his will.

Still, at some point near the end of the first decade of the seventeenth century Shakespeare moved back to Stratford for better or for worse. Why? Maybe he loved Stratford. Maybe – for better or for worse – he even loved Anne. One explanation of his 'return' to Stratford is he never really left in the first place. Throughout even his 'London years', he formally referred to himself in legal documents as a 'Gentleman of Stratford'. He only ever rented rooms in London, and it's easier to return if you've never really left.

(One thing that Shakespeare did not do in his 'retirement' is enter public service. His father, John, had been undone by the obligations of civic duty [see Chapter 2]. However well-off Shakespeare became, he prudently escaped his father's fate. Shakespeare was apparently not at home when the aldermen came knocking.)

If Shakespeare needed a sign that it was time to hang it up, he got it on 29 June 1613. The Globe burned down during a performance of *Henry VIII*. Some wadding from a discharged cannon lodged in the thatched roof and rapidly ran round the perimeter, turning Shakespeare's 'Wooden O' into a ring of fire. As omens go, the theatre catching fire during one of your plays is pretty clear cut.

By then, Shakespeare was likely back home in Stratford, so the news might have reached him a few days later. Though the company rebuilt rather quickly – this time, shrewdly, they used tile not thatch – it is not clear if Shakespeare contributed any capital. Maybe it looked like good money after bad. In any event, Shakespeare was busy reaping the winter fruit he had been sowing for some years.

*

There is risk in turning Shakespeare's life into a tale of there-and-back-again. A fairy-tale final act where everything lost is found again in the slanted light of his twilight years. Yet Shakespeare's work, with uncanny precision, describes the same dynamic. One traditional, though flawed, chronology begins with *Comedy of Errors*, where children leave home to find their parents, and ends with *The Tempest*, where an old man gives over his work so he can return home and worry about his daughter's marriage.

In 1930 Freud confided to Theodore Reik that he 'no longer believe[d] in the man from Stratford'.[8] Shakespeare did not believe in the man from Vienna either, but what is intriguing about the comment is the substitution of a place for a name. In fact, the loosely affiliated group of Shakespeare sceptics are called 'anti-Stratfordians', as though they doubt the place, not the poet. And while there are some unbelievable things about Stratford, it does actually exist. Just pick up the A40 north from London and drive until you're angry.

But the collapse of Shakespeare's name into the town of his birth reveals the power, even the hypnotic allure of Stratford in the Shakespeare narrative. 'The man from Stratford' is, if not his proper name, his proper sobriquet for Freud and his followers as well as pilgrims and sceptics the world over. The allure of the birthplace is so great that even Shakespeare could not resist it.

19

Shakespeare's Head

There's a special providence in the fall of a sparrow. What about a swan? William Shakespeare died on 23 April 1616. St George's Day. His own birthday. In dying on the day he was born Shakespeare follows Cassius, who points out at the end of *Julius Caesar* that 'This is my birthday: as this very day / Was Cassius born' (5.2.69–70), which can be paraphrased – as the actor John Harrell points out – as 'today is my birthday, since today is my birthday'. To Cassius, as to Shakespeare, or to Shakespeareans, birthdays seem like a good day to die, whosoever authors it. Shakespeare lived his life like a prophecy in reverse.

The rhyming dates make it seem that time itself had willed his life to be. Sometimes fate needs a helping hand, however, since it was not the hand of fate but the hands of man that forced the rhyme. Across the world, 23 April is celebrated as the birthday of William Shakespeare. Yet, for nearly one hundred and fifty years after Shakespeare's death, and for nearly two hundred years after his birth, Shakespeare's birthday was not celebrated at all, much less on 23 April. It was not until 1769, when David Garrick staged the Shakespeare Jubilee, that Bardolatry coalesced around prominent dates in the Shakespeare calendar.

If Shakespeare was not truly born until 1769, it would take still longer for 23 April to emerge as his 'birthday'. While records indicate that he was baptized on 26 April, no documents link his birth to the date of 23 April. This date, which can be traced back to an eighteenth-century scholar's mistake, has nonetheless proved appealing to biographers, since Shakespeare died on 23 April 1616. By celebrating his life, we are always, therefore, celebrating his death. In the year 2000, Easter fell on 23 April, but every day is Easter in the Shakespeare industry.

*

John Ward offers the only cause of death reported of Shakespeare: conviviality. 'Shakespear, Drayton and Ben Jonson had a merry meeting and it seems drank too hard, for Shakespear died of a fever there contracted.'[1] The report comes half-a-century after Shakespeare's death and so reeks of anecdote. Shakespeare, who had survived multiple tours of England, a dozen outbreaks of plague and a collaboration with George Wilkins, died of a hangover.

What Shakespeare could not survive, apparently, was a friendship with Ben Jonson, who drank him under the table, and then under the earth. But we do not know the cause of Shakespeare's death. His last signature on his will looks shaky, the scrawl of a man barely strong enough to hold a pen, though his handwriting was never very strong. He started work on his will in January 1616, so he knew the end was near. It suggests a decline in his health that even his capable son-in-law could not check. He died on or around 23 April and was put below the earth just a few days later.

Governed by assumptions about his retirements, it seems that Shakespeare died at a respectable age. He was done with his art, and so life was done with him. But the notion disguises the fact that Shakespeare died young. Not so young that we would call it 'tragic'. That label is reserved for those like Christopher Marlowe, dead in a knife fight at twenty-nine. But Shakespeare was only fifty-two when he passed. Not tragically young, but certainly premature. By today's standards even more obviously so. Fifty-two-year-old men today are usually getting a divorce, starting a podcast or writing a biography of Shakespeare. Shakespeare's mid-life crisis was that he died.

Was Shakespeare old for his age? Depends on how you count. Life expectancy – and *there's* an optimistic phrase – skewed young at the time because infant mortality was so high. As noted in Chapter 7, if you survived your childhood, you might expect to hit your late sixties or even seventies. (If you didn't, you couldn't. Remember Shakespeare's shadow, the butcher's boy of John Aubrey's *Brief Lives*?) Shakespeare outlived all his siblings but Joan, burying his last brother, Richard, in 1612. Like so much about Shakespeare's life and art, you can have it both ways. Shakespeare died both young and old.

There is an anecdotal tradition that Shakespeare played old men in his own plays: Adam in *As You Like It*, the aging Henry in *Henry IV*, perhaps Polonius in *Hamlet*, who cannot remember his lines – 'what was I about to say?' (2.1.30–1). This would set up a good gag in which the playwright pretends to forget himself, or at least the very lines that he himself had written. (Noël Coward wrote, 'I always forget, when I'm playing in my own plays, that I'm the author'.[2]) Given that he died at fifty-three – Richard Burbage at fifty-one, Middleton at forty-seven, Fletcher at forty-six – Shakespeare was 'middle aged' in his mid-twenties, and he acted like it.

Offstage, Shakespeare had been playing old men all his life. He was a husband and a father before he was out of his teens. He was planning for 'retirement' from his mid-twenties on. And when he looked in the mirror around the age of thirty, he saw a face 'beaten and chapped with time'. In sonnet 2 he dilates upon the ravages of time that 'forty winters' visit on a face. If Shakespeare was, as Jonson put it, 'the soul of the age', he was an old one.

If his death was a little 'early' it was not lonely. He was surrounded by relations, who all lived in Stratford. Anne was there of course, but so were his daughters and sons-in-law. He lived in London among players and patrons. He died in Stratford among family and friends.

After Shakespeare died, daughter Susanna and her husband John moved from Hall's Croft (which still stands) into New Place (which does not), where they lived the rest of their days. His younger daughter Judith had also wed, although less happily. She married Thomas Quiney, a vintner, on 10 February 1616, just months before Shakespeare died. At the time of his wedding to Judith, Thomas was about to become a father but not – unlike his father-in-law at the time of *his* wedding – by his wife. One Margaret Wheeler was with child by him. A month after the wedding, horribly, both Margaret and child died during delivery. If there had been a honeymoon for Judith and Tom, it may have been a short one. The couple's first child, Shakespeare Quiney, died as an infant in May 1617, and neither of their two sons lived past twenty-one.

Living well might be the best revenge, but living long might have done the trick for Anne had she resented Shakespeare's partial absenteeism during his life and full-time absenteeism after 23 April 1616. Anne died between the appearance of two memorials to Shakespeare, the bust of him in Holy Trinity and the printing of his complete works in 1623. She was sixty-seven years old.

In fact all of the women in Shakespeare's life outlasted their husbands. Susanna lived until the age of sixty-six and died on 11 July 1649. Judith outlived them all, dying on 9 February 1662 at the age of seventy-seven. His granddaughter – called his 'niece' in his will – died childless in 1670, putting a full stop to the Shakespeare line. The Shakespeare family plot in Holy Trinity gathers the family together again. Husband, wife and children. Reunited in death. (Only the unknown grave of Hamnet disrupts this reunion.) Itinerant Shakespeare, who'd gone here and there, found his final resting place in Stratford-upon-Avon next to Anne Shakespeare, née Hathaway, in a best bed made of earth.

*

It seems like an oversight that no-one took a photograph of Shakespeare during his life. To be fair, photography developed in the 1830s, so merely 250 years too late to give us a documentary account of Shakespeare's head. Still, a photograph would not provide the disclosure we desire. Instead, we have to settle for a handful of notional paintings and the one sure image we have of Shakespeare inside the first folio, the Droeshout image.

Martin Droeshout came from a Flemish clan of artists. His grandfather John came to London from Brussels in 1570, when Shakespeare was still a boy. Martin was just fifteen when Shakespeare died and so unlikely to have known or even seen the poet. He received the commission for the folio engraving when he was just twenty-one, so this old engraving is a young man's work. Shakespeare did not sit for Droeshout, so he presumably worked from a sketch or miniature. (Perhaps Richard Burbage, himself a fine artist, left a sketch behind, since he'd died in 1619.)

The curious thing about the Droeshout image is that it prompts the question it was drawn to answer: What did Shakespeare look like? Surely not this. A gigantic head on a ludicrously small torso. Even Ben Jonson was forced, finally, to look away at the end of his generous poem set opposite the engraving on the folio title page: 'Reader, look / Not on his picture, but his Book'. Jonson says the engraver did Will justice, though this is pretty faint praise. But then one of the most charming things about Ben Jonson is that he always ends up criticizing what he sets out to praise (that's how you know he means it). If you want to see Shakespeare, look at this book instead, he concludes.

There is a compulsion among biographers of Shakespeare to decry the inadequacy of the folio engraving. It is almost a contest. A certainty that it fails to live up to his life. Samuel Schoenbaum notes the bust's 'generous larding of adipose tissue' in what is actually an appreciation of Droeshout's work. A.L. Rowse describes Shakespeare's generous forehead as 'another dome of St. Paul's – plenty of room there …'. A 'sugar-loaf skull', another calls it. A 'horrible hydrocephalous development' still another notes. Northrop Frye pulled no punches. 'He looks like an idiot.'[3] For many the image of Shakespeare is too bad to be true.

In truth, the eyes are not bad, knowing and watchful with heavy bags beneath, as though from lack of sleep (all those bells, all those dreams; see *Macbeth* and sonnets 27, 28, 43, etc.). But for better or worse, the image is iconic. It is reproduced and imitated across the following folios: the second folio of 1632, the third of 1664, the fourth from 1685. It is augmented and altered over time. By the fourth folio the face has acquired a sheen, so that as it ages it takes on signs of life. There is even something of a five o'clock shadow sprouting on his chin, as though Shakespeare has been sitting for some time.

From Droeshout's engraving to the Felton Portrait to Pablo Picasso's minimalist sketch, artists are drawn to the head, which super-looms over the body as though a mind crammed with that many words must expand like a balloon pumped full of helium. (To the modern eye, Droeshout's engraving looks photoshopped.) In the Felton painting Shakespeare's forehead is so high it turns into his hind-head. Whether he was an actor before turning playwright or the other way around, the emphasis on the head at the expense of the rest settles the matter. Brain over body, playwright over performer, mind over matter.

To some, the bust of Shakespeare in Holy Trinity is also a bust. A botched job or a banal one. There's the usual contest to come up with disparagements. A 'pudding faced effigy', Dover Wilson called it. 'A self-satisfied pork-butcher.' His expression is 'suggestive of a man crunching a sour apple'.[4] Shakespeare's greatest biographer rallies to its defence, noting that 'not all middle-aged successful writers look delicately consumptive'.[5] For an image of Shakespeare as a delicate consumptive you can visit Southwark Cathedral. There, a semi-recumbent Shakespeare reclines in a field with London in the distance, descanting on a flower, his slight body exhausted from the effort of transporting his gigantic head from here to there.

Shakespeare's monument in Holy Trinity is five feet from the floor, so at eye level for his contemporaries. It memorializes Shakespeare's life, but its own history remembers Shakespeare as well. It too travelled from the Southbank to Stratford, presumably by boat or cart. It was carved in the workshop of Gerard Janssen, whose father Gheerhart emigrated to London from Amsterdam in 1567 (the parallels with the Droeshout clan are instructive). The Janssens worked in a yard quite close to The Globe and were tomb-makers to the stars. Their most renowned work memorialized the father of Shakespeare's early patron, the Earl of Southampton, at the family manse in Titchfield. If Shakespeare spent some time there in the mid-1590s (see Chapter 9), he knew the Janssens' work.

(Lena Orlin has recently argued that it was not Gerard but his brother Nicholas who prepared the monument. Since Nicholas worked on another statue in Holy Trinity, she claims, Shakespeare may have met him and commissioned the statue himself. The upshot being that the bust in Holy Trinity is *not* an image of a self-satisfied pork butcher. It is an image of a self-satisfied word monger.[6])

Whether it was Shakespeare himself or his family, they spared no expense, since the Janssens were tomb-makers to the rich and famous. Quite near Shakespeare's bust in Holy Trinity is another Nicholas Janssen product, the tomb of John Combe, who paid sixty pounds for his memorial. Shakespeare's monument therefore connects him with the tony circles he moved among in life and aspired to join, while possibly despising himself for doing so. The Shakespeares may not have spent quite that much since Combe got the full recumbent treatment. However lavishly they laid out for Shakespeare's memorial, his descendants decided not to spring for his legs.

There are a couple of oddities about Shakespeare's bust on the wall above his tomb, where he keeps his own grave under twenty-four-hour surveillance. There are twenty-nine tiny buttons on his doublet. (It's a wonder he wrote anything at all in between dressing in the morning and undressing at night.) Also, like John Combe's, most funeral statuary from the time shows the figure resting in peace, or at least repose. Shakespeare is not recumbent, he is rather upright. He has a pen in one hand and piece of paper in the other. The bust depicts a writer who does not take death lying down. Shakespeare keeps on writing, just like he might never stop. The effigy makes at least one thing clear: Shakespeare was a righty – his right-hand holds a quill, poised in composition. Oddly enough, there is no paper beneath. That is in his left hand, slightly folded, as if he has something to hide. In any event, there is no writing visible upon the 'paper'. Either he's just getting started or it's his will and he doesn't want Anne to see it. Perhaps we have surprised him writing, or maybe he is just taking a moment to compose himself.

The earliest image copied of this effigy included neither pen nor paper. William Dugdale sketched the bust in 1649 and got it interestingly wrong. It shows Shakespeare with a plump woolsack clutched firmly to his crotch or his lower stomach, like he just ate something bad, perhaps a sour apple. He looks like a wool merchant, not a writer. At least Dugdale copied the coat-of-arms correctly, which probably would have pleased Shakespeare given the trouble he took to acquire it. (Shakespeare's covering his crotch or stomach, but the falcon above him has nothing to hide. Its wings are displayed, not addorsed.)

The monument has been spruced up, whitewashed, desecrated and restored across the years. In 1746, a group of players performed *Othello* in the Stratford town hall to raise money to restore the bust. Led by John Ward, the anecdotalist and actor – but I repeat myself – the performance raised enough money to repair the original. This would not be the last time one of Shakespeare's plays was performed to restore his image.

*

Shakespeare's fans have always craved his likeness. As early as 1601, in the anonymous Cambridge play *Return from Parnassus*, Gullio enthuses, 'O sweet Mr Shakespeare! I'll have his picture in my study at the court'. Gullio is a dunce, but the desire to have a picture of Shakespeare is common. No less a poet than John Dryden rhapsodized over his copy of the 'Chandos Portrait' of Shakespeare. He asked 'his blessing e're I write'.[7] Why we wish to look a poet in the face is a question beyond the scope of this book (or the grasp of its writer). It must have something to do with a desire to meet our maker.

There are a number of decent candidates for portraits of Shakespeare: the Flower, the Chandos, the Felton, the Janssen, the Ashebourne, the Grafton and so forth. (Portraits are often named after the rich people who own them not the poor ones who paint them. The 'Flower Portrait' is named for the wealthy brewing family who also funded the Shakespeare Memorial Theatre, now the RSC. All those pints add up to pounds.)

The National Portrait Gallery in London has a couple of images of Shakespeare with reasonable claims to authenticity. The Chandos Portrait of Shakespeare was the image that founded their collection, and it gives us much that Droeshout does not, not least some colour.[8] If the folio engraving shows Shakespeare as a stuffed shirt – or starched ruff – the Chandos loosens him up a bit. The laces of his doublet are slightly undone – like a modern businessman loosening his tie – and he wears a rakish earring. The image is slightly louche and has proven appealing across the years.

It also has an appropriately theatrical provenance. It has even been ascribed, however dubiously, to the King's Man Joseph Taylor (1586–1652). The later playwright and proud Shakespeare bastard William Davenant might have owned it for a bit, and it more certainly came into the hands of Thomas Betterton, the leading actor of the Restoration stage. He passed it on to Elizabeth Barry, renowned for her Desdemona, etc. Eventually it made its way into the family of the Duke of Chandos, and then the Earl of Ellesmere, who liked it so much – or the opposite – that he gave it to the Portrait Gallery in 1856.

The 'Janssen Portrait' of 1610 is the best of the lot, which in this case means the most flattering. Shakespeare looks urbane, refined and sensitive. A feathered ruff spreads exquisitely beneath his chin, as though his head has been dropped into a drift of soft snow. He is expensively dressed, more like a patron than a poet, the kind who might scatter a few coins in the path of the boho poet of the Chandos Portrait.

One art historian thought that the Earl of Southampton – Shakespeare's first patron – might have commissioned Janssen to paint the portrait, which now hangs at the Folger Shakespeare Library. Still others doubt that it is of Shakespeare at all. Janssen was only sixteen or seventeen at the time of the painting if its '1610' inscription is accurate, and the Earl had an eye for precocious talent. But this is unlikely. An audit of paintings in Titchfield House in 1731 recorded none of Shakespeare.

There are still others with claims to authenticity, paintings whose provenances prove as colourful as the portraits themselves. Just as biographers must repeat anecdotes of Shakespeare's life that are not true (Queen Elizabeth commissions *Merry Wives* etc.), art historians spend a lot of time rehearsing provenances whose credibility crumble in their hands. And so just as biographies – this one included – contain things about Shakespeare that are not true, the Exhibition Hall at the Folger Shakespeare Library hangs portraits of Shakespeare that are not. As a representative case, we can turn to the words of Giles Dawson, past curator of rare books and manuscripts at the Folger. Reviewing the 'Felton Portrait' in 1967 he declared it – in the jargon that makes scholarship so impenetrable – 'mighty fishy'.[9]

It is a rough rule of thumb that the better the portrait the less likely it is to be of Shakespeare. Still, every once in a while another candidate emerges and attracts lively interest. Part of the problem is that – lacking photographic images – any sixteenth- or seventeenth-century portrait of a man with a ruff, goatee and receding hairline can claim to depict Shakespeare. A brief stroll through London's National Portrait Gallery quickly reveals that a dismayingly large number – roughly all – of Englishmen back then featured at least two of the three attributes. To go without a beard in the period seems roughly akin to going without trousers today.

Whether engraving, portrait or bust, these are the images we have of Shakespeare, as opaque as they are revealing. They all leave us wanting. Susan Sontag has suggested that,

'Between two fantastic alternatives, that Holbein the Younger had lived long enough to have painted Shakespeare or that a prototype of the camera had been invented early enough to have photographed him, most Bardolators would choose the photograph.'[10] If there *was* a photograph of Shakespeare it wouldn't look like what we want it to look like. It would look like the photos on our drivers' licences that look nothing like us (but capture our soul).

Sontag concludes that 'having a photograph of Shakespeare would be like having a nail from the true cross'.[11] For Sontag, a photo would be a nail *in* not a piece *of* the cross itself. A photograph would hang Shakespeare on the crux of the real. Sontag speaks for many, though, in that the quest for Shakespeare, the desire for his life, his image, his touch begins where he ended, at the place of his death.

*

Shakespeare's tomb has attracted visitors for centuries, many of whom took their interest a step too far. According to William Hall, who came to pay his respects in 1694, Shakespeare was buried 'full seventeen foot deep, deep enough to secure him'.[12] Hall was overly optimistic. Shakespeare's tomb has been disturbed despite his watchful effigy and his warning epitaph, which reads: 'Good friend, for Jesus' sake forebear to dig the bones interred here. / Blessed be the man that spares these stones, / And cursed be he that moves my bones'. The malediction is designed to prevent the sort of bone-play Shakespeare scripted in *Hamlet*, where a couple of gravediggers disinter old bones to make way for new ones. It didn't work. In 1794, according to Victorian anecdote, a few biographers came digging for signs of life:

The men had dug to the depth of three feet, and I now watched narrowly, for, by the clogging of the darker earth, and that peculiar humid state – smell I can hardly call it – which sextons and earth-grubbers so well understand,

I knew we were nearing the level where the body had formerly mouldered. 'No shovels but the hands,' I whispered, 'and feel for a skull.' There was a long pause as the fellows, sinking in the loose mud, slid their horny palms over fragments of bone. Presently, 'I got him,' said Cud, 'but he's fine and heavy'. Delving to the armpits with both hands, he tugged for some seconds, and then brought up a huge grey stone, like that with which the church is built. I began to be sceptical, when Tom Dyer, who was groping some two feet away from where the skull ought to have been, according to the position of the slab, came upon it, and lifted it out, diving again for the jaw. I handled Shakespeare's skull at last, and gazed at it only for a moment, for time was precious. It was smaller than I expected, and in formation not much like what I remembered of the effigy above our heads. ... My men were surprised at the care which I bestowed upon the venerable article. 'Any skull from the charnel-house close by,' they remarked, 'would have answered fully as well, without the labour.' 'Every man has his fancy,' I replied; 'this is mine.'[13]

This tale includes the usual confusion. The skull may or may not have been Shakespeare's but, if it was, according to at least one disappointed grave-robber, it was 'smaller than I expected' and did not look like his effigy. The failure of a poet to measure up to his effigy is just one more reason why it's best to let them lie.

Ultimately, the story of Shakespeare's stolen head resolves into ambiguity. The skull was stolen – of that the anecdote is sure – but it is not clear whether it was ever returned. It is not even clear the robbers got the right one, but then Hamlet does not recognize Yorick at first either. Apparently the tomb-raiders started to dig up the wrong grave at first, because 'they were illiterate and could not read the name on the tombstone'. At this point, the anecdote almost eats itself, since the only reason you'd want to open Shakespeare's tomb is because of what's written there. (Shakespeare's bust was desecrated as well, on 2

SHAKESPEARE'S HEAD   225

October 1973, when vandals chipped away at Shakespeare in search of, the police reported, 'valuable manuscripts written by the Bard'.[14]) Incidentally, you may find a group of illiterate grave-robbers digging in the wrong place for Shakespeare's head to be a highly suggestive image of his biographers, but I don't.

This account sounds implausible, not least because it reads more like a gothic novel than a crime report. And so we might want to file it under the category of '*dubia*' with those many anecdotes about Shakespeare's life, and afterlife.

Except.

A story often dismissed as wild fiction, that 18th-century grave robbers stole Shakespeare's skull, appears to be true, archaeologists have said. The first archaeological investigation of Shakespeare's grave at Holy Trinity church in Stratford-on-Avon has been carried out for a documentary to be broadcast by Channel 4 on Saturday. The most striking conclusion is that Shakespeare's head appears to be missing and that the skull was probably stolen from what is a shallow grave by trophy hunters.

Kevin Colls, the archaeologist who led the team, said the grave was not as they had expected. 'We came across this very odd, strange thing at the head end. It was very obvious, within all the data we were getting, that there was something different going on at that particular spot. We have concluded it is signs of disturbance, of material being dug out and put back again …'. All of that gives credence, Colls said, to a story published in the Argosy magazine in 1879 that Shakespeare's skull was stolen from Holy Trinity in 1794.[15]

The archaeologist offers a forensic assessment when he concludes that, 'something different' was going on at the 'particular spot' of Shakespeare's head, but that opinion is shared by literary historians, theatre fans and the ages yet to come. Something definitely 'different' went on in Shakespeare's head, which, when you come right down to it, is why tourists flock to his tomb and biographers to his life.

The account appeared in the *Guardian* on 23 March 2016. Pity the paper did not sit on the story for one more month. They could have run it to mark the four-hundredth anniversary of Shakespeare's death. For whether the evidence is anecdotal or archaeological, the suggestion is strong that were we to roll back the stone on Shakespeare's tomb, we might find he is not there.

Epilogue: Yellow Leaves

In the late nineteenth century, the Shakespearean actor Henry Irving went to visit the 'Stratford Shrine'. He may or may not have been inspired, but the pilgrimage produced an anecdote he dined out on for years. The shortest version goes like this,

> Mr. Irving tells with infectious humour a story of one of his visits to the Stratford Shrine – the Shakespeare house. 'We met a native,' said he, 'just opposite Shakespeare's house, and asked him whose place that was over there. "Dunno," he said. "Come, come, you must know who lives there. Is his name Shakespeare?" "Dunno," "But can't you tell whether he's alive now?" "Dunno." "But surely you know whether he was famous – whether he ever did anything?" "Yees, he-he-he-" "Well, what did he do?" "He writ summut." "That's it – we were sure you knew all about him. What did he write?" "He writ a Boible."'[1]

Shakespeare did not write the Bible, but he did something equally unbelievable. By the numbers alone it beggars belief. There are the long, early, narrative poems. There are the sonnets he produced throughout his life. And then there are the plays, preeminently the plays. Thirty-seven and counting, depending upon the edition you consult (and seemingly the day you consult it). Remarkably, the sonnets were written at the same time as the plays. In other words – and stay with me here – Shakespeare was writing *while he was writing*.

So the industry is unbelievable, but the numbers alone hardly tell the whole story. Some of Shakespeare's contemporaries produced as much or more. Thomas Middleton, Ben Jonson, Thomas Heywood, who claimed to have had 'an entire hand, or at least a main finger' in two hundred and twenty plays, which is definitely a strange way to put it. Shakespeare's complete works is bigger than Christopher Marlowe's, but rescaled to annual output Marlowe's complete works is bigger. Put another way, Shakespeare's complete works is not bigger than Marlowe's, there's just more of it.

What about the unbelievable vocabulary? The prestigious internet will tell you that Shakespeare 'invented' 10,000 words or so, as though what constitutes creative writing is neologistic fecundity. This is an odd notion since the goal of most writers is to use words the audience already knows, albeit in inventive sequences. In any event, in the time it takes to read this paragraph, you could probably, with sufficient bandwidth, find an earlier usage for any one of the 10,000 words Shakespeare is credited with inventing. It is hard to say exactly how many words Shakespeare 'invented' but you should place a bet on a number ending in zero, and beginning with it as well.

Turns out, the *Oxford English Dictionary* gives to Shakespeare so many 'first usages' because his work was one of the main places they looked. That is because his work is so well known but also because Shakespeare left a large print legacy: the folio, of course, but also quartos and octavos full of plays, and sonnets and narrative poems. There are not many other writers of the period with a commensurate foot-print – pun intended, if not appreciated. The parallels are Middleton and Jonson, who both published widely during their working lifetimes. And here is the obvious but disappointing kicker: they have similarly large vocabularies, which is to reach the inevitable conclusion that to have a large vocabulary you have to write a lot.

It is the quality that counts in the end, and the plays are unbelievably good. Shakespeare wrote a dozen or so of the greatest plays ever written (and some other ones). There is a canon within the canon, the 'A-sides' that get played over and over and over again, but even his B-sides are hits. In this year alone, there will be more performances of Shakespeare's plays than there were during his entire lifetime.

This looks, in hindsight, like a miracle. It was, in fact, inevitable. When one thinks of all the writers, then and now, who were not Shakespeare, the wonder is not that there was one Shakespeare but that there were not more. Thinking about Einstein's brain, Stephen Jay Gould concluded that, 'I am, somehow, less interested in the weight and convolutions of Einstein's brain than in the near certainty that people of equal talent have lived and died in cotton fields and sweatshops.'[2] Gould's notion returns us to John Aubrey's other son of Stratford, the talented butcher's boy who – every bit Shakespeare's rival but in health – did not survive his childhood. Shakespeare was unbelievably talented. And unbelievably, almost Biblically lucky.

*

Shakespeare did not write the Bible but Irving's classist anecdote gets at something true. Shakespeare's plays and poetry are no longer literature. They are liturgy. We do not read and perform them to recover their meaning. We read and perform them to produce it.

Where does that leave his life? Henry Irving's contemporary, the archbishop of Westminster, Cardinal Wiseman, found time away from writing Latin acrostics, playing badminton with his nieces and re-animating the Catholic community in England to dilate on something familiar in

the mystery of Shakespeare's life. It reminded him of the mystery which hides what all generations of men would have liked to know about the Founder of the Christian Faith; and in their vain anxiety have endeavoured to interpret by traditionary fables. How did the carpenter's reputed Son live, and employ Himself, up to the time when His ministry commenced? Reliable history gives no answer. What was

Shakespeare's common life? Did he hold horses in his youth outside The Theatre? Did he steal deer in Mr Lucy's park? Was he a fond or faithless husband? Did he ever serve in the wars, and go abroad? Were his writings ever corrected by himself? Was he a free liver in his old age, and did death come upon him after a drinking bout at a marriage feast? What was his height and average weight? And we might add many more questions, only to be answered by conjecture.[3]

The Victorians saw something in the parallel, or parable, between the life of Jesus and the life of Shakespeare, since on his three-hundredth birthday (Shakespeare's) an article in *The Times* laid out the full Shakespeare-of-Nazareth allegory:

in all the ages, we cannot point to any man who, for a mere human achievement, has been remembered one century after his birth as the child born at Stratford-on-Avon is now remembered after the lapse of the three longest centuries in the history of mankind. It is the son of a homely alderman whose birth we celebrate – the son of a grazier, who was bred among the cows and the calves; but his intellectual work has raised him to a throne recognized from continent to continent and lasting from age to age.

Shakespeare's father was not named 'Joseph' though his mother *was* named 'Mary'. Still, he was a town boy, not bred 'among the cows and calves'. *The Times* does not claim that he was born in a manger, but the humble origins are essential to his ascension to his 'throne'.

This is one of the appealing dynamics of the Shakespeare myths – the humble beginning, the lofty achievements. Compared to the sprawling excess of his plays – too many characters, too many scenes, too many too long speeches – the tiny house in Stratford with wattle-and-daub walls and a low ceiling seems impossibly cramped. With such low origins, the sky was the only limit. (Maybe this is what Shakespeare was thinking of in *Henry V* when he calls himself a 'bending author'. Maybe no room could hold him.)

It was this over-ripe strain of Victorian worship that goaded George Bernard Shaw to coin the term 'Bardolatry' (rhymes with 'idolatry'). If there is a Shakespeare theology, it is the theology of the exemplary individual, whose life is subsequently rewritten to fit his letters. And that, finally, is the mystery that Wiseman is thinking of: How did Shakespeare get from here to there? From immaturity to immortality?

In his poem 'To Shakespeare After Three-Hundred Years', written the same year as Wiseman's review, Thomas Hardy called him 'bright baffling soul, least capturable of themes'. Shakespeare's ineffability, his illusory nature has been troped into a theme by troupes of biographers who have emphasized their own heroism in flinging their nets at Shakespeare. But what, in the end, is so baffling about the 'Bard'? He was the luckiest and most talented of men – born in the right time and place, at the cross-hairs of time and eternity.

The coincidence of dates here – Wiseman, *The Times*, Hardy – is not coincidental. It is hard to pinpoint precisely *when* it happened, but by his three-hundredth birthday Shakespeare had left this earth, with or without his head. It helps explain why Henry Irving and countless others visit the 'Shakespeare Shrine', the 'Birthplace'. If David Garrick's jubilee beatified Shakespeare for his two-hundredth birthday, by his three-hundredth he had been fully canonized.

Shakespeare was born on 23 April 1564. He was born again on 23 April 1616. In less exalted, less Biblical terms, he died on 23 April 1616. And nothing happened. Or nothing happened *yet*, because his orbit was complete, but it was not finished.

NOTES

Preface

1   Peter Atkinson, 'Spiritual Studies', in *The Arden Research Handbook of Contemporary Shakespeare Criticism*, ed. Evelyn Gajowski (London: Arden Shakespeare, 2021), pp. 222–32, esp. p. 226.

2   Geoff Dyer, *Working the Room: Essays and Reviews: 1999–2010* (Edinburgh: Canongate Books, 2010), p. 175.

3   David Mamet, *Three Uses of the Knife: On the Nature and Purpose of Drama* (New York: Random House, 1998), p. 12.

4   See James Shapiro, *Contested Will: Who Wrote Shakespeare?* (New York: Simon & Schuster, 2010).

5   Lytton Strachey, *Eminent Victorians* (New York: Penguin Classics, 1990), p. 5.

Chapter 1

1   https://shakespearedocumented.folger.edu/resource/document/manuscript-marginalia-gabriel-harvey-refers-hamlet-lucrece-and-venus-and-adonis.

2   Clare Gittings, *Death, Burial and the Individual in Early Modern England* (London: Routledge, 1998), p. 190.

3   Ralph Houlbrooke, *Death, Religion, and the Family in England 1480–1750* (Oxford: Clarendon Press, 1998), pp. 166–7.

4   Katy Mair, 'An Archival and Material Reading of Shakespeare's Will', in *Shakespeare on the Record: Researching an Early Modern Life*, ed. Hannah Leah Crummé (London: Bloomsbury, 2019), pp. 179–98, esp. p. 184.

5   Samuel Schoenbaum, *William Shakespeare: A Compact
    Documentary Life* (Oxford: Oxford University Press, 1987), p. 302.

6   E.K. Chambers, *William Shakespeare: A Study of Facts and
    Problems*, 2 vols. (Oxford: Clarendon Press, 1930), Vol. 2, p. 136.

7   Mair, 'An Archival and Material Reading of Shakespeare's Will',
    p. 179.

8   William West, *The First Part of Simboleography* (London:
    Thomas Wright, 1603), sig. Oo3ᵛ.

9   David Cressy, *Birth, Marriage, and Death: Ritual, Religion, and
    the Life Cycle in Tudor and Stuart England* (Oxford: Oxford
    University Press, 1999), p. 392.

10 Cressy, *Birth, Marriage, and Death*, p. 427.

11 Thomas North, *English Bells and Bell Lore: A Book on Bells by
    the Late Thomas North* (Leek: T. Mark, 1888), p. 128.

12 Cressy, *Birth, Marriage, and Death*, p. 426.

13 Thomas Browne, *Hydriotaphia Urn-Burial, or, A Brief
    Discourse of the Sepulchrall Urnes Lately Found in Norfolk*
    (New York: New Directions, 2010), p. 58.

14 Gittings, *Death, Burial and the Individual in Early Modern
    England*, p. 93.

15 C.M. Ingelby, *Shakespeare Allusion-Book: A Collection of
    Allusions to Shakespeare from 1591 to 1700*, 2 vols. (London:
    Humphrey Millford, 1909), Vol. 1, p. 269.

16 Nicholas Rowe, *Works of Mr. William Shakespear* (London:
    Jacob Tonson, 1709), pp. 1–2.

17 Jeremy Lopez, 'Elder Brother, Younger Brother: Shakespeare,
    Fletcher, Beaumont', unpublished manuscript.

Chapter 2

1   John Aubrey, *Brief Lives* (London: Penguin Books, 2000), p. 289.

2   Chambers, *Facts and Problems*, Vol. 2, p. 34.

3   *The Book of Common Prayer: The Texts of 1549, 1559, and
    1662*, ed. Brian Cummings (Oxford: Oxford University Press,
    2011), p. 141.

4   All quotations from Shakespeare's plays refer to *The Arden Shakespeare: Complete Works*, eds. Richard Proudfoot, Ann Thomspon and David Scott Kastan (London: Thomson Learning, 2007).

5   http://www.guildchapel.org.uk/the-wall-paintings/, accessed 20 July 2021.

6   https://www.dimev.net/record.php?recID=1170, accessed 17 June 2020. *

Chapter 3

1   Samuel Schoenbaum, *Shakespeare's Lives* (Oxford: Clarendon Press, 1970), p. 729.

2   Thomas Spencer Baynes, 'What Shakespeare Learnt at School', in *Shakespeare Studies, and Essay on English Dictionaries* (London: Longmans, Green, and Co., 1894), p. 741.

3   Jonathan Bate, *Soul of the Age: A Biography of the Mind of William Shakespeare* (New York: Random House, 2010), p. 7.

4   Ewan Fernie, *Spiritual Shakespeares* (London: Routledge, 2005), p. 7.

5   Lena Orlin, *The Private Life of William Shakespeare* (Oxford: Oxford University Press, 2021), p. 30.

6   Rowe, *Works of Mr. William Shakespear*, pp. iii–iv.

Chapter 4

1   See Jonathan Hope and Laura Wright, 'Female Education in Shakespeare's Stratford and Stratfordian Contacts in Shakespeare's London', *Notes and Queries* 248, no. 2 (June 1996), pp. 149–50.

2   *Shakespeare's Sonnets*, ed. Katherine Duncan-Jones (London: Thomson Learning, 1997).

3   William Harrington, *The Commendations of Matrimony* (London, n.d.), sig. A4^V.

4   Schoenbaum, *William Shakespeare: A Compact Documentary Life*, p. 71.

5   Schoenbaum, *Shakespeare's Lives*, p. 25.

6   Schoenbaum, *William Shakespeare: A Compact Documentary Life*, p. 83.

7   Augustine Skottowe, *The Life of Shakespeare; Enquiries into the Originality of His Dramatic Plots and Characters; and Essays on the Ancient Theatres and Theatrical Uses* (London: Longman, Hurst, Rees, Orme, Brown and Green, 1824), I, 1–2.

8   Schoenbaum, *Shakespeare's Lives*, p. 313.

9   Richard Grant White, *Memoirs of the Life of William Shakespeare, with an Essay toward the Expression of His Genius, and an Account of the Rise and Progress of the English Drama* (Boston: Little Brown, 1865), p. 147.

10 Archana Srinivasan, *Sixteenth and Seventeenth Century Writers* (Chennai: T. Khrishna Press, 2006), p. 12.

11 Anthony Burgess, *Shakespeare* (New York: Vintage, 1996), p. 54.

Chapter 5

1   Robert Bearman, 'Was William Shakespeare William Shakeshafte?' *Shakespeare Quarterly* 53 (2002), pp. 83–94.

2   Bearman, 'Was William Shakespeare William Shakeshafte?' p. 93.

3   The image of Shakespeare at his father's knee is sourced from the account of R. Willis who, later in life, recalled a performance of *The Cradle of Security* in Gloucestershire: 'At such a play, my father tooke me with him and made mee stand between his legs, as he sate upon one of the benches where we saw and heard very well.' *Mount Tabor, or private exercises of a pentitent sinner* (London, Printed by R[ichard] B[adger] for P. Stephens and C. Meredith, at the gilded Lion in S. Paul's Church-yard, 1639), p. 110.

4   https://shakespearedocumented.folger.edu/resource/document/court-kings-bench-coram-rege-roll-complaint-john-shakespeare-against-john-lambert.

Chapter 6

1   https://www.nytimes.com/2018/07/13/books/review/lord-of-the-rings-fellowship-of-the-ring-jrr-tolkien-wh-auden.html.

2   Schoenbaum, *Shakespeare's Lives*, p. 366.

3   Schoenbaum, *Shakespeare's Lives*, p. 751.

4   David Ellis, *The Truth about William Shakespeare: Fact, Fiction, and Modern Biographies* (Edinburgh: Edinburgh University Press, 2013), p. 44.

5   Rowe, *Works of Mr. William Shakespear*, p. 5.

6   Schoenbaum, *William Shakespeare: A Compact Documentary Life*, p. 98.

7   Margreta de Grazia, 'Shakespeare's Anecdotal Character', *Shakespeare Survey* 68 (2015), pp. 1–14, esp. p. 1.

8   Mark Brayshay, *Land Travel and Communications in Tudor and Stuart England: Achieving a Joined-Up Realm* (Edinburgh: University of Edinburgh Press, 2014), p. 183.

9   J.O. Halliwell-Phillipps, *Outlines of the Life of Shakespeare* (London: Longman, Green, and Co., 1883), p. 556.

10 *Remarks and Collections of Thomas Hearne*, ed. C.E. Doble (Oxford: Clarendon Press, 1886), Vol. 2, p. 228.

11 *The Comedies of Merchant of Venice and As You Like It*, ed. Ambrose Eccles (Dublin: John Jones, 1805), Vol. 1, p. 255.

Chapter 7

1   Charles Nicholl, *The Lodger: Shakespeare, His Life in Silver Street* (New York: Viking, 2008).

2   Duncan Salkeld, *Shakespeare and London* (Oxford: Oxford University Press, 2018).

3   Qtd. in Jacqueline Vanhoutte, *Age in Love: Shakespeare and the Elizabethan Court* (Lincoln, NE: University of Nebraska Press, 2019), p. 15.

4   https://shakespeareauthorship.com/bd/.

5   E.A.J. Honigmann and Susan Brock, *Playhouse Wills, 1558–1642* (Manchester: Manchester University Press, 2015).

6   John Astington, *Actors and Acting in Shakespeare's Time: The Art of Stage Playing* (Cambridge: Cambridge University Press, 2010).

7   Imtiaz H. Habib, *Black Lives in the English Archives, 1500–1677: Imprints of the Invisible* (London: Routledge, 2007).

Chapter 8

1   P.J. Finkelpearl, 'John Davies', *Oxford Dictionary of National Biography*.

2   *The Routledge Anthology of Early Modern Drama*, gen. ed. Jeremy Lopez (London: Routledge, 2020).

3   David Thompson, *The Whole Equation: A History of Hollywood* (New York: Vintage, 2006), p. 164.

4   *The Cambridge Edition of the Works of Ben Jonson*, gen. eds. David Bevington, Martin Butler and Ian Donaldson, 7 vols. (Cambridge and New York: Cambridge University Press, 2012), Vol. 7.

5   G.E. Bentley, *The Profession of Dramatist in Shakespeare's Time, 1590–1642* (Princeton: Princeton University Press, 1971).

6   Sarah Lewis, 'John Fletcher', in *The Cambridge Guide to the Worlds of Shakespeare*, eds. Bruce Smith, Katherine Rowe, Ton Hoenselaars, Akiko Kusunoki, Andrew Murphy and Aimara Da Cunha Resende (Cambridge: Cambridge University Press, 2016), pp. 958–63.

7   Folger Shakespeare Library Scrapbook B.133.2 'Theatrical Miscellany'.

8   John Jowett, 'Johannes Factotum: Henry Chettle and Greene's Groatsworth of Wit', *Papers of the Bibliographical Society of America* 87 (1993), pp. 469–70.

9   https://shakespearedocumented.folger.edu/resource/document/greenes-groats-worth-witte-first-printed-allusion-shakespeare-playwright.

10 Alan Bennett, *Writing Home* (New York: Picador, 1994), p. xiii.

11 *English Professional Theatre, 1530–1660*, eds. Glynne
    Wickham, Herbert Berry and William Ingram (Cambridge:
    Cambridge University Press, 2000), p. 84.

Chapter 9

1   Qtd. in Katherine Duncan-Jones, 'Much Ado with Red and White:
    The Earliest Readers of Shakespeare's *Venus & Adonis* (1593)',
    Review of English Studies 44 (1993), pp. 479–501, esp. p. 490.

2   Chambers, *Facts and Problems,* Vol. 2, p. 197.

3   Katherine Duncan-Jones and Henry Woudhuysen, *Shakespeare's
    Poems: Venus and Adonis, The Rape of Lucrece and the Shorter
    Poems* (London: Bloomsbury, 2007).

4   *Henslowe's Diary*, ed. R.A. Foakes and R.T. Rickert
    (Cambridge: Cambridge University Press, 1961), p. 21.

5   This dating follows Paul Edmondson and Stanley Wells, eds. *All
    the Sonnets of Shakespeare* (Cambridge: Cambridge University
    Press, 2020), esp. p. 25.

6   Aubrey, *Brief Lives*, p. 156.

7   See Donald Foster, 'Master W.H., R.I.P.', *PMLA* 102 (1987),
    pp. 42–54. Also see the entry on 'W. H. (Mr. W. H.)' in the
    Oxford Dictionary of National Biography.

8   Bruce Smith, *Homosexual Desire in Shakespeare's England:
    A Cultural Poetics* (Chicago: University of Chicago Press, 1991),
    p. 65.

9   Kim F. Hall, *Things of Darkness: Economies of Race and
    Gender in Early Modern England* (Ithaca, NY: Cornell
    University Press, 1995), p. 2.

10 Francis Meres, *Palladis Tamia*, fols. 281^v–282^r.

Chapter 10

1   https://henslowe-alleyn.org.uk/catalogue/mss-1/article-009/.

2   https://henslowe-alleyn.org.uk/essays/henslowes-diary-1591-
    1609/?highlight=newington.

3   Andrew Gurr, *The Shakespeare Company 1594–1642*
    (Cambridge: Cambridge University Press, 2010), p. 94.

4   https://shakespearedocumented.folger.edu/resource/document/
    augustine-phillips-last-will-and-testament-original-copy.

5   John Dennis, *An essay on the genius and writings of Shakespear:
    with some letters of criticism to The spectator* (London: Printed
    for W. Mears, 1712), p. 33.

6   https://shakespearedocumented.folger.edu/resource/document/
    john-aubreys-notes-shakespeare.

7   Christopher Matusiak, 'Was Shakespeare "not a company
    keeper"?: William Beeston and MS Aubrey 8, fol. 45v',
    Shakespeare Quarterly 68 (2017), pp. 351–73.

8   https://shakespearedocumented.folger.edu/resource/document/
    shakespeare-roisterer-tabard-inn.

9   John A. Astington, 'His Theatre Friends: The Burbages', in *The
    Shakespeare Circle: An Alternative Biography*, eds. Stanley Wells
    and Paul Edmondson (Cambridge: Cambridge University Press,
    2015), pp. 248–60, esp. p. 248.

10 Lois Potter, *The Life of William Shakespeare* (London:
    Blackwell, 2017), p. 288.

11 Schoenbaum, *William Shakespeare: A Compact Documentary
    Life*, p. 205.

12 Antony Sher, *Year of the King: An Actor's Diary and Sketchbook*
    (New York: Limelight, 1999), p. 21.

13 John Stockwood, *A Sermon Preached at Paul's Cross* (1578),
    p. 134.

Chapter 11

1   See Park Honan, *Shakespeare: A Life* (London: Clarendon,
    1998), pp. 268–9, and David Kathman, 'Six Biographical
    Records "Re-Discovered": Some Neglected Contemporary
    References to Shakespeare', *Shakespeare Newsletter* 45 (Winter
    1995), pp. 73–8.

2   Eric W. Nye, *Pounds Sterling to Dollars: Historical Conversions
    of Currency*, https://www.uwyo.edu/numimage/currency.htm.

Chapter 12

1   Folger Shakespeare Library Scrapbook, B.130.2 Theatrical Clippings.

2   Richard Dutton, *Shakespeare, Court Dramatist* (Oxford: Oxford University Press, 2016).

3   https://shakespearedocumented.folger.edu/resource/document/king-james-establishes-kings-men-warrant-under-privy-seal.

4   Rowe, *Works of Mr. William Shakespear*, pp. viii–ix.

5   https://thehareonline.com/tags/lois-potter.

Chapter 13

1   https://shakespearedocumented.folger.edu/resource/document/allen-v-burbage.

2   Samuel Rowlands, *The Letting of Humours Blood in the Head-Vaine. With a new Morissco, daunced by seauen Satyres, vpon the bottome of Diogines Tubbe* (London, printed by W. White for W. F., 1600), epig. 7.

3   Lucy Munro, 'Who Owned the Blackfriars Playhouse?' *Shakespeare Quarterly* 70 (2019), pp. 247–69, esp. p. 251.

4   Walter Raleigh, *The History of the World* (London, printed for Walter Burre, 1614), C2v; John Donne, *The Sermons of John Donne*, eds. George R. Potter and Evelyn Simpson (Berkeley: University of California Press, 1953), p. 207; John Webster, *The Routledge Anthology of Early Modern Drama* (London: Routledge, 2020).

5   Schoenbaum, *William Shakespeare: A Compact Documentary Life*, pp. 134–5.

6   https://shakespearedocumented.folger.edu/resource/document/neighbors-petition-november-1596-against-playhouse-blackfriars.

7   *The Spectator*, 17 December 1864, p. 149.

Chapter 14

1   Chambers, *Facts and Problems*, Vol. 2, p. 97.

2   https://shakespearedocumented.folger.edu/resource/document/
    note-chamberlain-s-account-submitted-stratford-corporation-
    payment-mr-shaxspere-10.

3   Robert Bearman, *Shakespeare's Money: How Much Did He
    Make and What Did This Mean?* (Oxford: Oxford University
    Press, 2016), p. 61.

4   Bearman, *Shakespeare's Money*, p. 147.

5   John Berger, *Selected Essays* (New York: Vintage, 2003), p. 215.

6   Meres, *Palladis Tamia*, fol. 282^r.

7   See *The Return from Parnassus* (1600); https://
    shakespearedocumented.folger.edu/resource/document/
    pilgrimage-parnassus-and-return-parnassus-multiple-
    references-shakespeare.

8   Katharine Eisaman Maus, unpublished lecture. For an expansion
    on this theme, see Maus' introduction to *The Alchemist* in
    English Renaissance Drama: A Norton Anthology, eds. David
    Bevington, Eric Rasmussen, Katharine Eisaman Maus and Lars
    Engle (New York: W. W. Norton & Co., 2002).

9   Graham Holderness, 'His Son Hamnet Shakespeare' in *The
    Shakespeare Circle: An Alternative Biography*, eds. Stanley Wells
    and Paul Edmonson (Cambridge: Cambridge University Press,
    2015), pp. 101–9, esp. p. 104.

Chapter 15

1   *The Diary of John Manningham of the Middle Temple,
    1602–1603*, ed. Robert Sorlien (South Kingston: University of
    Rhode Island Press, 1976), pp. 205–6, 209.

2   Thomas Dekker, *The Wonderful Year* (London, printed by
    Thomas Creede, 1603), p. 44.

3   Dutton, *Shakespeare, Court Dramatist*, p. 36.

4   Folger Shakespeare Library Scrapbook A.7.1 London, Drury
    Lane, 1663–1847 (Beaufoy Coll.)

5   Matthieu Chapman, *Anti-Black Racism in Early Modern
    English Drama: The Other 'Other'* (London and New York:
    Routledge, 2016), p. 53.

Chapter 16

1   https://shakespearedocumented.folger.edu/node/126

2   Gabriel Egan claims an early allusion to the *Macbeth*
    superstition in Richard Brome and Thomas Heywood's *The
    Late Lancashire Witches*, but the allusion is opaque (see
    http://gabrielegan.com/publications/Egan2002k.htm). See
    also Lina Perkins Wilder's 'An Alternate Form of the *Macbeth*
    Superstition', *Notes and Queries* 57 (2010), pp. 393–5.

3   Folger Shakespeare Library Scrapbook B.51.1 Peters, Frank
    9 January 1898.

4   Alan Stewart, *The Cradle King: The Life of James VI & I, The
    First Monarch of a United Great Britain* (New York: St Martin's
    Press, 2003), p. 209

5   https://shakespearedocumented.folger.edu/resource/document/
    parish-register-entry-recording-edward-shakespeares-burial

6   https://shakespearedocumented.folger.edu/resource/document/
    parish-register-entry-recording-edmund-shakespeares-burial

7   Kenneth Tynan, *Curtains* (New York: Atheneum, 1961), p. 61.

8   *HMC Report on the Calendar of MSS of the Marquess of
    Salisbury* (1933), Vol. 16, p. 415.

Chapter 17

1   James Shapiro, *The Year of Lear: Shakespeare in 1606*
    (New York: Simon & Schuster, 2015), p. 15.

2   Algernon Charles Swinburne, *Harper's Monthly Magazine*,
    Vol. 101, No. 631 (1902), p. 3.

3   Shapiro, *Year of Lear*, p. 45.

Chapter 18

1   Alexander Cockburn, 'Introduction', in *The Code of the
    Woosters* (New York: Knopf Doubleday, 1976).

2   Schoenbaum, *William Shakespeare: A Compact Documentary
    Life*, p. 271.

3   *All the Sonnets of Shakespeare*, eds. Paul Edmondson and
    Stanley Wells (Cambridge: Cambridge University Press, 2020);
    Peter Holland, 'Shakespeare and the DNB', in *Shakespeare,
    Marlowe, Jonson: New Directions in Biography*, eds. Takashi
    Kozuka and J.R. Mulryne (Burlington: Ashgate, 2006), pp.
    139–49, esp. p. 147.

4   Stanley Wells, https://www.shakespeare.org.uk/explore-
    shakespeare/podcasts/what-was-shakespeare-really/what-
    sonnets-tell-about-shakespeare/.

5   Jane Kingsley-Smith, *The Afterlife of Shakespeare's Sonnets*
    (Cambridge: Cambridge University Press, 2021).

6   Munro, 'Who Owned the Blackfriars?' p. 257.

7   Sarah Dustagheer, *Shakespeare's Two Playhouses: Repertory
    and Theatre Space at the Globe and Blackfriars, 1599–1613*
    (Cambridge: Cambridge University Press, 2017), p. 82.

8   Schoenbaum, *Shakespeare's Lives*, p. 609.

Chapter 19

1   Schoenbaum, *William Shakespeare: A Compact Documentary
    Life*, p. 296.

2   Hal Burton, *Great Acting* (London: BBC, 1967).

3   Samuel Schoenbaum, *William Shakespeare: Records and Images*
    (Oxford: Oxford University Press, 1981), pp. 11, 13, 287.

4   Schoenbaum, *William Shakespeare: Records and Images*, p. 161.

5   Schoenbaum, *William Shakespeare: Records and Images*, p. 369.

6   Lena Orlin, *The Private Life of William Shakespeare* (Oxford: Oxford University Press, 2021), pp. 196–252.

7   Schoenbaum, *William Shakespeare: Records and Images*, p. 177.

8   Tanya Cooper, *Searching for Shakespeare* (New Haven, CT: Yale University Press, 2006), pp. 54–61.

9   Schoenbaum, *William Shakespeare: Records and Images*, p. 177.

10 Susan Sontag, *On Photography* (New York: Picador, 2001), p. 154.

11 Sontag, *On Photography*, p. 154.

12 Chambers, *Facts and Problems*, Vol. 2, p. 260.

13 *How Shakespeare's Skull Was Stolen and Found* (London: Elliot Stock, 1879).

14 Schoenbaum, *William Shakespeare: A Compact Documentary Life*, p. 313.

15 'Shakespeare's Skull Probably Stolen by Grave Robbers, Study Finds', *Guardian*, 23 March 2016.

Epilogue

1   Folger Shakespeare Library Scrapbook B.34.1 Irving, Henry; Terry, Ellen.

2   Stephen Jay Gould, 'Wide Hats and Narrow Minds', *New Scientist*, 8 March 1979, p. 777, rpt. in *The Panda's Thumb: More Reflections in Natural History* (New York: W.W. Norton, 1992), p. 151.

3   Review of 'William Shakespeare', *The Era*, May 1865.

INDEX